# Develop Microsoft HoloLens Apps Now

Allen G. Taylor

**Apress®**

*Develop Microsoft HoloLens Apps Now*

Allen G. Taylor
Oregon City, Oregon
USA

ISBN-13 (pbk): 978-1-4842-2201-0          ISBN-13 (electronic): 978-1-4842-2202-7
DOI 10.1007/978-1-4842-2202-7

Library of Congress Control Number: 2016957156

Managing Director: Welmoed Spahr
Acquisitions Editor: Todd Green
Technical Reviewer: Reid Blomquist
Editorial Board: Steve Anglin, Pramila Balan, Laura Berendson, Aaron Black, Louise Corrigan, Jonathan Gennick, Todd Green, Robert Hutchinson, Celestin Suresh John, Nikhil Karkal, James Markham, Susan McDermott, Matthew Moodie, Natalie Pao, Gwenan Spearing
Coordinating Editor: Nancy Chen
Copy Editor: April Rondeau
Compositor: SPi Global
Indexer: SPi Global
Artist: SPi Global
Cover Image: Courtesy of Freepik

Distributed to the book trade worldwide by Springer Science+Business Media New York, 233 Spring Street, 6th Floor, New York, NY 10013. Phone 1-800-SPRINGER, fax (201) 348-4505, e-mail orders-ny@springer-sbm.com, or visit www.springer.com. Apress Media, LLC is a California LLC and the sole member (owner) is Springer Science + Business Media Finance Inc (SSBM Finance Inc). SSBM Finance Inc is a Delaware corporation.

For information on translations, please e-mail rights@apress.com, or visit www.apress.com.

Apress and friends of ED books may be purchased in bulk for academic, corporate, or promotional use. eBook versions and licenses are also available for most titles. For more information, reference our Special Bulk Sales–eBook Licensing web page at www.apress.com/bulk-sales.

Any source code or other supplementary materials referenced by the author in this text are available to readers at www.apress.com. For detailed information about how to locate your book's source code, go to www.apress.com/source-code/. Readers can also access source code at SpringerLink in the Supplementary Material section for each chapter.

Printed on acid-free paper

*This book is dedicated to the artists of the world.*

*Pursue your art with passion.*

# Contents at a Glance

# Contents

# About the Author

**Allen G. Taylor** is an independent software developer, educator, and early adopter of HoloLens technology. He is the author of more than 40 books and speaks internationally on science and technology and their impact on society. Allen can be reached at allen.taylor@ieee.org. He blogs at allengtaylor.com and posts items of interest at moontube.wordpress.com. Allen's Twitter handle is @SQLwriter.

# About the Technical Reviewer

**Reid Blomquist** is a creative technologist living in Portland, OR. Attached to pretty much anything shiny, new, and electronic, Reid spends his time exploring new and exciting ways to leverage technology. Fortunate to have been exposed to computers and programming from a young age, he has professional experience that spans from full-stack web development to building immersive VR and AR experiences with Unity3D.

# Acknowledgments

I would like to thank Andy Mingo, Thomas Wester, Reid Blomquist, Sonya Neunzert, and Philip Modin for their help in making this book possible. Thanks also to the Apress editorial staff that helped with the production of the book, and, as always, to my literary agent, Carole Jelen of Waterside Productions.

# Introduction

Ever since Microsoft first announced it in January of 2015, there has been a tremendous amount of excitement about the Microsoft HoloLens mixed-reality device. It seamlessly integrates holographic objects into the user's world, making it sometimes difficult to distinguish between what is real and what is virtual. The HoloLens has ushered in a whole new realm of experience.

The HoloLens provides a platform for the development of applications in many different fields that would benefit from being able to place a user within an environment that is completely real, but that also has holographic elements that seem real, even though they are not.

Microsoft is making a major bet that augmented reality—or mixed reality, as they call it—will become a new mass market, rivalling what happened to the smartphone after Apple's introduction of the original iPhone. If they are right, as was the case with the smartphone, the opportunity for independent developers promises to be huge. Every new app increases the value of the HoloLens platform, thus drawing more customers to it and making the pie bigger for all HoloLens developers.

This book is a manual for how to get started as an application developer for the HoloLens. It's a great time to start, because you are starting on an equal footing with everyone else. The technology is brand new, so nobody has much of an edge over you, even if you are just starting out as a developer. Most of the resources you will need in order to get started as a developer are either free downloads or an inexpensive investment. When you consider the potential return on investment, getting into HoloLens development now should be an easy decision.

In the first part of this book, I describe the HoloLens device and how it fits in with the other devices of the Windows 10 platform. I tell you exactly what you will need as a HoloLens developer and give step-by-step instructions on how to configure your development system. Connecting your development system to your HoloLens device and establishing communication between the two comes next. Once you have developed your app, you will want to upload it onto your HoloLens to test it out.

The second part of this book talks about the kinds of applications that are particularly well suited for mixed reality in general and the HoloLens in particular. It also covers the kind of development team that is most likely to be successful at producing an app that meets a real need in the marketplace.

The third part of the book takes you through the process of actually developing an application for the HoloLens using the tool chain recommended by Microsoft.

Part Four starts with a deep dive into the details of the HoloLens hardware to help you get a sense of what is available to you and what some of your constraints are as a developer. It continues with a description of the mixed-reality environment and the types of holograms that you can create within it.

Part Five walks you through the creation of a simple application, followed by a recounting of the myriad ways you must test it to make sure it does what it is supposed to do, under every possible condition that you can think of.

Part Six considers what it will take to become a professional HoloLens developer, and what opportunities lie just over the horizon for people who enter the field today.

# PART I

# The Windows 10 Development Environment and HoloLens

# CHAPTER 1

■ ■ ■

# What Is the Microsoft HoloLens?

It's hard to say what the HoloLens is like, because it is not like anything that you might want to compare it to. Microsoft calls it a stand-alone, fully untethered, holographic computer, but what does that mean?

- *Stand-alone* and *untethered* mean that the HoloLens does not need to be connected, either wired or wirelessly, to any external computer or other device.

- *Holographic* means that the user can see three-dimensional virtual objects and even walk around them, viewing them from every angle. The holograms created by a HoloLens device go beyond that by also enabling the user to interact with them. They also interact realistically with their real-world surroundings.

- *Computer* means that this device contains a powerful and fully functional computing system.

HoloLens is usually mentioned in the press in the context of virtual reality and augmented reality, but it is separate and distinct from both of those technologies. It is creating a new category that will alter our perception of what is real.

## Virtual Reality, Augmented Reality, and Mixed Reality

On the surface, virtual reality sounds like an oxymoron. If something is virtual, by definition it is not real. If it is real, it cannot be virtual. However, there is some logic to the terminology. By immersing oneself in a virtual world, one is, in a sense, entering a new and different reality. When you enter a virtual world, as far as your sight and hearing are concerned, it becomes your reality. Virtual reality completely replaces what we have come to consider normal reality.

With virtual reality gear on your head, you can turn completely around, 360 degrees, and see a world that bears no resemblance to the physical world that you inhabited before you donned that gear. You may also hear sounds that don't match the soundscape of your normal world. However, you better not start walking around. If you do, you will probably walk into an obstacle that is part of the real world, which you have never really left. It only seems like you have. Worst case, you might step off a cliff or into an elevator shaft. Either way, your virtual reality experience will end rather abruptly.

---

**Electronic supplementary material** The online version of this chapter (doi:10.1007/978-1-4842-2202-7_1) contains supplementary material, which is available to authorized users.

Augmented reality is different in that you do not lose sight of the real world, but instead add something to it. Augmented reality has been around for quite a while, most notably in the heads-up displays of fighter pilots. These displays put critical information into the pilot's field of view without obscuring the reality around her, which could very well be a deadly combat situation. There is no need to look away from the action to view a value on a gauge in the cockpit. That value is right there in her field of view. Thus, augmented reality is an overlay on top of what a person normally sees. It looks like icons, symbols, or numbers displayed on a transparent virtual screen.

Microsoft does not like to refer to their HoloLens technology as either virtual or augmented reality, although it does have elements of both. They prefer to call the technology mixed reality. Rather than being superimposed on top of normal reality, as is done with augmented reality, the HoloLens experience blends the two realities together to create a new mixed reality. This new mixed reality is an example of the combination being greater than the sum of its parts. The real and the virtual work together to create an amped-up world that you can move through and interact with in unprecedented ways. The virtual part of your world responds to your hand gestures and to voice commands. The real part of your world is always there to anchor your perceptions.

# The HoloLens Headset

The HoloLens headset consists of a band that encircles your head, with a visor in the front that you look through. Figure 1-1 shows what it looks like.

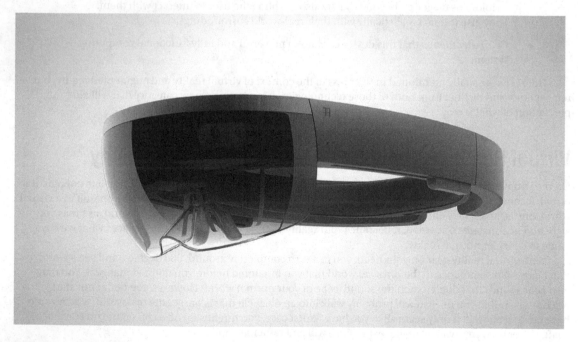

***Figure 1-1.*** *Microsoft HoloLens*

The band does not rest on your ears, and at about one and a quarter pounds, it feels like you are wearing a football helmet. It doesn't take long for you to forget that you are wearing anything, however. Your mind becomes engaged with what is in front of you, both real and virtual.

## The headband

The headband can be adjusted to fit any adult head, both in terms of circumference and the placement of the lenses right in front of the eyes. All of the electronics, processors, memory, cameras, speakers—everything—is contained within the headband. Miniaturization has made all these things lightweight and compact. The weight of all "the works" is evenly distributed around the head, so that no undue pressure is applied to either the ears or the nose. A removable nosepiece is provided, but can be left off. If you don't use it, there is no pressure on your nose at all. Even if you do use it, you can adjust the headband to minimize pressure on the nose.

The bottom line of these considerations is that a person could wear a HoloLens for several hours without feeling any discomfort. Surgeons could perform operations, assembly-line workers could perform assembly or inspection tasks, or designers could collaborate, all while being helped by the addition of three-dimensional virtual objects to the real environment they are working in. Oh, and gamers could battle killer robots breaking through the walls of the room or monsters erupting out of the floor.

## Speakers and spatial sound

There is a small, unobtrusive speaker attached to the headband above each ear. You can make it appear to the wearer that sounds are coming from the virtual assets you create by adjusting the phase of the sound waves going to each ear. This mimics the phase of sound waves that would be coming from a virtual asset as if it were actually making those sounds.

Although the wearer can only see the virtual items that are right in front of her in her field of view, she can hear sounds made by virtual objects behind her or off to the side. Swiveling around to face them will bring them into view.

## Controls

There are only three controls on the HoloLens device itself: a power switch, a sound volume control, and a contrast control for the holographic lenses. The user controls what the application does primarily with gestures and voice commands. Some apps, particularly games, may also use a hand-held controller (the Clicker) that communicates with the HoloLens via Bluetooth.

## The processors

Generating realistic, rapidly changing, three-dimensional holographic images in the user's field of view requires a lot of processing power, and those three requirements (realistic, rapidly changing, three-dimensional holographic) each place three different kinds of demand on the processing system. To handle the load, the HoloLens has three different processors: a central processing unit (CPU), a graphics processing unit (GPU), and a holographic processing unit (HPU). Processing tasks are divided up among the three, and the result is combined to give the user an integrated, high-fidelity experience.

## The Inertial Measurement Unit (IMU)

The IMU includes an accelerometer, a gyroscope, and a magnetometer. These sensors, along with head-tracking cameras, track where your head is and how it is moving. This information is integrated with what HoloLens knows about the space you are moving through to render the virtual objects in your field of view from the right perspective, with the right sizing, and at the right apparent distance from you.

## The cameras

The HoloLens includes five visible-wavelength cameras, one looking straight ahead plus two on the left and two on the right. These cameras track your head movements with respect to your surroundings, and the one in the center can take either videos or still images. In addition, there is an infrared camera facing straight ahead and an infrared laser projector facing the same way. The laser is used to scan objects, which reflect the infrared light back to the infrared camera. This provides a laser-ranging capability that enables the HoloLens to map the distance to everything in the room. A quick 360 degree pirouette will map out a room and everything in it. That map gets refined as the user moves around and interacts with the environment.

## The microphone

The HoloLens includes a microphone so that the user can provide input to the running app with voice commands. As an example, a user could start an app running with a voice command and terminate execution with another voice command.

## Other input devices

In addition to cameras sensing hand gestures and the microphone sensing voice commands, a cordless game controller or a cordless mouse can also be used as an input device.

## The lenses

The lenses of the HoloLens device are transparent so the user can see right through them. However, they also contain an array of very fine, invisible grooves that direct the virtual images generated by the app into the user's eyes, making it appear that virtual objects are at various positions and distances in the room. The illusion is very effective. The virtual objects can appear solid or semi-transparent, with background (real) objects showing though from behind them.

# Sensor Fusion

The HoloLens uses its IMU to track the movements of the user and the infrared laser and camera to map out the local environment. These two streams of data are combined so that the virtual objects mesh accurately with the real environment. Virtual objects change in appearance appropriately as the user moves around. They get smaller as the user moves away and larger as she approaches the object. A user can walk completely around a virtual object and see what it looks like from all sides.

# How HoloLens Differs from Virtual Reality and Ordinary Augmented Reality

There is a proliferation of products on the market that can be classified as either virtual-reality devices or augmented-reality devices. Virtual-reality devices immerse the user in a virtual world. The virtual world completely replaces the real world of sight and sound. In augmented reality, the real world remains visible and audible. A transparent screen is overlaid upon it, which can display words, icons, symbols, or other virtual 2-D objects. A military pilot's heads-up display is an example of augmented reality.

Microsoft's HoloLens is neither a virtual-reality nor an augmented-reality device. It is the first example of a new category, which they call mixed reality. 3-D virtual objects are added to the real environment. They are three dimensional and are located where either the running app or the user places them. They can be hung on a wall of the room, placed on a table, or they can fly through the air. They can even appear to break through the walls of the room and fly into the room beyond. The user remains in the real world, as is true with augmented reality, but can also deal with three-dimensional virtual objects that seem real enough to touch.

# Summary

This chapter is a quick overview of the new Microsoft HoloLens mixed-reality device. We will get into much more detail later about the device, some of the promising uses for it, and how to develop applications for it.

The HoloLens, among other things, is a full 64-bit computer running the Universal Windows 10 operating system. As such, you can run programs on it that were originally targeted at other Windows 10 devices, such as desktops, laptops, tablets, and phones. We'll discuss that in the next chapter.

■ ■ ■

# CHAPTER 2

# The Windows 10 Platform

After widespread criticism of the user interface for Windows 8, Microsoft decided to start with a clean slate in the next version of Windows to be released. What would have become Windows 9 was abandoned without ever seeing the light of day. The next Windows release was given the moniker Windows 10 to put some distance between it and the much-maligned Windows 8.

Since Microsoft was starting from scratch anyway, and since the marketplace had changed dramatically from the PC-centric world that the original Windows was born into, Windows 10 was designed as a universal platform. That means that apps that you develop for one device, such as a Surface Pro or a Windows Phone, will run on any other Windows 10 device as well. One consequence of this is that any app developed for any Microsoft platform, from Xbox One to PC, will also run on HoloLens. That being said, if you want an app you develop to deliver a good mixed-reality user experience, you should probably design it specifically with HoloLens in mind.

## The Windows 10 User Interface

One of the biggest objections to the Windows 8 user interface was the removal of the Start menu, which had been standard in previous versions of Windows, and replacing it with Live Tiles. Live Tiles are great for devices with touch screens but make things harder for desktops and laptops that rely on a mouse or touchpad. In Windows 10, the Start menu returns, but in a different form, as shown in Figure 2-1.

© Allen G. Taylor 2016
A. G. Taylor, *Develop Microsoft HoloLens Apps Now*, DOI 10.1007/978-1-4842-2202-7_2

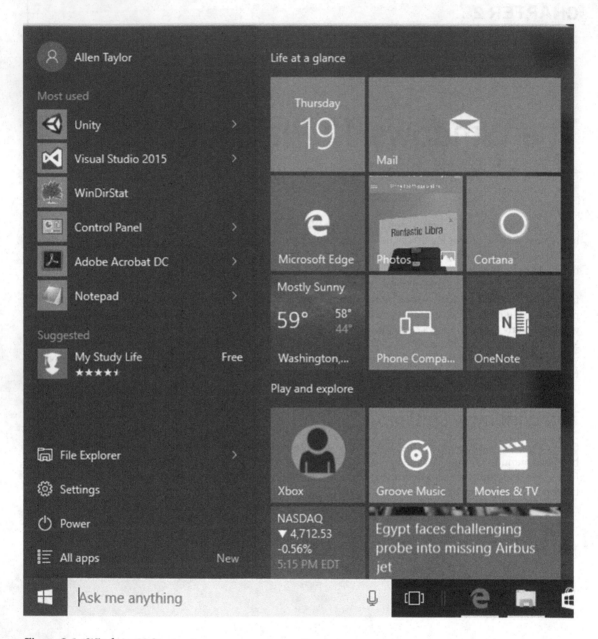

**Figure 2-1.** *Windows 10 Start menu*

Frequently used apps appear at the upper left, and the often used File Explorer, Settings, Power, and All apps options appear at the lower left. On the right is the Action Center, a new incarnation of Live Tiles that gives you access to notifications of various sorts and other things that you might want to access, such as your photos or games. As Windows 10 becomes increasingly familiar with your normal operations, it will display the tiles for the operations that you are most likely to want to use.

Windows 10 also includes the new DirectX 12 gaming API. It provides a software layer that frees game developers from having to know exactly what hardware they are running on. Thus, a game developed for a tablet, for example, could run on a HoloLens without having to be rewritten. Differences between hardware devices are hidden from the programmer's view by the DirectX 12 API.

## Differences between Windows 7 and Windows 10

The design of the user interface of Windows 8 was so different from that of Windows 7 in order to accommodate tablets and other devices with touch screens. Windows 7 did not handle touch screens well at all. Windows 8 was a lot better for touch-screen devices, but was roundly hated by anyone with a traditional desktop PC or a non-touch-screen laptop. The goal for Windows 10 was to run on and be appropriate for all Microsoft devices, from phones to desktops and beyond, even to the Internet of Things (IoT). It was not possible to revert to the well-accepted Windows 7 user interface, but it was also necessary to separate Windows 10 from the negative vibes that surrounded Windows 8. Windows 10 ended up being a blend of what people liked about Windows 7 with some of the aspects of Windows 8 that were supportive of the goal of running across a wide spectrum of Microsoft devices, including those with touch screens.

Advantages of Windows 10 that it carried over from Windows 8 include a significantly faster boot-up time than Windows 7, better hardware acceleration, faster navigation between apps, and even a little better battery life for mobile devices.

Windows 7 included a search function on the Start menu. Windows 10 has a separate search box, which in addition to searching the device's storage, will also search Windows Store apps and the Web.

Another significant improvement over Windows 7 is an upgraded File Explorer, with a ribbon of controls up top and a helpful layout; frequently used folders and recent files have their own highly visible sections, and there is a familiar quick-access strip on the left-hand side.

## Differences between Windows 8 and Windows 10

The most visible difference between Windows 8 and Windows 10 is that Windows 10 has eliminated the full-screen Start screen, replacing it with the Start menu mentioned previously. The Windows 8 full-screen Start screen never made sense when used with a keyboard and mouse, slowing down operations and making it harder to find what you wanted. The Start menu that Windows 10 uses in place of the Start screen does include a small number of Live Tiles, but they are the ones you are most likely to use, rather than filling the screen with a checkerboard of tiles that you rarely use, if ever. More important, the columnar Start menu is back, with the options you are most likely to need being displayed.

## New Capabilities of Windows 10

The most significant new capability of Windows 10 stems from the fact that you can develop universal applications with it. This means that the code for a Windows Phone app is the same as that for a Windows PC app or even a HoloLens app. Different hardware platforms have different displays and different capabilities, so your app needs to be able to sense what platform it is on, but once it does, it can run in a manner appropriate for that platform.

Cortana has been added to Windows 10. This personal digital assistant accepts voice commands as well as text ones. Besides answering questions for you, she also monitors your email and calendar, reminding you of new messages and upcoming appointments.

## Summary

The Windows 10 platform is a major upgrade from the versions of Windows that preceded it. In addition to a more intuitive user interface, performance improvements, and the Cortana digital assistant, it gives developers cross-platform operation for their apps.

# CHAPTER 3

■ ■ ■

# The Universal Windows Platform (UWP)

Windows 10 represents a major departure from previous versions of Windows. A number of different devices run Windows 10 with a variety of different form factors and characteristics, ranging from phones to desktop PCs and everything in between. For the first time since there has been such a diversity of devices, one operating system runs on all of the different platforms. This means that an application written to run on one Windows 10 device could potentially run on all of them. The HoloLens runs a variant of Windows 10 named Windows Holographic. When you develop for Windows Holographic, you can access and activate all of the capabilities of the HoloLens.

## Device Families

One of the biggest objections to the Windows 8 user interface was the removal of the Start menu, which had been standard in previous versions of Windows, and replacing it with Live Tiles. Live Tiles are great for devices with touch screens but make things harder for desktops and laptops that rely on a mouse or touchpad. In Windows 10, the Start menu returns, but in a different form.

Rather than targeting an app at an operating system (Windows 10), developers now should target their app at a specific device family. Devices that are similar to each other are clustered together into families. All the devices in one family share some capabilities with all the devices in the other families, but they also share some additional capabilities with the other devices in their own family. Thus, if you write to the common core APIs that are common to all families, your app will run anywhere. If you want to take advantage of the special capabilities of the devices in a particular family, you can do so with the extended APIs that are specific to that family. To run on devices in families that do not share those particular extended APIs, you will need to make your build or app adaptive.

This new architecture impacts how apps are written in the following ways:

- One app can be run across multiple device families, which means it must be able to adapt to the characteristics of whichever device it is running on.

- The form that user inputs take may vary from one device family to another. The app must be able to handle the input forms that are allowed on the devices that it runs on.

- Only one SDK and one set of tools is needed to support all the devices that run Windows 10.

- There is only one Windows store, which is where apps for all Windows 10 devices are sold.

- There is only one Dev Center, which is where information and tools for Windows 10 app development may be obtained.

© Allen G. Taylor 2016
A. G. Taylor, *Develop Microsoft HoloLens Apps Now*, DOI 10.1007/978-1-4842-2202-7_3

The granddaddy of device families is the desktop computer family. It features a multiplicity of screen resolutions, some of which are larger than what you will find in other device families. Other families include the mobile device family, the Xbox Live device family, the IoT (Internet of Things) device family, the IoT headless device family, and of course the holographic device family. Overseeing all of these is the Universal device family (Figure 3-1).

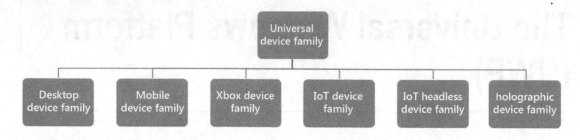

***Figure 3-1.*** *The Windows 10 device families*

# The Universal Device Family

The Universal device family is the parent of all the specific device families. The set of APIs in the Universal device family are inherited by all the child device families. This means that if you restrict your app to using only the APIs of the Universal device family, it will run on any Windows 10 device, regardless of which device family it belongs to. Each child device family adds its own specific APIs to those it inherits from the Universal device family in order to enable functionality that is specific to that device family. Your app can run across family boundaries by using adaptive code that detects the family of the device it is running on and calls the APIs that are appropriate for that family. In this way, your app may have different capabilities, depending on the family of the device it is running on. The set of APIs your app uses, both universal and specific, will determine on which devices the app can be installed. If you are targeting multiple device families, you can enclose the invocation of features specific to a device family within a conditional statement. The API in question will only be invoked if the app is running on a device that supports it.

Because an app designed to run on the Universal device family can run on any Windows 10 device, the app must have a highly adaptable user interface that can conform to the form factor and characteristics of whatever device it is running on. It must also be able to accept input from a full range of input devices, including keyboard, mouse, pen, touch screen, voice, and more.

# Developing for a Specific Device Family

When you choose to develop primarily for a specific device family, you can call the APIs that are specific to that device family unconditionally. The app will run on all the devices in that family. To run on devices in other families, the APIs specific to those other families must be enclosed in conditional statements that only allow access to those APIs when running on devices in those other families.

For example, when developing for the mobile device family, you must include APIs that are specific to mobile devices, such as phones and tablets, but you need not include the APIs for input devices that are not found on those devices.

You should note that an app developed for the IoT device family can only be installed on IoT devices. That being the case, it can assume all IoT APIs are present, and there is no need to include APIs for any other device family.

# The Holographic Device Family

The HoloLens device is the first representative of the holographic device family. Although the HoloLens relies primarily on gaze, gesture, and voice for user input, it also can accept input from other input devices, such as a mouse, and other Windows 10 devices that are not in the holographic device family can accept input from gaze, gesture, and voice—assuming, of course, that they have a way of sensing those inputs.

Because the experience of using the HoloLens is so different from the experience of using any of the devices in the other device families, the HoloLens app developer's job in many cases will be easier than that of developers of apps for other device families. The HoloLens developer can concentrate of running on HoloLens, since although a HoloLens app may be run on other devices, it will not give the user anything like the same experience. At this point, no other device can track gaze, and PCs, tablets, and phones don't track gestures either.

- When you write an app, you target device families rather than an OS. The members of a device family will have common APIs, system characteristics, and behaviors. Your app can be written specifically for the devices you intend it to run on.

- All UWP apps are packaged and distributed as AppX packages. This standardized distribution and installation mechanism ensures a smooth deployment and update experience.

- Although there are multiple device families on the Universal Windows Platform, a set of core APIs will run on all of them. If you stick to those core APIs with your applications, they will run on any Windows 10 device.

- In addition to the core APIs, there are specialized APIs for each device family. If your app is intended for a specific device family, you can invoke a device's full functionality, making use of the extension SDK that gives you the tools you need in order to use the specialized APIs.

# Summary

The HoloLens is radically different from any other device running Windows 10, or for that matter any other device running anything. Even so, apps written for other Windows 10 devices that stick to the core APIs will run on HoloLens with no more than a little minor tweaking. This means that users will be able to experience some of their favorite apps from other platforms in an entirely new way.

# CHAPTER 4

■ ■ ■

# The Development Edition

The HoloLens Development Edition contains almost everything you will need in order to begin developing applications for the HoloLens. The only other things you will need can be downloaded from the Web for free, including instructions on how to set up your development environment and the order in which to do it.

## Development System Requirements

The first thing that a HoloLens developer must provide is development hardware and operating software that supports HoloLens development. Required are the following:

- A 64-bit PC with a minimum of four cores, plus SLAT and DEP, that supports virtualization in its BIOS
- Windows 10 Pro or Enterprise Edition with Hyper-V virtualization support
- At least 8 GB of RAM in the PC

Windows 10 Home Edition will not work, nor will a version of Visual Studio earlier than Visual Studio 2015, Update 3.

## The Development Edition

As shown in Figure 4-1, the Microsoft HoloLens Development Edition includes:

- HoloLens device
- Clicker
- USB cable and power supply
- Extra nosepiece
- Startup instruction booklet (not pictured)
- Carrying case

© Allen G. Taylor 2016
A. G. Taylor, *Develop Microsoft HoloLens Apps Now*, DOI 10.1007/978-1-4842-2202-7_4

***Figure 4-1.*** *Microsoft HoloLens Development Edition*

It may seem like you are not getting very much for your $3,000 purchase price, but this is really all you need. Everything else required to get you up and running as a HoloLens developer can be downloaded for free from the Web. In addition to the things you can download, the Windows Holographic Developer Forum is an invaluable resource. No matter what problem you run into, there is probably someone on the forum who has encountered it and solved it already. Developers are happy to share their experiences.

# Required Tools

Aside from the Development Edition itself, you will need to install Visual Studio 2015 Update 3. The Community Edition of this development tool can be downloaded from Microsoft's MSDN Web site for free. You will also require the latest version of the special edition of the Unity platform, which includes support for holographic development not normally found in the standard version.

Before your Development Edition arrives, you can use the HoloLens Emulator on your development machine. You can become familiar with the process of creating, building, and deploying applications. Even after your HoloLens arrives, using the Emulator will enable you to iterate builds and debug your code quickly without having to load your app onto the HoloLens headset every time you make a change.

Microsoft's Holographic Academy has a sequence of tutorials that introduces you to the controls that you will need to build into your apps to give them their functionality. After completing the setup steps and going through the tutorials, you will be in a position to start developing your own holographic applications for the HoloLens.

A tool that is not strictly required but can potentially be helpful to developers is Visual Studio Tools for Unity (VSTU), which can be downloaded at `https://visualstudiogallery.msdn.microsoft.com/8d26236e-4a64-4d64-8486-7df95156aba9`

# Summary

This chapter provides an overview of what is included in the HoloLens Development Edition as well as the software tools that you will need in order to start developing applications. Chapter 5 will go into detail on exactly what is needed and how to get it all working. The holographic development tutorials available on Microsoft's online Holographic Academy take you step by step through the major features and capabilities of the HoloLens and of holographic development.

# CHAPTER 5

# Getting Started with HoloLens Development

To create holographic applications, you will need an appropriately equipped development machine. This means you need a Windows 10 PC, but not just any old Windows 10 PC. You will need to be able to run the HoloLens Emulator, which will run on a virtual machine that is running under your primary operating system. You need the Emulator so that you can test your code as soon as you make an update or change without having to upload it to a HoloLens every time. You will also want a system with a fast enough processor and sufficient memory. Here's what you will need:

- 64-bit Windows 10 in the Pro, Enterprise, or Education Edition. The Home Edition does not support virtualization with Hyper-V.

- A CPU with four or more cores, or multiple CPUs with a total of at least four cores.

- 8 GB or more of RAM

- A BIOS where the following features are supported and enabled:

  - Hardware-assisted virtualization

  - Second Level Address Translation (SLAT)

  - Hardware-based Data Execution Prevention (DEP)

- Supported GPU with the following:

  - DirectX 11.0 or later

  - WDDM 1.2 driver or later

## Configuring Your Windows 10 Computer for Development

To develop holographic applications for HoloLens, you need a sufficiently powerful PC, which must be a 64-bit (X64) model with at least 8 GB of RAM, sufficient storage to hold not only the Developers Kit and all the associated tools, but also whatever media you will be creating as a project. In addition, make sure that your video card is compatible with Windows 10. Not all of them are.

© Allen G. Taylor 2016
A. G. Taylor, *Develop Microsoft HoloLens Apps Now*, DOI 10.1007/978-1-4842-2202-7_5

## Confirm that your computer BIOS supports HoloLens development

Even if your computer supports virtualization, that support is probably disabled by default. This is controlled by an option switch in the BIOS. Boot up your computer and interrupt the boot process to enter the BIOS control panel. Terminology differs from one computer manufacturer to another, but there should be an option somewhere for you to either enable or disable virtualization. Be sure this is set to Enable and then save the new setting.

## Install Hyper-V support

It is not enough to have the BIOS enable virtualization. The operating system must enable it too. Once again, the default is for virtualization to be disabled. To enable virtualization at the Windows 10 level, enter "Windows Features" into the Search/Cortana box. This will display the Windows Features window shown in Figure 5-1.

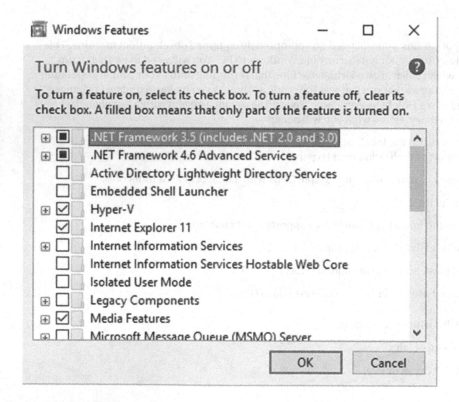

***Figure 5-1.*** *Windows Features window*

Make sure the **Hyper-V** box is checked, as shown in the figure, then click on OK to set the feature on.

## Enable Developer mode on your development machine

When in Developer mode, Windows 10 turns on some capabilities that you will need. By default, Developer mode is turned off, so you will have to turn it on. Here's how:

- From the Start menu, select **Settings**.

- In the window that appears, select **Update & Security**.

- From the menu on the left edge, select **For developers**.

- Select **Developer mode**.

Figure 5-2 shows what you want to see.

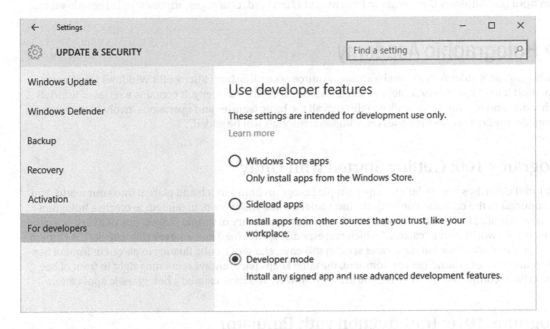

***Figure 5-2.*** *You must be in Developer mode to develop apps for HoloLens*

## Install Visual Studio 2015 Community Edition, Update 3

Update 3 of Visual Studio 2015 contains support for building holographic apps. Previous versions may not work for what we are trying to do. Make sure you have at least Visual Studio Update 2. All editions are supported, including the Community Edition, which can be downloaded for free from Microsoft or from www.visualstudio.com.

## Install the HoloLens Emulator

Within the Resources Setup folder, find the Emulator folder, and from it launch EmulatorSetup.exe.

After the successful completion of all of the preceding operations in the order described, your development machine will be ready to start developing holographic apps for the HoloLens. You will want to get your apps running consistently and flawlessly on the HoloLens Emulator before uploading the app to your HoloLens device. If there is a problem with your app, it will be a lot easier to diagnose and fix with the Emulator than it would be with the HoloLens.

App development is accomplished with a combination of Unity, Visual Studio 2015, and the HoloLens Emulator. Creating an app in Unity, building it in Visual Studio, and deploying it to the Emulator is a complex process that is easy to do incorrectly. A large number of operations must be done correctly and in the right order in order for your efforts to be crowned with success.

## Install Unity

The version of Unity that you need includes special features that specifically support HoloLens development. If you already have Unity on your development machine, you will want to replace it with the one that is specifically for use with the HoloLens. You can have both on the same machine. Just be sure you launch the correct one when you want to work on a holographic app. You can download the holographic version from the Windows Dev Center or from `https://unity3d.com/pages/windows/hololens#download`.

# The Holographic Academy

The Holographic Academy is a virtual learning resource accessible from Microsoft's Windows Dev Center. You can find it at `https://dev.windows.com/en-us/holographic/academy`. It contains a series of tutorials in both video and text form that walk you through all the basic features and operations involved in creating a holographic application. As time goes on, additional tutorials will be added.

## Holograms 100: Getting Started with Unity

This tutorial describes how to build a super-simple hologram from scratch and place it into your world. You are introduced to the combination of Unity and Visual Studio, which work in tandem to create a hologram that you will be able to see with a HoloLens. Unity includes a library of simple shapes, one of which is a cube. Unity views the world with a "camera," which corresponds to the HoloLens wearer's point of view. A camera on the HoloLens takes in what the wearer sees. In this case, she sees a cube floating in air out in front of her. As the wearer moves around her environment, the cube keeps pace, always remaining right in front of her. Once you have completed this tutorial, you are on your way. You have created a holographic application.

## Holograms 101e: Introduction with Emulator

This tutorial gives you a step-by-step procedure to create, build, and deploy a holographic application to the HoloLens Emulator. The application, named Origami, is built up from pre-existing assets, including holograms and C# scripts. The tutorial is about combining those assets into a complete and functioning application. Using the Emulator enables a developer to create and iterate versions without having to export repeatedly to a HoloLens device. This is particularly helpful in situations where there are more developers working than there are available HoloLens devices.

The process of creating, building, and deploying an application is highly detailed, so a developer new to HoloLens development will save much time and avoid frustration by following this tutorial carefully. In addition to creating holographic objects, this tutorial covers interacting with those objects with gaze, gesture, and voice. It also adds an audio component to the objects with spatial sound and enables the user to place the objects in one of several sample "rooms" with spatial mapping.

---

■ **Warning**   Even if you follow the procedure in the tutorial *very* carefully, it is all too easy to misunderstand an instruction, miss a step, or do something slightly out of the specified order. Sometimes this will not cause a problem. However, at other times it can suck you into a frustrating spiral of incomprehensible failure modes that differ from one attempt at progress to the next. If this happens to you, the best thing to do is abandon the project you have been working on and download the tutorial files afresh to a new directory, then start from scratch.

---

## Holograms 101: Introduction with HoloLens Device

This tutorial is exactly like the Holograms 101e tutorial, except for the fact that you deploy the Origami app to your HoloLens device rather than to the HoloLens Emulator. The create and build portions of the procedure are identical to what they are in Holograms 101e. After you deploy Origami to your HoloLens, you will be able to see it in front of you, then walk around it and see it from every angle. You will also be able to interact with it via gaze, gesture, and voice. Spatial sound and spatial mapping will now operate in the real room that you are physically in.

■ **Note**    Before you can deploy your first app to your HoloLens, you will need to identify it to your development machine with its IP address. How to do this is described later, in the section titled "Setting Up the HoloLens."

## Holograms 210: Gaze

Gaze is one of the three ways in which a HoloLens user communicates with the app running on her device. The other two are gesture and voice, which are covered in Holograms 211 and 212, respectively. This tutorial displays an astronaut in a space suit floating out in space. You can add gaze functionality incrementally as you alternate between adding scripts and deploying the result to your HoloLens. Observe the result of each change to make sure you have not introduced any bugs from one deployment to the next.

■ **Note**    Although the tutorials in the 200 series—none of which are designed for use with the HoloLens Emulator—do not include the letter *e* as tutorial 101e does, you can deploy them to the Emulator if you do not have ready access to a HoloLens device. The Emulator cannot tell where your gaze is directed, nor can it see any gestures that you make. Nonetheless, deploying to the Emulator will tell you whether the app you are building is basically working. After you have added all the pieces to the app, deploying to the HoloLens will enable you to test full functionality.

■ **Tip**    As of this writing, a deployment will sometimes abort with an error message, preventing you from continuing. Depending on what caused the problem, you may be able to get around this. Without disconnecting your HoloLens (or, if you are deploying to the HoloLens Emulator, without exiting the emulator), try deploying again by selecting **Debug/Start without Debugging** in Visual Studio. Oftentimes, the deployment will work on the second try, and sometimes on the third.

You can indicate where the user is looking by adding a cursor to your app. When the cursor is located on a hologram, your app can cause a change of some kind to the hologram. C# scripts, such as GazeManager. cs and CursorManager.cs, provide functionality. Additional scripts, such as InteractibleManager.cs, Interactible.cs, and InteractibleAction.cs, provide interactivity. The source code for these scripts is provided with the tutorial, so you can modify the code as you desire to see how behavior changes.

## Holograms 211: Gesture

This tutorial is a continuation of HoloGrams 210, adding gesture functionality and also exercising voice commands a little bit. As noted previously, if you are deploying to the HoloLens Emulator, it cannot see any hand gestures that you might make. You can, however, see whether all expected elements are present, and you can exercise a couple of voice commands, observing how the app responds to them.

## Holograms 212: Voice

Aside from gaze and gesture, the other way a HoloLens user can affect the holograms she sees is with voice. The HoloLens includes a microphone so that the user can issue voice commands. This tutorial tells how to configure an app so that the microphone is active. It also describes how to write apps so that they respond to voice commands. As with the gaze and gesture tutorials, the app shows an astronaut floating in space. The user can speak to the astronaut with verbal messages as well as send commands to the app to cause it to perform various functions.

---

■ **Tip**    To maximize the chance that the voice-recognition mechanism correctly interprets what you say, be sure to speak clearly and distinctly. Use common rather than obscure words. Use multisyllabic commands, which are easier to differentiate from other communications, and avoid the use of any of the reserved words, such as *Select*, which is used to perform an action on whichever hologram element currently has the focus of the user's gaze.

---

## Holograms 220: Spatial Sound

Seeing holograms as three-dimensional objects in your world can put you in the middle of the action. Hearing sounds that appear to be coming from them makes them seem even more real. Adding to the sense of reality is what spatial sound is all about.

In the real world, we know where a sound is coming from because the sound waves coming from a sound source arrive at one of our ears before arriving at the other ear. Our brains do some math and determine where in space the sound is coming from. This is the basis for traditional stereophonic sound systems. The sound coming out of the speaker on your left hits your left ear before it hits your right ear, and because it is closer, it is a little louder in the left ear than in the right. Correspondingly, the sound coming out of the speaker on your right hits your right ear sooner and is louder than what your left ear hears.

Spatial sound one-ups stereo by making the virtual sound environment sound much more like sounds you would hear coming from real sound sources. Unlike stereo, where to hear the best sound you must sit midway between the left and right speakers, with spatial sound you can move around in a room and, no matter where you are, the sound you hear appears to be coming from the locations of the holograms that are generating those sounds. As you move toward a sound source, what you hear becomes louder. As you move away, it becomes fainter. If the sound source is on your left, when you turn toward it, not only does the hologram that is generating it become centered in your field of view, but also the sound it is making seems to be coming from right in front of you.

This tutorial demonstrates the difference between stereo sound and spatial sound and leads you to turn toward the place where a sound seems to be coming from. Since you can't actually touch a hologram and feel anything, audio cues can instead inform you when you have selected a holographic object or when your hand has come into view or made a gesture.

One cool thing you could do is place yourself in the middle of a holographic symphony orchestra. If you want to hear more from the violins, you could walk over toward the string section. Their part would get louder and the percussion would get softer. Spatial sound could provide an opportunity to experience music in new and entirely different ways. As an audience member, you could not walk into the middle of a symphony orchestra or your favorite rock band, but if a holographic recording of a performance has been made, you could.

## Holograms 230: Spatial Mapping

Spatial mapping is the technology that enables a HoloLens to place holographic objects into the context of the real world. By making a scan of its surroundings, the HoloLens learns where the walls, floor, and ceiling are, as well as any furniture or other objects that are in the room. This enables holographic characters to sit on your sofa and place their drink on your coffee table. It also, for example, enables you to see holographic pointers and highlights on the automatic transmission you are trying to reassemble in your Automotive 131 class.

Spatial mapping is the key technology that produces the illusion that holographic objects are actually present in the real world. You can control how detailed you want a scan to be. The more detailed the scan, the more accurate the placement of holograms and the more convincing the illusion will be. However, there is a tradeoff in performance. The more detailed the scan, the longer it will take to complete it. On the plus side, once you have scanned a room in detail, you don't have to do another full scan the next time you enter that room. You need only update the things that have changed.

Once you have scanned an area, you can alter its appearance with one of the shaders in Unity. Once an area has been scanned and shaded, processing can be used to simplify the representation with no loss of realism. This reduces the number of calculations that must be made to keep the representation of the room up to date, reducing the processing load and thus improving performance.

Another calculation illustrated in this tutorial determines whether a hologram will fit into a spot in the real world without colliding with something. It's not cool if you place a holographic character into a chair that a real person is already sitting on.

Occlusion is also covered in this tutorial. If a hologram is located behind a real object in the room, you should not be able to see it. However, when it passes in front of such an object, it should remain visible. This means that the HoloLens must know how far away things are as well as where they are so as to know how much of a hologram to show as it moves out from behind a real-world object.

## Holograms 240: Sharing Holograms

One of the really useful aspects of the mixed reality that HoloLens provides is the fact that you can share a virtual landscape with someone who could be miles away from you, provided you are both hooked into the Internet and both wearing a HoloLens. This is accomplished by establishing a reference point and then sharing coordinates with everyone who will be sharing in the experience. The leader of the experience will scan her environment and all action will take place in that environment. Other participants will appear as avatars in the scanned space. Real-world physics will apply, with moving holograms bouncing off walls and other surfaces when they encounter them. All participants will be able to interact with the holograms using gaze, gesture, and voice. Beyond multiplayer games, this capability can also be used in educational situations or conferences. The possibilities are virtually limitless. (No pun intended.)

# Development with Unity

Unity, well known to developers as a game-development platform, is the primary tool for developing HoloLens applications of all types. The standard Unity toolchain and pipeline have been updated to incorporate support for HoloLens functions such as gaze, gesture, and voice input as well as spatial mapping, spatial audio, and the ability to anchor holographic objects to specific locations in the real world. Unity is the main toolset endorsed and recommended by Microsoft for the development of HoloLens applications. Direct3D is the API used with Unity for HoloLens application development.

# The Windows Device Portal

The Windows Device Portal is the channel through which your development PC communicates with your HoloLens. To set up this connection, you must pair the devices. This is a fairly involved procedure, which I will walk you through in the next several sections.

## Setting up the HoloLens

Although you can do quite a bit of learning and even app development using the HoloLens Emulator on your development PC, at some point you will want to start using your HoloLens device. In order to do that, you will need to establish a communication link between your HoloLens and your development PC using the Windows Device Portal.

To start the setup procedure, power up your HoloLens device and put it on. Then follow these steps:

1. With you hand clearly in your field of view, perform the bloom gesture, which is a hand with fingers pinched together that then opens like the petals of a flower, with the fingers splayed apart. This should start the operating system and display the Start Pins menu shown in Figure 5-3.

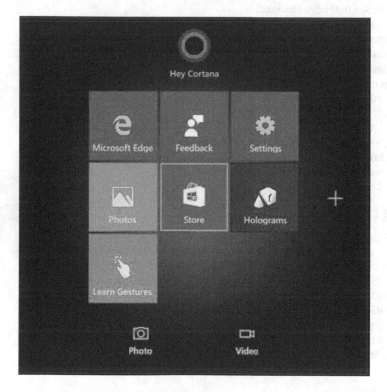

***Figure 5-3.*** *Start Pins menu*

2. Gaze at the Settings tile in the upper-right corner and perform the air tap gesture to select it. You perform the air tap gesture by holding your thumb and your index finger apart and then bringing them together. This launches the Settings app. When the cursor is over a tile that can be selected, it will be shaped like a torus or doughnut. Otherwise, it will just be a dot of light.

3. Select the **Update menu** item.

4. Select **For developers**. This will display the screen shown in Figure 5-4.

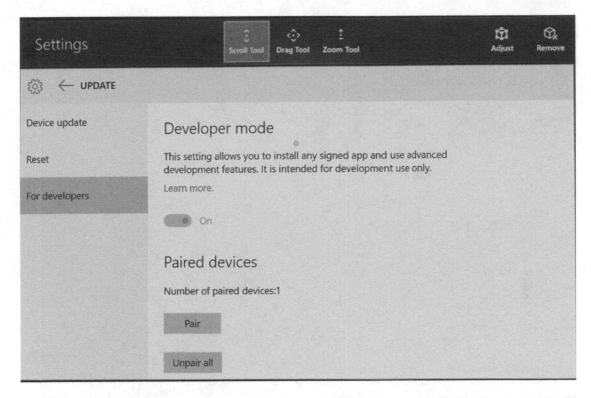

*Figure 5-4.* *HoloLens setup*

5.  Make sure that the Developer mode switch is set to the On position.

6.  Scroll down below the Paired devices section (below what is shown in Figure 5-4) and make sure the Device Portal switch is set to the On position.

## Connecting the HoloLens to the development machine

There are two ways to connect your HoloLens to your development PC: over Wi-Fi or via a USB cable. At least one of these is necessary, of course, so that you can upload the app that you have developed to your HoloLens.

### Connecting via Wi-Fi

Before you can upload your app to a HoloLens using Wi-Fi, you must connect your HoloLens to the Wi-Fi network. Here's the procedure for doing that:

1.  Perform the bloom gesture to display the Start Pins main menu.

2.  Select the Settings app in the upper-right-hand corner.

3.  When the Settings menu appears, gaze at the Network & Internet symbol and select it with an air tap.

4.  Make sure Wi-Fi is turned on, as shown in Figure 5-5.

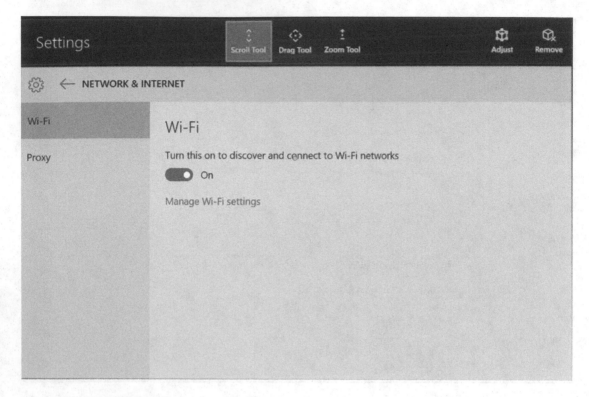

***Figure 5-5.*** *Turn on Wi-Fi discovery and connection*

5. Select the network you want to connect to.

6. If needed, enter the network password.

7. Find the HoloLens's IPv4 IP address. You can do this by finding it under Settings ➤ Network & Internet ➤ Wi-Fi ➤ Advanced Options.

---

■ **Warning**    Some Microsoft documentation says that you can also get this IP address by asking Cortana to give it to you by saying "Hey Cortana, what is my IP address?" As of this writing, this is incorrect. The IP address that Cortana gives you is not the one you need. Use the one given by the Settings menu.

---

8. From your PC's web browser, go to https://<YOUR_HOLOLENS_IP_ADDRESS>

The browser will probably display a message similar to "There is a problem with this Website's security certificate." You can ignore this warning, since the security certificates for HoloLens are not set up during the current development phase of the product. If you continue on in spite of the warning, you will be taken to the Home screen of the Device Portal.

## Connecting via USB

Connecting your HoloLens to your development PC with a micro-USB cable is simpler than connecting over Wi-Fi. All you need to do is send your PC's Web browser to http://<YOUR_HOLOLENS_IP_ADDRESS>, as determined in the previous section.

## Identifying yourself with a username and password

The HoloLens is like any other Windows 10 PC in that it tailors what it presents to you based on who you are. That means that it must identify you based on credentials that you present to it. The credentials it looks for are a username and a password. There is a little back and forth involved in doing this:

1.  Enter the IP address of your HoloLens into a Web browser on your PC. This will bring up the Set Up Access page.

2.  Click or tap the Request Pin button. Your HoloLens will display the PIN that has been generated.

3.  Enter the PIN into the "Pin displayed on your device" textbox.

4.  Enter the username you have chosen for connecting to the Device Portal into the "New user name" textbox.

5.  Enter a password into the "New password" textbox. It must be at least seven characters long.

6.  Enter the same password into the "Confirm password" textbox.

7.  Click on the Pair button to connect the HoloLens to the Windows Device Portal.

You can always add new users or change the credentials of an existing user by following this procedure after clicking on the "Security" link in the top-right corner of the Start Pins menu and then navigating to https://<YOUR_HOLOLENS_IP_ADDRESS>/devicesecurity.htm.

## Creating a security certificate

When a PC connects to an external device such as a HoloLens, it wants to know that it can trust that device. This trust is established with a security certificate. Each HoloLens generates a unique self-signed certificate for its SSL connection. By default, your PC will not recognize or trust this certificate and will issue a certificate error message. This situation can be remedied by uploading the certificate from the HoloLens to the PC, using either a USB cable or a Wi-Fi link. Once the PC trusts the certificate, you can securely connect the two devices.

---

■ **Warning**   If you make this trusted connection over Wi-Fi, be sure that it is a connection you trust. Among other things, that means don't establish the trust relationship over a Starbucks Wi-Fi network or any other unsecured network.

---

Here's the procedure:

1.  Download your HoloLens's security certificate from the Security page, which is accessed by clicking on the Security tab on the Device Portal's Home ribbon, shown in Figure 5-6.

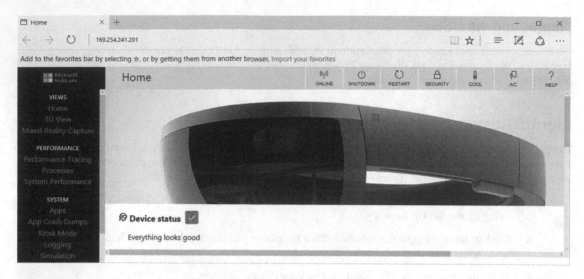

**Figure 5-6.** *Select Security from the Home ribbon*

You can also reach this page by navigating to

`https://<YOUR_HOLOLENS_IP_ADDRESS?/devicesecurity.htm`

2. Follow the directions on the Security page shown in Figure 5-7 to retrieve the security certificate you need and install it in the Trusted Root Certification Authorities store.

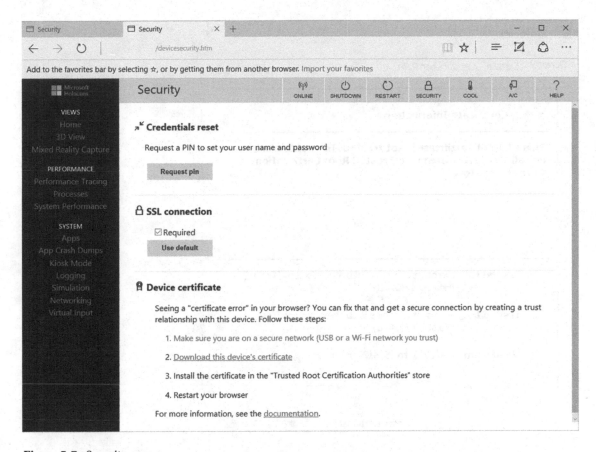

***Figure 5-7.*** *Security page*

When you download the certificate, it will appear in a window, tell you it is not yet trusted, and encourage you to install it in the Trusted Root Certification Authorities store, as shown in Figure 5-8.

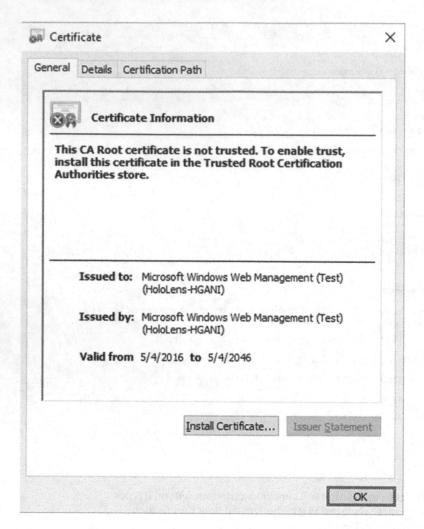

*Figure 5-8.* *Trust certificate*

3. Import the certificate using the Certificate Import Wizard, shown in Figure 5-9.

*Figure 5-9.* *Certificate Import Wizard*

4.   Restart your browser.

## Device Portal features

The Device Portal is the connecting link between your HoloLens and your development PC. It enables you to set parameters on your HoloLens and gives you a wealth of performance data as well as other information. The Device Portal consists of multiple pages, beginning with the Home page.

## Home page

The Home page, the top portion of which is shown in Figure 5-10, contains a lot of information and has text boxes into which you can enter more information.

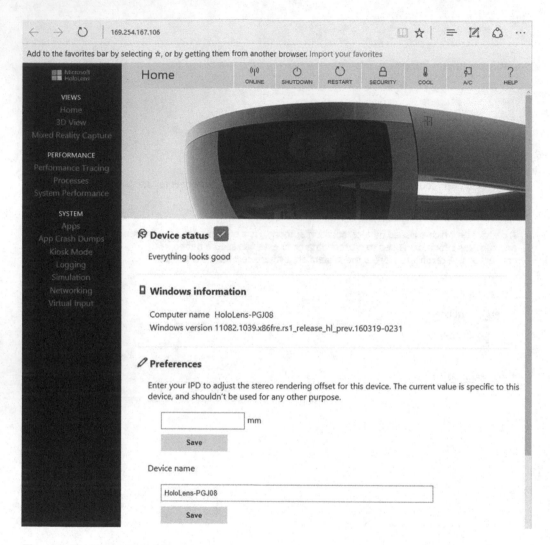

*Figure 5-10.* *Device Portal Home page*

The toolbar across the top of the page, shown in Figure 5-11, contains important indicators and controls.

*Figure 5-11.* *Device Portal toolbar*

ONLINE tells you whether your HoloLens is connected to your PC via Wi-Fi. If it indicates you are not, and you are not connected by USB cable either, then the Device Portal is not talking to your HoloLens.

SHUTDOWN turns off your HoloLens (assuming it is connected to the Device Portal by either Wi-Fi or USB cable.

RESTART reboots the HoloLens.

SECURITY opens the Device Security page, shown in Figure 5-12.

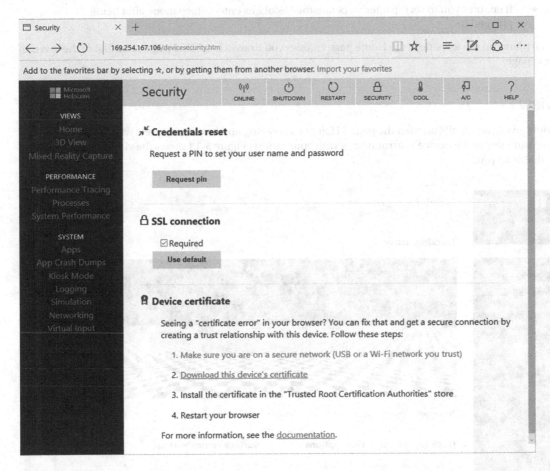

***Figure 5-12.*** *Device Security page*

On this page, you can set up a trust relationship between a user and the HoloLens and between the HoloLens and the development PC.

COOL gives you a temperature reading on the HoloLens. If it gets too hot, it will shut down, so this gives you a heads-up that perhaps you should suspend a compute-intensive activity until things cool off.

A/C tells you whether the device is plugged in and charging via its USB cable. You should be able to do that just by looking at the device, the PC, and the cable between them, but I guess this would tell you whether you have a defective cable that is not charging the device.

HELP opens the REST interface documentation page.

In addition to the toolbar, the Home page does a number of other things:

- It gives you a device status.

- It tells you the name of your HoloLens and the version of Windows it is running.

- It asks you to enter your inter-pupillary distance (IPD) in millimeters.

- It gives you the option of changing the default device name.

- It enables you to set the interval before the HoloLens enters Sleep mode after a period of inaction.

- It enables you to set the interval before the HoloLens enters Sleep mode after being plugged in.

The menu on the left side of the Home page enables you to switch to other pages. The first of these is the 3D View page.

## 3D view

This view gives you details on what the paired HoloLens is seeing and how it interprets what it sees. You can change your view of the device's surroundings with your mouse. Figure 5-13 shows the viewing options that are available to you.

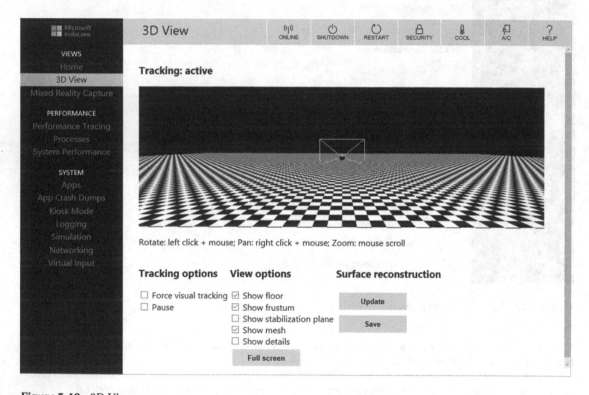

*Figure 5-13.* *3D View page*

Click on the **Force visual tracking** box to turn on continuous visual tracking. Click on the **Pause** box to turn visual tracking off. The View options determine what is displayed in the view area when tracking is active, as follows:

- Show floor: When this option is checked, the checkerboard floor is displayed.

- Show frustum: The green rectangular box shows the view frustum, which is the area within which holograms are visible to the user.

- Show stabilization plane: This shows the plane, perpendicular to the checkerboard floor, that the HoloLens uses to stabilize motion.

- Show mesh: Displays the surface mapping mesh that represents the user's surroundings.

- Show details: This option displays hand positions, head rotation quaternions, and the device origin vector as they change when the user moves her hands and head.

- Full Screen button: Expands the view of the space around the user to fill the PC's screen

Click the Update button to update the spatial mapping mesh of the area around the user. You must click the Update button to get the latest mesh from the HoloLens device. Click the Save button to save the new mesh as an obj file on the PC.

## Mixed reality capture

With HoloLens, you can not only experience a holographically augmented world in real time, you can also record the experience and replay it later. You can specify whether you want to capture holographic, video, photo, or audio information, or any combination of them. Figure 5-14 shows the media-capture options and displays any previously captured media that you can play, save, or upload to your paired PC.

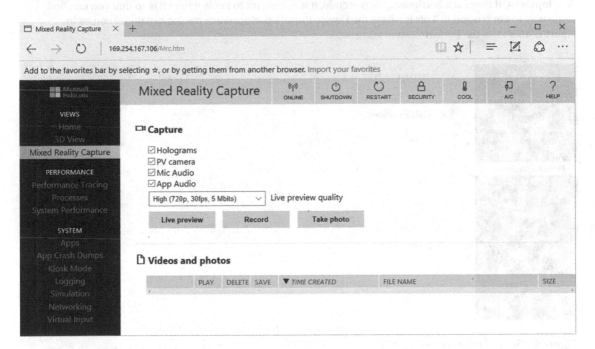

*Figure 5-14.* *Mixed Reality Capture page*

Available options include the following:

- The Holograms option enables you to capture just the holographic content of the video stream. This content is rendered in mono rather than stereo, so it will not appear doubled when viewed on the PC.

- The PV Camera option captures the full video stream from the photo/video camera.

- The Mic Audio option captures the audio signal picked up by the HoloLens microphone array.

- The App Audio option captures any audio signal generated by the app that is running.

- The "Live preview quality" dropdown menu enables you to select the screen resolution, frame rate, and streaming rate of the live preview.

If you click the Live Preview button, the capture stream will be displayed. While the live preview is running, the Live Preview button becomes the Stop Live Preview button. Clicking the Record button starts recording the mixed-reality stream. Clicking it again stops the recording. Clicking the Take Photo button captures a still image from the capture stream. Finally, the Videos and photos section at the bottom of the page lists the media that have already been captured.

## Performance tracing

To optimize the user's experience while running your HoloLens app, you want to make sure that a bottleneck in either computation, memory, storage, or I/O does not impact the performance of the app. During development, if there is a bottleneck in your code, it is important to know where it is so that you can find some way to get around it. This is where the Device Portal's performance tracing capability comes in. Figure 5-15 shows the Performance tracing page.

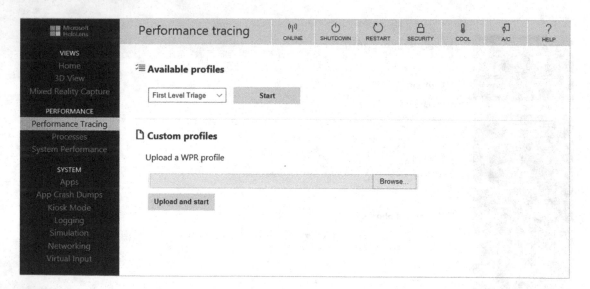

***Figure 5-15.*** *Performance tracing page*

Initially, you can run a First Level Triage trace to isolate the problem to either system activity, computation, storage, or memory. Based on what you see there, you can drill down with a more targeted trace of the part of the system that seems to be causing the problem. In addition to the standard computation, memory, and I/O profiles, you can upload a custom profile to examine the exact parameters that concern you the most.

## Processes

The Processes page, shown in Figure 5-16, lists all the processes that are currently running on the HoloLens device and what percentage of system resources each process is consuming. This can be an important clue to what might be slowing down the performance of your application.

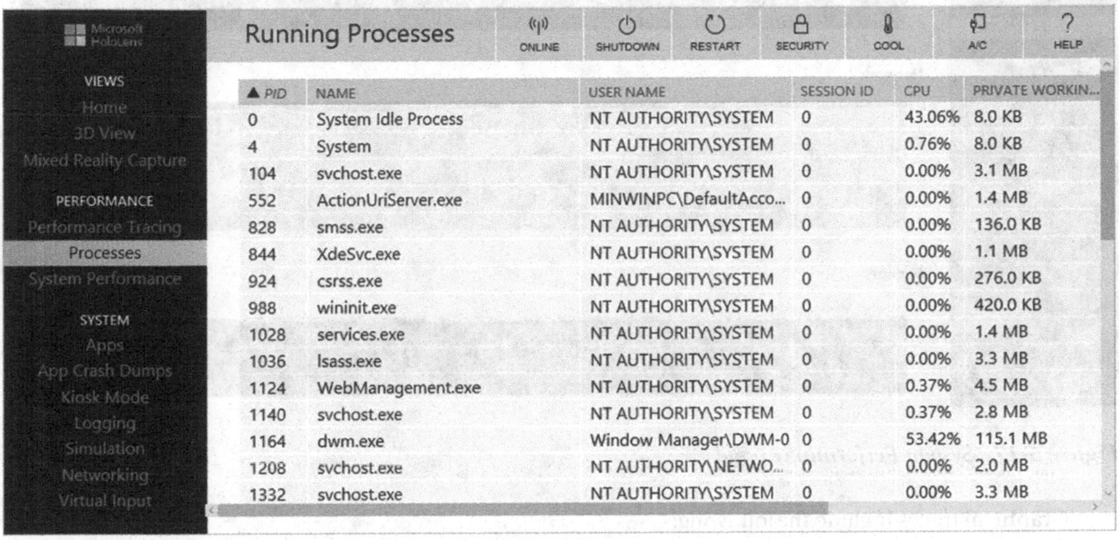
Running Processes
ONLINE
SHUTDOWN
RESTART
SECURITY
COOL
A/C
HELP
VIEWS
Home
3D View
Mixed Reality Capture
PERFORMANCE
Performance Tracing
Processes
System Performance
SYSTEM
Apps
App Crash Dumps
Kiosk Mode
Logging
Simulation
Networking
Virtual Input
PID | NAME | USER NAME | SESSION ID | CPU | PRIVATE WORKIN...
0 | System Idle Process | NT AUTHORITY\SYSTEM | 0 | 43.06% | 8.0 KB
4 | System | NT AUTHORITY\SYSTEM | 0 | 0.76% | 8.0 KB
104 | svchost.exe | NT AUTHORITY\SYSTEM | 0 | 0.00% | 3.1 MB
552 | ActionUriServer.exe | MINWINPC\DefaultAcco... | 0 | 0.00% | 1.4 MB
828 | smss.exe | NT AUTHORITY\SYSTEM | 0 | 0.00% | 136.0 KB
844 | XdeSvc.exe | NT AUTHORITY\SYSTEM | 0 | 0.00% | 1.1 MB
924 | csrss.exe | NT AUTHORITY\SYSTEM | 0 | 0.00% | 276.0 KB
988 | wininit.exe | NT AUTHORITY\SYSTEM | 0 | 0.00% | 420.0 KB
1028 | services.exe | NT AUTHORITY\SYSTEM | 0 | 0.00% | 1.4 MB
1036 | lsass.exe | NT AUTHORITY\SYSTEM | 0 | 0.00% | 3.3 MB
1124 | WebManagement.exe | NT AUTHORITY\SYSTEM | 0 | 0.37% | 4.5 MB
1140 | svchost.exe | NT AUTHORITY\SYSTEM | 0 | 0.37% | 2.8 MB
1164 | dwm.exe | Window Manager\DWM-0 | 0 | 53.42% | 115.1 MB
1208 | svchost.exe | NT AUTHORITY\NETWO... | 0 | 0.00% | 2.0 MB
1332 | svchost.exe | NT AUTHORITY\SYSTEM | 0 | 0.00% | 3.3 MB

***Figure 5-16.** Processes page*

## System performance

The System Performance page gives you a graphical snapshot, on an instant-to-instant basis, of the performance of the major components of the HoloLens device, including power usage, frame rate, CPU usage, GPU usage, I/O reads and writes, network traffic, and memory usage. Figure 5-17 shows several of these graphical traces.

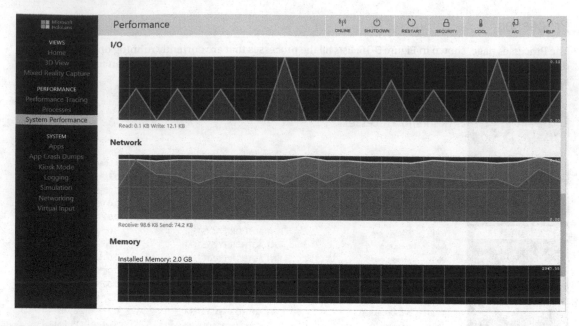

**Figure 5-17.** *System Performance page*

Graphical traces include the following:

- The SoC Power trace shows the instantaneous system-on-chip power usage, averaged over one minute.

- The System Power trace shows the instantaneous system power usage, averaged over one minute.

- The Frame Rate trace shows the number of frames per second being served, the missed VBlanks per second, and the consecutive missed VBlanks.

- The CPU trace shows the percentage of the CPU's capacity that is being used.

- The GPU trace shows the percentage of the GPU's capacity that is being used.

- The I/O trace shows the number of reads and writes being executed.

- The Network trace shows the number of bytes being received and sent over the network connection.

- The Memory trace shows the amount of memory installed and how much of it is currently in use.

## Apps

The App Manager tells you which apps are installed and which are currently running. It also is the tool you use to install a new app and to install any files that the app may depend upon. Once you have specified the new app and its dependencies, clicking the Go button will deploy it to the HoloLens. Figure 5-18 shows the App Manager page.

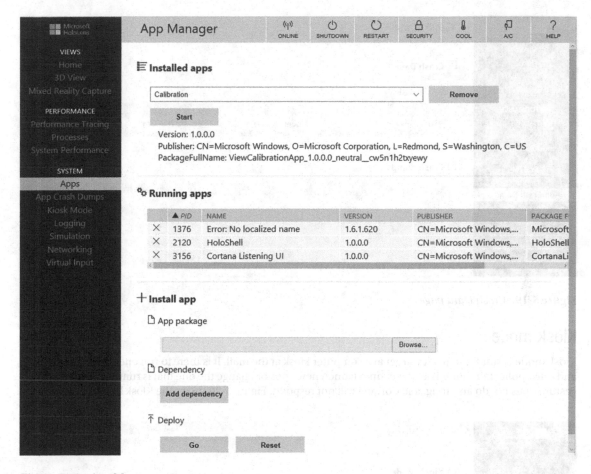

**Figure 5-18.** *App Manager page*

## App crash dumps

Sometimes you can tell what is wrong with an application by looking at a crash dump. It will at least show you the point at which the application failed, if not quite what caused the failure. Figure 5-19 shows the Crash Data page. It shows the currently running app and gives you the opportunity to specify that you want to enable the crash dump facility for that application. It also lists dumps that it has saved in the past, along with their size and when they were executed.

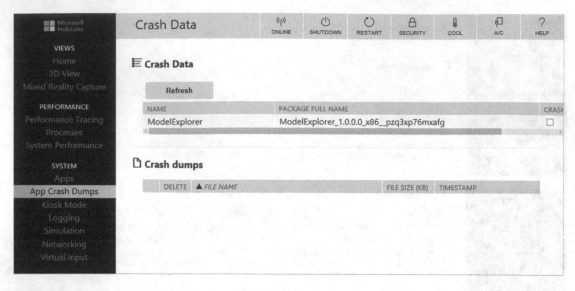

*Figure 5-19.* *Crash Data page*

# Kiosk mode

Kiosk mode is similar to what you get at a computer kiosk at the mall. It is there to run one application and one application only. The user cannot launch new apps or change the one that is running. The bloom gesture does not do anything, and Cortana will not respond. Figure 5-20 shows the Kiosk Mode page.

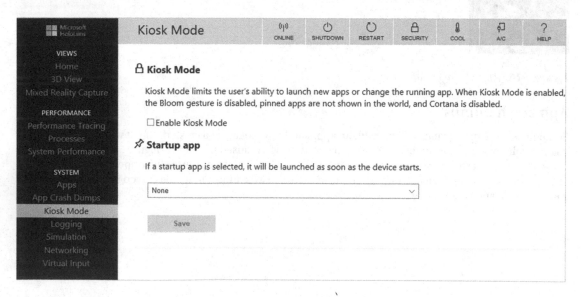

*Figure 5-20.* *Kiosk Mode page*

Checking the **Enable Kiosk Mode** box will put the HoloLens into kiosk mode. Select an app to run at startup from the "Startup app" dropdown menu and click on the Save button. The next time the HoloLens is started, it will start in Kiosk mode. It will stay in that mode until you come back to this page, uncheck the **Enable Kiosk Mode** checkbox, and then click the Save button.

---

■ **Note** Kiosk mode was removed at one point during the beta program and may not be a part of the released product. Don't count on it being available.

---

## Logging

The Realtime ETW Tracing page manages realtime Event Tracing for Windows (ETW) on the HoloLens. A wide variety of variables can be traced, chosen from a list of registered providers. Figure 5-21 shows the places where you specify which provider of data you want to use and the level of detail you want to trace to show.

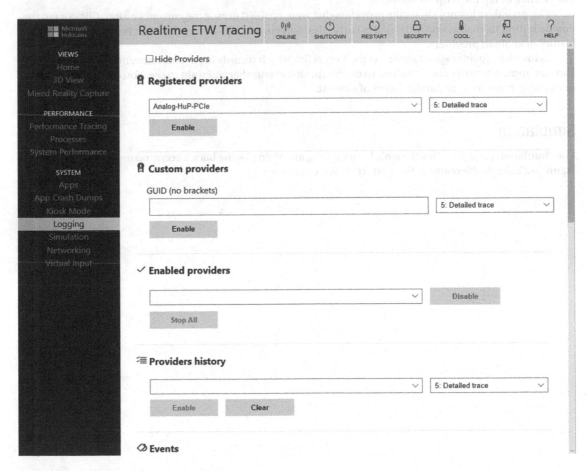

*Figure 5-21. Realtime ETW Tracing page*

From the list of registered providers, select one, along with the tracing level you want. Levels are as follows:

1. Abnormal exit or termination

2. Severe errors

3. Warnings

4. Non-error warnings

5. Detailed trace

Click or tap the Enable button to start the trace. When you do this, the registered provider you have specified is added to the "Enabled Providers" dropdown list.

Instead of a registered provider, you can specify a custom ETW provider and tracing level. Identify the provider by its GUID (Globally Unique Identifier). Don't include brackets in the GUID. Click the Enable button to add your custom provider to the list of enabled providers.

Enabled providers are providers that are actively performing a trace. To stop a trace, click or tap the Disable button, with the selected provider showing in the field to the left of the Disable button. To stop all traces, click or tap the Stop All button.

The providers history shows the providers that were enabled during the current session. Click or tap the Enable button to enable a provider that is currently disabled, and click or tap the Clear button to clear the history of enabled providers.

Below the provider specifications is the Events list, which records the events encountered by a trace. You can apply filters to events to home in on the specific events that you want to see. You can set either single or multiple criteria to sift out the events of interest.

## Simulation

The simulation page provides the tools for recording and then playing back a scene taking place in a room. Figure 5-22 shows the controls that perform these operations.

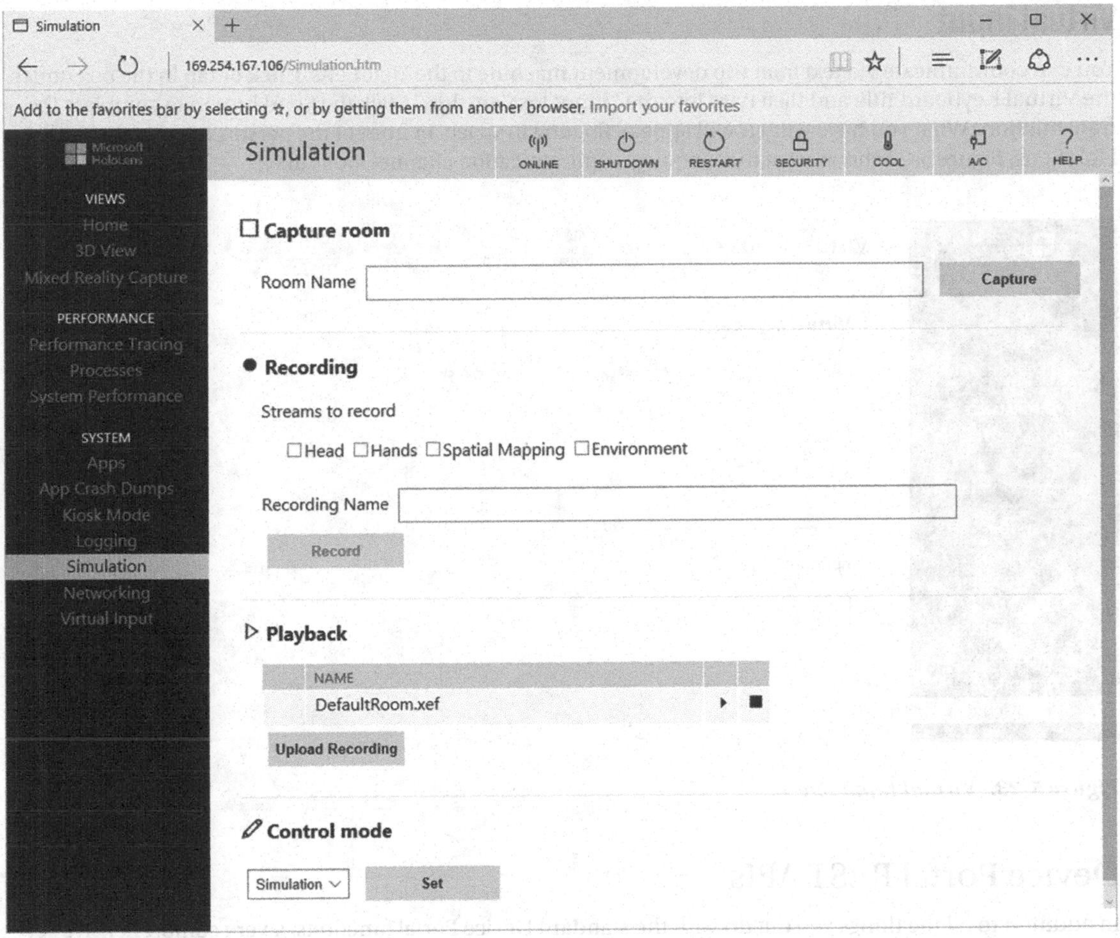

*Figure 5-22.* *Simulation page*

The HoloLens device can capture multiple streams of information with its array of sensors. It can capture the user's head movement, hand gestures, spatial-mapping information, and the visible and audible environment.

To capture a room, tick the **Capture room** box, fill in a room name, and then click on the Capture button. Specify which streams of information you want to record: Head, Hands, Spatial Mapping, or Environment. Then give the recording a name and click the Record button.

Once you have made and saved a recording, you can play it back either on the HoloLens Emulator or on the HoloLens device itself. To play it back on the HoloLens, click the Upload Recording button.

The Control mode can be in one of two possible modes: Simulation or Default. In the Simulation mode, the HoloLens sensors are disabled and the Emulator or device is playing back a recording. In the default state, sensors are enabled and functioning and no recording is being played.

## Networking

The Networking page shows the Wi-Fi network adapters available on the development PC and gives you the opportunity to select one with which to connect your HoloLens to the PC. You can also connect the two via the USB cable supplied with the HoloLens Development Kit, but that would remove the advantages of being untethered.

45

## Virtual input

You can communicate via text from the development machine to the HoloLens. Click or tap in the box under the Virtual Keyboard title and then type into the "Input text" textbox. Click the Send button to complete the transmission. What you have written will appear, floating in space, in front of the person wearing the paired HoloLens. Figure 5-23 shows what this one-way communication channel looks like.

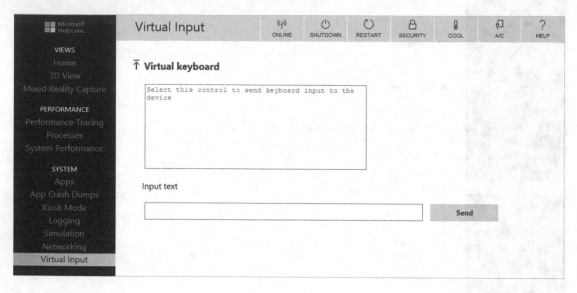

***Figure 5-23.*** *Virtual Input screen*

## Device Portal REST APIs

In addition to all the things you can do with the standard Device Portal functions, a very comprehensive set of APIs gives you fine-grained control over just about every aspect of HoloLens operation that you might want to affect.

# Summary

This chapter gives you detailed instructions on what hardware and software you need in order to create holographic applications and describes how to install and configure them. It introduces you to the tutorials available on Microsoft's online Holographic Academy and describes the intricacies of connecting your HoloLens to your development PC. The Device Portal is a source of a wealth of information about the performance of your HoloLens as well as a means of passing applications back and forth between the HoloLens and the development PC.

Once you have set up the hardware, gone through all the tutorials, and explored the nooks and crannies of the HoloLens that are described here, you are ready to move forward and tackle a real project. That is what Part II of this book is all about–creating and building applications. The first step in that journey is to select a project to tackle.

**PART II**

# Building Apps

# CHAPTER 6

■ ■ ■

# Choosing a Project to Tackle

Since you are reading this book, it's a pretty good bet that you would like to develop applications that will run on the Microsoft HoloLens. The HoloLens is an exciting platform with potential applications that nobody has thought of yet. This is a ground-floor opportunity for software developers. The $3,000 price tag for a Developer's Kit means that a mass-market consumer version of the HoloLens is probably several years away. In the meantime, there are plenty of enterprise-level use cases for a device that can embed realistic three-dimensional holograms into the user's surroundings. Retailers can use the technology to help customers visualize how a product would look in their home, changing colors or features at will. The educational and training applications are many. Holographic images of complex objects, such as jet engines, can be examined in detail and even disassembled to enable scrutiny of individual parts. Step-by-step maintenance and repair operations can be practiced with a holographic representation superimposed on top of a device, requiring minimal intervention from a human instructor.

The application you choose to develop for your first project will probably depend to some extent on the kinds of applications that you have developed in the past. Microsoft initially envisioned the HoloLens as a game platform and entertainment device. They worked with the Unity development environment, popular with game developers, to create the tools for developing holographic applications for the HoloLens. As a result, the first people to get excited about the possibilities opened up by the HoloLens were game developers. With the HoloLens, game action, rather than being restricted to the flat panel of a video screen, can take place in a full three dimensions in a room, a series of rooms, or even outdoors. HoloLens is a good platform not only for any of the traditional types of games that people are accustomed to, but also for entirely new types of games that have yet to be conceived.

## It Isn't All About Games

Although game developers were among the first to get excited about the potential of the HoloLens, use cases in business, government, research, and education may have a greater impact than games do. Two HoloLens devices are already in use on the International Space Station. Currently, walking an astronaut through a complex maintenance procedure via an audio uplink from Mission Control is time consuming and subject to error. An astronaut wearing a HoloLens would be able to see right in front of her what needs to be done, and see how the holograms she sees mesh with the physical device she is working on.

## The First Applications: Industrial, Commercial, and Educational

The first release of the HoloLens is the $3,000 Developer Edition. As we are still at the beginning, there are only a handful of apps available, so it is doubtful that many end users would buy one. However, there is quite a bit of diversity among developers. Some developers will be game developers who work for

© Allen G. Taylor 2016
A. G. Taylor, *Develop Microsoft HoloLens Apps Now*, DOI 10.1007/978-1-4842-2202-7_6

large game-development companies. Others will be independent game developers who sense a ground-floor opportunity. Some will be non-game-application developers who envision business or educational applications that would benefit from the ability to interact with both virtual and physical objects.

## Industrial applications

A new product design, such as an automobile drive train, can be walked around and viewed from all angles before any metal is actually bent. This can save time and money by reducing the number of times a prototype must be rebuilt. Figure 6-1 shows such a design at the Volvo design center.

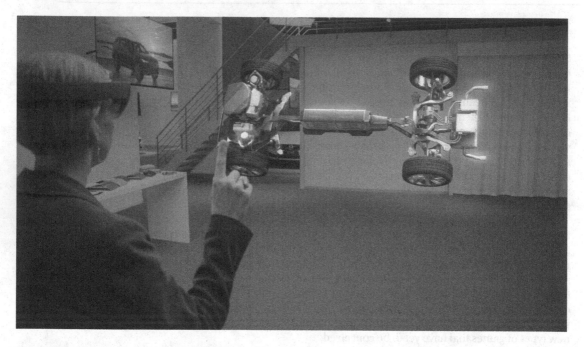

**Figure 6-1.** *Examining a prototype drive train*

In many different work situations, an employee must perform a complex procedure of some kind. If she hasn't performed this particular procedure in a while, she may have to refer to written work instructions or a procedure manual. This entails looking back and forth between the instructions and the item she is working on. Sometimes it is not crystal clear how the text in the manual relates to what must be done. If it were possible to show exactly what needs to be done, step by step, with both a virtual representation and the physical object right in front of the worker, there would be much less possibility of error and the job could be completed more quickly, perhaps much more quickly. Figure 6-2 shows both virtual information and a physical car door directly in front of an automotive assembly worker.

**Figure 6-2.** *HoloLens on the assembly line*

An even bigger advantage occurs if a technical expert at a remote location can Skype in to the on-site employee and see exactly what the on-site employee is looking at. It is almost like having the expert looking over the employee's shoulder and giving step-by-step instructions on what to do to complete the operation at hand. Since the HoloLens is a fully functional Windows 10 computer with a built-in video camera, it can easily support this kind of cooperative operation.

## Commercial applications

In a sales situation, "try before you buy" gives a potential customer a much better idea of what a product would actually be like than would be possible from seeing the product on a store shelf, a catalog page, or a Web site screen. In an early commercial application, Microsoft is partnering with the Lowe's home improvement chain to help sell kitchen remodeling. The HoloLens-wearing customer enters a relatively bare showroom, and holograms show various configurations and textures of countertops, tables, and cabinets, all at actual size. People can see, rather than having to imagine, how appliances and room elements might look within a room. Figure 6-3 shows a customer designing her new kitchen at her local Lowe's home improvement center.

***Figure 6-3.*** *HoloLens helps you visualize and then design a room*

## Educational applications

Probably the biggest early application of HoloLens technology will be in educational and training applications. HoloLens is unique in its ability to enable an instructor to direct the attention of students to holographic details and animations overlaid upon physical items such as jet engines or automatic transmissions. Archaeology professors can show students what the insides of a Mayan pyramid or Pompeiian villa were like at their height hundreds or thousands of years ago, overlaid on top of the ruins that remain today. New employees can be brought up to speed on how to do their jobs in a way that seems real but without the need for individualized instruction from a human expert. Human anatomy can be experienced in a way that goes beyond what you get from illustrations in books or on life-size posters, as shown in Figure 6-4.

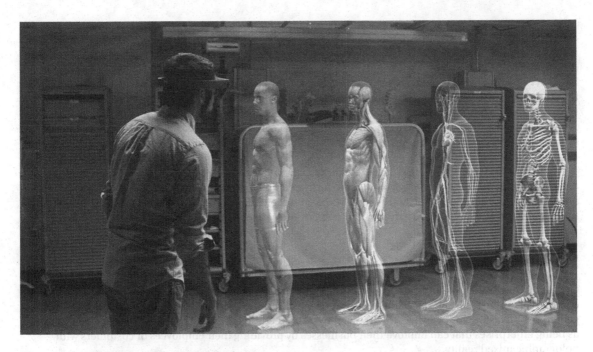

*Figure 6-4. The systems of the human body*

Educational institutions such as Carnegie Mellon University, Dartmouth College, Virginia Tech, Clackamas Community College, and the University of California–Berkeley are using HoloLenses in a diverse array of fields, including interactive art, augmented reality for the visually impaired, data analysis, trade-based education, and control of airborne drones.

# Tearing Down and Reassembling an Automatic Transmission

There are around 260 million passenger cars on the road in the United States, not counting trucks of any kind. Nearly all of those cars contain an automatic transmission, as manual transmissions have become an endangered species restricted to the vehicles of automotive purists and those who want to save a couple of hundred bucks. Most young adults today have never learned how to operate a manual transmission car.

An automobile transmission, like an automobile engine, is an expensive part of a car, and thus is often repaired rather than replaced and scrapped when it ceases to work. With 260 million cars on the road, a significant number at any given time will be having transmission problems, making transmission repair a much needed subspecialty of the trade of automobile mechanic.

Community colleges and other educational institutions that teach job skills in the trades favor a hands-on approach. In the case of automobile maintenance, physical contact with the systems and subassemblies being taught is critical. It is difficult to switch back and forth between an engine or a transmission being disassembled and a thick service manual on the bench nearby, particularly if the mechanic has greasy hands. With relevant information being holographically displayed right above the piece being worked on, the student can move through a disassembly or reassembly procedure without having to pause to consult the manual and without putting oily fingerprints on manual pages or computer keyboard.

An automatic transmission is a complex assembly of gears, clutches, gaskets, shafts, and other parts that fit together like a puzzle. Planetary gears operate in different modes depending on which gear (first, second, third, etc.) is selected.

The HoloLens can enable the student to see an exploded view of all of these parts and then control an animation of the parts all coming together to form a complete transmission. Callouts and labels can be added at appropriate places and times, and a verbal commentary from an instructor can help the student to understand the purpose of each part and how it contributes to the function of the complete assembly.

# Summary

Originally conceived as a new gaming device, the HoloLens has evolved into a device aimed squarely at commercial, industrial, and educational institutions. Use cases in these areas can justify a higher cost than gamers are accustomed to paying. Anyone can buy a HoloLens, but Microsoft sees their best customers as being enterprises that can improve their businesses by providing their employees or customers with holographic mixed reality.

Once you have chosen a project to tackle, the next step is to assemble a team of people to bring that project into existence. This requires people with talents in a variety of disciplines who can work together to create a holographic application that fills a need.

# CHAPTER 7

■ ■ ■

# Forming Project Teams

The days of the lone programmer, much like those of the lone scientist, are receding into the past. There are too many specialties, and they are too complex for one person to master to the extent necessary to produce a commercial-quality application. Application development today is a team endeavor. Tasks are broken up by specialty, with a major division between those who create the application's graphical and audible assets and those who write the code that puts those assets into a functional context. Graphics and sound designers create the assets that make up the substance of the application. Programmers generate the code that gives those assets the behaviors that bring the application alive.

## The Project Leader

It goes without saying that project success hinges on having a clear idea of what the final product will be. Anyone on the team can contribute to this idea, but there should be one person charged with making sure that all objectives are met. That person is the project leader.

It is the responsibility of the project leader to be aware of the status and progress of the various components of the project and to provide any needed support to team members working on the various aspects of the project. This person should be a generalist who is reasonably familiar with all the specialties involved in producing a holographic application without being a world-class expert in any one of them. She should also be a good planner and organizer.

The project leader must ensure that every aspect of the project is properly documented, including all the false starts and ideas that were considered but ultimately not pursued. Ongoing maintenance of the app will depend on this knowledge after responsibility for the app is turned over by the development team to the ongoing maintenance team.

## The Design Team

The first team to swing into action on a new development project is the design team. These are the people who hammer out exactly what the application will look like, what it will do, and how it will do it. It has members representing both the creative and the technical sides of the project. This ensures that the design that is produced not only meets project objectives, but is also feasible given the staffing, budget, and schedule that the team must work within. Once the design is frozen, the members of this team can migrate to the teams that perform the actual implementation.

© Allen G. Taylor 2016
A. G. Taylor, *Develop Microsoft HoloLens Apps Now*, DOI 10.1007/978-1-4842-2202-7_7

# The Computer Graphics Team

A holographic application must, by definition, include holograms. These holograms are the assets created by the computer graphics team. The mixed reality produced by a HoloLens device includes holograms that have locations and behaviors. The graphics specialists on this team create the holograms using a tool such as Maya. Anyone familiar with 3D design, consisting of 3D meshes, vertices, triangles, and normals, already knows how to do this. They bake in most of the animations too. The programming specialists put the holograms into the desired context. The two types of professionals work together to produce a compelling experience for the person running the app.

# The Computer Vision Team

The computer vision team works with the HoloLens spatial-mapping capability to match the holograms created by the computer graphics team to the contours of the space where the user will experience the application. The application must be able to adapt itself to whatever space it finds itself in when it is launched. This team will be primarily made up of programming specialists.

# The Audio Team

A hologram can have spatial sound associated with it. Spatial sound is sound that appears to be coming from the hologram that is "generating" the sound. This is achieved by modifying the phase of the sound fed into each ear by the HoloLens speakers. Sound can be music, sound effects of various sorts, speech, or any combination of the three. Sound can be very important in making holograms seem more like real, physical objects. They can also help to propel a narrative. Games, for example, depend heavily on music to help set the mood of the action taking place at any given moment.

# The QA Team

Before releasing a new application to customers, or even to beta testers, it must be thoroughly thrashed by the internal quality assurance (QA) team. Users are bound to do things with a new application that the developers never conceived would be possible. Users will find a way to put it into an obscure operating mode or stress it in innumerable ways. It is important to put the app through the wringer before customers can get their hands on it.

It helps if the QA team can mimic the mind of the naïve or even clueless user and make every mistake possible. They should purposely violate every recommendation in the user's manual. Speaking of the user's manual, they should also check that it explains everything in the simplest possible way, in addition to being accurate and grammatically correct.

# Parallel Development Paths

At least some of the work of most of the project teams can be done in parallel, as long as that work does not depend on work that has already been completed by another team. Even before the design team completes its work, everyone should have a general sense of what the final app will be expected to do and how it will do it. With that as a basis, people can start investigating the kinds of things they will need once the design has been finalized and they are given the go-ahead to start producing the pieces that will make up the final product.

The design team is the one that will move into serious production mode first. All the other teams depend on what the design team comes up with. From a staffing viewpoint it may make sense to wait until the design team has substantially completed their work before staffing up the other teams. As their work is completed, they can join the newly forming computer graphics team, computer vision team, and audio team. The QA team can form later yet, after an early prototype has been developed by the other teams.

## Intergroup Communication

Some of the best applications have been the product of relatively small project teams. Communication among all the members of the team, regardless of the subteam they belong to, is critical to success, and if communication breaks down because the team is too large or its members are remote from each other, success is very difficult to achieve. Team members should be comfortable with each other, and it is also good if they can socialize outside of the work context. A relaxed, friendly atmosphere encourages creativity, communication, and productivity.

## Summary

In this chapter, we explored the different aspects of a holographic development project and the people who would perform the various jobs that such an effort requires. Also emphasized was the importance of communication among group members.

Once your team is in place, it's time to actually start developing your first holographic application. That is what the next chapter is all about.

# PART III

# Developing with the Unity Framework

# CHAPTER 8

■ ■ ■

# Create a Hologram with Unity and Visual Studio

Mixed-reality devices such as the Microsoft HoloLens represent an entirely new medium. As a result, there are no pre-existing software tools that are specifically designed to create holographic applications. However, there are tools that have been developed for other media that can be adapted to develop holographic apps.

Holograms are three-dimensional images that can be viewed from any angle, giving the impression of being actually present in space. Three-dimensional designs have been around for a number of years in animated motion pictures, video games, and models for fabrication with 3-D printers. The tools used to create these 3-D models can be used to create holograms too.

Video games give us not just three-dimensional objects, but also three-dimensional characters that move and have a variety of behaviors. These characters and other objects are similar to holograms except for the fact that they exist on a two-dimensional screen rather than in three-dimensional space.

We can use the tools that have been developed for creating 3-D models to develop holographic assets and then apply the tools used for developing action-oriented video games to give those assets behaviors that bring them alive.

## Development System Requirements

The first thing that a HoloLens developer must provide is development hardware and operating software that support HoloLens development. Required are the following:

- A 64-bit PC that supports virtualization in its BIOS

- Windows 10 Pro, Education, or Enterprise Edition with Hyper-V virtualization support; Windows 10 Home Edition will not work, nor will a version of Visual Studio earlier than Visual Studio 2015, Update 1.

- At least 8 GB of RAM in the PC

- Support for DirectX 11 or above

## Develop Apps without Hardcore Programming Skills

In the early days of computers, programmers had to explicitly set every bit of every instruction to the appropriate one or zero value. Assemblers and compilers raised things to a higher level of abstraction, making the programmer's job much easier. Game-development environments such as the Unity framework raise the abstraction level even higher. Although those who program the behavior of game objects still must

© Allen G. Taylor 2016
A. G. Taylor, *Develop Microsoft HoloLens Apps Now*, DOI 10.1007/978-1-4842-2202-7_8

know the basics of the computer language used by Unity or other similar platforms, it is no longer necessary to dive down to the nuts-and-bolts level. Much of the code you would need in order to give your characters and environments the behaviors you want has already been written. You just need to place it piece by piece into the context of your application.

The development tools available today have had the effect of democratizing the application-development profession. Unity is an example of an application-development platform that enables you to create rich and dynamic worlds. Visual Studio is a full-featured programming environment that interfaces smoothly with Unity to provide an integrated tool chain for moving from concept to fully featured application. The latest versions of Unity and Visual Studio support the development of holographic applications in addition to the desktop and mobile apps that they have been supporting for many years now.

# Installing Unity and Visual Studio

Unity Technologies, at unity3D.com, is in business to make a profit. They earn revenue by licensing their development software for a fee. However, they also realize that aspiring developers need to be able to learn to use the Unity framework before they start earning enough to pay for a license. As a result, there are two versions of Unity: the Personal Edition and the Professional Edition. The Personal Edition is full featured and includes everything you need in order to learn how to develop holographic applications. It is a free download.

The Professional Edition includes everything that the Personal Edition does, along with additional features that you will need if you want to sell commercial applications that you build on top of the Unity framework. Once you go Pro, Unity will collect a monthly fee from you for the use of their platform.

Installing Unity Personal Edition is as simple as clicking on the FREE DOWNLOAD button on the Unity Web site. From there, just follow the instructions. For HoloLens use, you will want to download the beta version that includes holographic support.

Microsoft's Visual Studio is an integrated development environment that you can use to build applications for Windows, Android, and iOS, as well as Web- and cloud-service applications. Oh, and you can also use it to build holographic applications in combination with Unity.

Like Unity, Microsoft is also in business to make money, and, like Unity, they realize that to sell software services they must have customers who know how to use those services. Visual Studio 2015 Community is a free download that you can use as long as you are learning. When you start needing the tools and services that will enable you to develop commercial applications, Visual Studio Professional will give you what you need for a monthly fee. For large development teams working on complex projects, Visual Studio Enterprise is the product for you, at a larger fee. This book is about learning how to create holographic apps with a combination of Unity and Visual Studio. For that job, the free Visual Studio Community is all you need. You can download it from www.visualstudio.com.

# Quick Tour of the Unity Framework

When you launch Unity to start the development of a new application, it presents you with the screen shown in Figure 8-1.

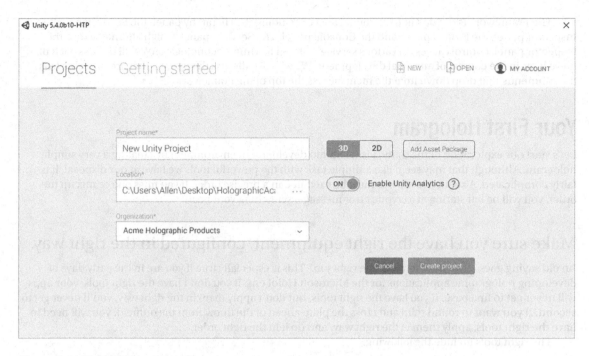

*Figure 8-1.* *Unity Getting Started screen*

Give your new project a name, a location in storage, and the name of your organization. In addition, specify 3D from the 3D/2D toggle and enable Unity analytics. When all that is done, click the Create Project button. This creates your project and displays the development environment shown in Figure 8-2.

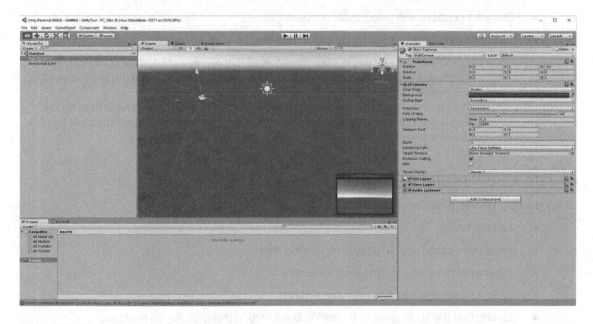

*Figure 8-2.* *Unity Framework development environment*

The Framework is divided into functional areas, including the Hierarchy panel, the Scene panel, the Inspector panel, the Project panel, and the Console panel. The Services panel, which alternates with the Inspector panel, controls access to various services offered by Unity Technologies. We will discuss each of these later in the context of an actual development. We will also discuss the options that are available from the submenus that drop down from the menu across the top of the Framework.

# Your First Hologram

Let's start our exploration of the Unity/Visual Studio development environment by creating a very simple hologram. Although that may seem like a simple task with the powerful tools we have at our disposal, it is fairly complicated. A sequence of steps must be executed in a precise order. If you miss one or mix up the order, you will be left staring at a cryptic error message, scratching your head.

## Make sure you have the right equipment, configured in the right way

An old saying goes, "The right tools for the right job." This is especially true if you are in the early days of developing holographic applications for the Microsoft HoloLens. If you don't have the right tools, your apps will never get to first base. If you have the right tools, but don't apply them in the right way, you'll never get to second. If you want to round third and cross the plate ahead of the throw from the outfield, you will need to have the right tools, apply them in the right way, and do it in the right order.

The right tools include the following:

- A PC with at least 8 GB of RAM
- DirectX 11 or above video card support
- Windows 10 Pro or Enterprise
- Hyper-V support in your PC
- Unity 5.4 or above with holographic support
- Visual Studio Community 2015, Update 2 or above

Applying the right tools in the right way is sometimes not all that obvious a task. That is why carefully following the steps in this book or in online tutorials is critical to success. Since many of the steps depend on the steps that have gone before, applying them in the right order is also important.

Considering all the places where a slight misstep could lead to failure, when you make it through the entire process, don your HoloLens, and actually view a hologram that you have created, sitting there in all its 3-D glory, it is an occasion for major rejoicing.

## Create a new project in Unity

Here's the step-by-step procedure to follow:

- Launch Unity.
- From the window shown in Figure 8-1, select **New**.
- Enter a project name, such as FirstHologram.
- Enter a location in which to save your project.
- Ensure that the 3D toggle switch position is selected, rather than the 2D position.
- Click on the Create Project button.

## Place the camera

All holograms that you create will be located at a position relative to the main camera. The main camera is at the position of the person wearing the HoloLens. Figure 8-2 shows the main camera at its default location of X = 0, Y = 1, and Z = -10 in the Scene pane.

- Select **Main Camera** in the Hierarchy panel and then look at the Inspector panel, shown in Figure 8-3.

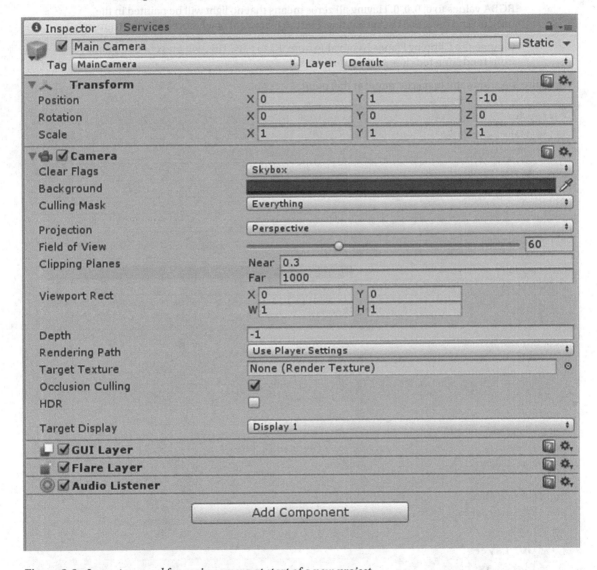

***Figure 8-3.*** *Inspector panel for main camera at start of a new project*

- Note in the Transform section of the Inspector that the position of the main camera shows it to be at x = 0, Y = 1, and Z = -10.

- Note that the values for Rotation are X = 0, Y = 0, and Z = 0, and the values for Scale are 1, 1, and 1.

65

We now need to change some of these values, as follows:

- In the Transform section of the Inspector, change the Position coordinates from 0, 1, -10, to 0, 0, 0.

- In the Camera section of the Inspector, change the "Clear Flags" dropdown from **Skybox** to **Solid Color**.

- Click in the Background area to display the Color window, and then change the RGBA values to 0, 0, 0, 0. Having all zeros means that no light will be painted in the background area. The background will be the real world of whatever room you are in.

- Change the Clipping Planes Near value from 0.3 to 0.85. This will prevent holograms from rendering too close to the user's eyes.

Figure 8-4 shows the Inspector panel at this point.

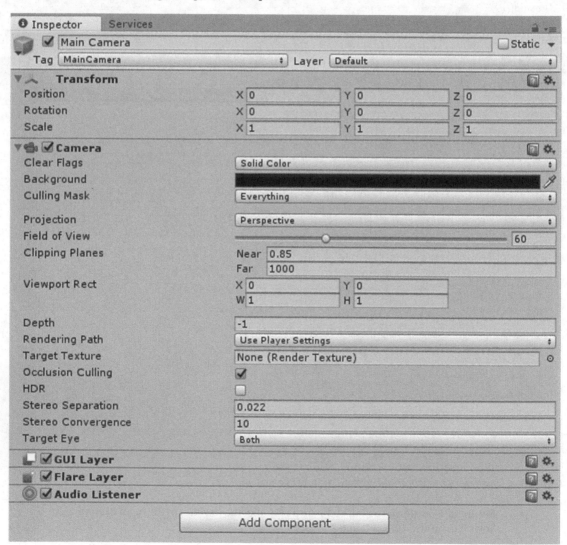

***Figure 8-4.*** *Inspector panel after environment has been set up*

## Create a hologram

Now that the Unity environment is set up, we can create a hologram.

- In the top-left corner of the Hierarchy panel, click on the Create button, and from the menu that drops down, choose **3D Object** and then **Cylinder**.

- Select the newly created cylinder in the Hierarchy panel.

- In the Inspector, change Position to x = 0, Y = 0, Z = 2. This will position the hologram two meters in front of the user's starting position.

- Change Rotation to X = 30, Y = 30, Z = 30 and scale to X = .25, Y = .25, and Z = .25. This gives the cylinder a dimension of .25 meters along each axis.

- Click the Play button (a right-pointing triangle) above the Scene panel to change to Scene mode and view the cylinder you have created. Figure 8-5 shows what this looks like in the Scene panel.

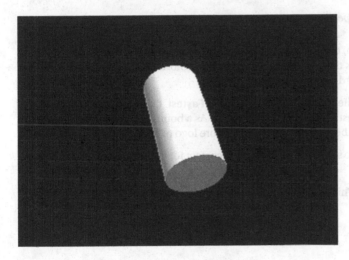

***Figure 8-5.*** *Cylinder asset in Scene panel*

- Click the Play button again to exit Scene mode.

- Save the scene by selecting File > Save Scene, naming the scene, and then clicking Save again.

# Export Your Project to Visual Studio

The next step in the process of creating a holographic application is to export the project to Visual Studio. To do that, follow these steps:

- From the main menu at the upper left, select Edit ➤ Project Settings ➤ Quality. This displays the Quality Settings panel of the Inspector, shown in Figure 8-6.

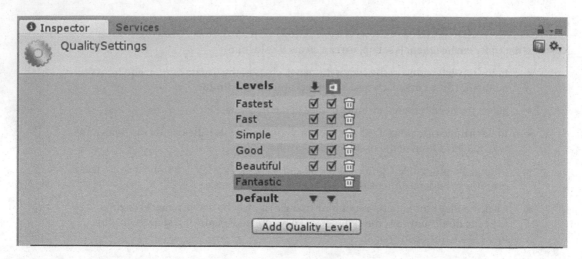

***Figure 8-6.*** *Quality Settings panel of the Inspector*

Various quality levels are shown, from Fastest all the way to Fantastic. Above the second column of checkboxes is the green logo of the Windows Store. At the bottom, in the Default row, is a downward-pointing triangle.

- Click on the triangle to display the Quality menu, then select **Fastest**. Our hologram is not very complex, so the Fastest setting will work just fine. As a bonus, it will be fast. This will cause the Fastest checkbox under the Windows Store logo to turn green.

We now want to make sure that what we send to Visual Studio is correct for creating a holographic application.

- Click on File ➤ Build Settings. This will display the Build Settings window, shown in Figure 8-7.

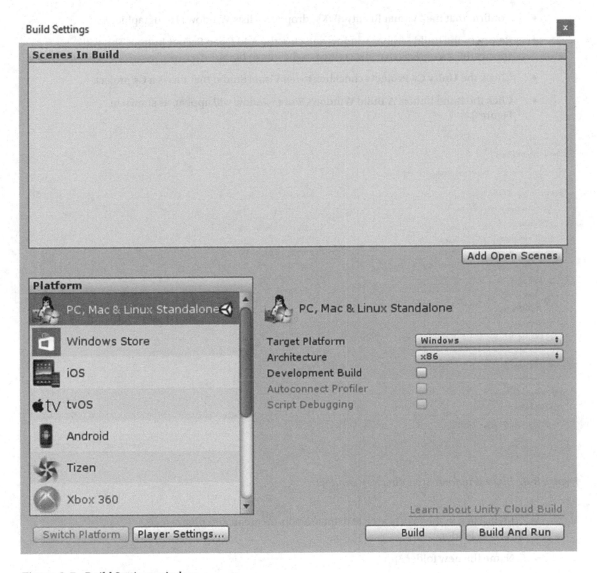

*Figure 8-7. Build Settings window*

- In the Platform menu, select **Windows Store**.

- Click the Switch Platform button.

- Set SDK to Windows 10.

- Set UWP Build Type to D3D.

- Click on the Player Settings button. This will display the Player Settings panel in the Inspector.

- In the Settings for Windows Store area of the Player Settings panel, in the Other Settings group, locate the Rendering section.

- Check the **Virtual Reality Supported** box.

- Confirm that the "Virtual Reality SDKs" dropdown lists Windows Holographic.

- Return to the Build Settings window and click the Add Open Scenes button. This will specify the scene you have just created as the one to build.

- Check the **Unity C# Projects** checkbox to tell Visual Studio that this is a C# project.

- Click the Build button. A Build Windows Store window will appear, as shown in Figure 8-8.

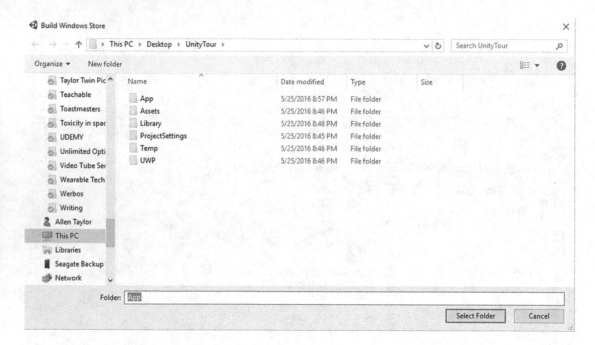

***Figure 8-8.*** *Build Windows Store directory window*

- Right-click in the folders area to display a pop-up menu and then select New ➤ Folder.

- Name the new folder App.

- With the App folder selected, click on the Select Folder button. This will start the build operation. Progress is shown in the Building Player progress bar. When the build process completes, the project's directory will reappear, as shown in Figure 8-9.

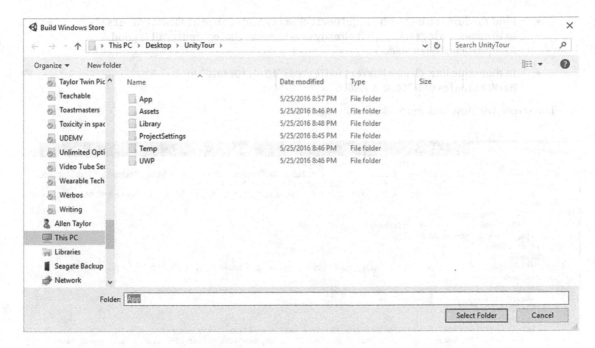

**Figure 8-9.** *Project directory with folders*

- Double-click on the App folder to select it. This shows what is now in the App folder (Figure 8-10).

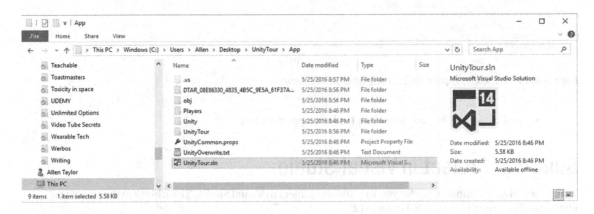

**Figure 8-10.** *App folder contents*

- Double-click on the .sln file. I named my project Unity Tour, so my file is UnityTour. sln. Yours will be whatever you named your project. This launches Visual Studio.

- Visual Studio's error list may show some warnings. You can usually ignore these.

- In the Solution Explorer, right-click on Package.appxmanifest and select **View Code** from the menu that pops up.

- Find the line starting with `TargetDeviceFamily` and change `Windows.Universal` to `Windows.Holographic`. (If it already says `Windows.Holographic`, all is good. An update has been made.)

- In that same line, change `MaxVersionTested="10.0.10240.0"` to `MaxVersionTested="10.0.10586.0"`.

The screen will now look much like that in Figure 8-11.

```
Package.appxmanifest ⇌ ×
    <?xml version="1.0" encoding="utf-8"?>
  <Package xmlns:mp="http://schemas.microsoft.com/appx/2014/phone/manifest" xmlns:uap="http://schemas.microsoft.com/ap
    <Identity Name="UnityTour" Publisher="CN=DefaultCompany" Version="1.0.0.0" />
    <mp:PhoneIdentity PhoneProductId="715f29f4-2293-4efe-84d6-cd09f3c17f68" PhonePublisherId="00000000-0000-0000-
    <Properties>
      <DisplayName>UnityTour</DisplayName>
      <PublisherDisplayName>DefaultCompany</PublisherDisplayName>
      <Logo>Assets\StoreLogo.png</Logo>
    </Properties>
    <Dependencies>
      <TargetDeviceFamily Name="Windows.Holographic" MinVersion="10.0.10240.0" MaxVersionTested="10.0.10586.0" />
    </Dependencies>
    <Resources>
      <Resource Language="x-generate" />
    </Resources>
    <Applications>
      <Application Id="App" Executable="$targetnametoken$.exe" EntryPoint="UnityTour.App">
        <uap:VisualElements DisplayName="UnityTour" Square150x150Logo="Assets\Square150x150Logo.png" Square44x44Logo="
          <uap:DefaultTile Wide310x150Logo="Assets\Wide310x150Logo.png" />
          <uap:SplashScreen Image="Assets\SplashScreen.png" BackgroundColor="#FFFFFF" />
          <uap:InitialRotationPreference>
            <uap:Rotation Preference="landscape" />
            <uap:Rotation Preference="landscapeFlipped" />
            <uap:Rotation Preference="portrait" />
            <uap:Rotation Preference="portraitFlipped" />
          </uap:InitialRotationPreference>
        </uap:VisualElements>
      </Application>
    </Applications>
  </Package>
```

*Figure 8-11.* *Package.appxmanifest code after modifications*

- Click on File ➤ Save All to save Package.appxmanifest.

# Build the Project in Visual Studio

Now everything is almost ready for you to build the project in Visual Studio. The ribbon at the top of the Visual Studio screen is shown in Figure 8-12.

*Figure 8-12.* *Visual Studio menu and function ribbon*

Note that the dropdown menus in the ribbon show Debug, ARM, and Device.

- Change these entries to **Release**, **X86**, and **Remote Machine**.

A Remote Connections dialog box will appear, as shown in Figure 8-13.

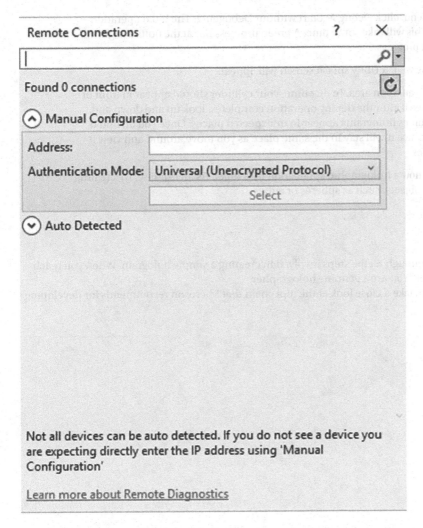

*Figure 8-13. Remote Connections dialog box*

- Under Manual Configuration, enter the DHCP network address of your HoloLens device. This assumes that you have already paired your HoloLens to your development PC as discussed in Chapter 5, and that you know its DHCP network address. The Authentication Mode dropdown should be left as **Universal (Unencrypted Protocol)**.

- Click the Select button.

## Deploy Your Project to the HoloLens

At last, you can send your project via Wi-Fi to your HoloLens.

- Don your HoloLens and make sure it is on and active.

- From the main menu, click Debug ➤ Start without Debugging. The build operation will commence. This will take some time. A green progress bar at the bottom right will inform you of progress.

- If things have gone well, a Unity splash screen will appear.

- Aim your gaze into an open area. In due time, your cylinder should appear in front of you. If you don't see it after the deploy operation completes, look up and down and all around. Sometimes holograms appear in unexpected places. Once you do find it, though, you will notice it will stay in the same place as you move around and view it from various angles.

Congratulations! You are now a holographic application developer. As an exercise, try creating holograms of other geometric objects, such as spheres or cubes.

## Summary

In this chapter, we have gone through all the steps involved in creating a simple hologram. When you reach this point, congratulate yourself. You are a genuine holographer.

In the next chapter, we will take a close look at the tool chain that Microsoft recommends for developing holographic applications.

# CHAPTER 9

∎ ∎ ∎

# Developing with Unity and Visual Studio

Building holographic applications is a new endeavor, as it was pioneered by Microsoft HoloLens developers. As such, there are no software tools that have been specifically designed to build and deploy such applications. However, 3D holographic applications are similar in many ways to 3D computer games.

The major difference is that holograms really are 3D objects located in 3D space, while 3D computer games look like they are three dimensional, but in reality are confined to a 2D screen. Because of their similarity, tools that have been developed for creating computer games and video games have been modified to create holographic applications for the HoloLens. These applications could be holographic games, such as Microsoft's Robo Raid, Fragments, or Young Conker, or they could be industrial, commercial, or educational applications.

## Combining Scripts from Visual Studio with Assets in Unity Project Explorer

Unity, being primarily a game engine, gives you the tools you need to create rich and complex game environments as well as characters and artifacts to place in those environments. It depends on small computer programs called scripts to imbue assets, such as characters and artifacts, with behaviors. Those scripts could be written in either C#, which is a Microsoft language, or JavaScript. Not surprisingly, Microsoft recommends the use of C# in developing holographic applications for the HoloLens.

Visual Studio is Microsoft's major tool for developing applications of all kinds, using a wide array of languages, one of which is C#. There is tight integration between the latest versions of Unity and Visual Studio such that a new script created in Visual Studio can be ported directly into a Unity project in an intuitive and seamless manner. The application we built in Chapter 8 to create a holographic cylinder did not use any scripts to give the cylinder any behaviors. It just hangs there suspended in space. However, C# scripts were running "under the covers and out of sight" to bring the hologram to life. More elaborate projects, such as those we will cover later in this book, will use scripts to give behaviors to the holograms we create.

## Giving Objects Behaviors Using Scripts

A static hologram floating in front of you in three-dimensional space in and of itself is a pretty amazing thing that people have dreamed about for decades. However, much cooler and a great deal more useful would be a hologram that had behaviors, such as obeying the laws of physics, moving, changing shape, emitting sounds, or responding to the actions of people.

© Allen G. Taylor 2016
A. G. Taylor, *Develop Microsoft HoloLens Apps Now*, DOI 10.1007/978-1-4842-2202-7_9

Game platforms such as Unity have been giving behaviors to characters in their video games for quite a while now. This is achieved by attaching scripts written in a programming language to those characters or other game objects. The same basic technology that works for game objects confined to a screen will work for holograms in space. Multiple scripts can endow a hologram with multiple behaviors.

In Unity, game objects are controlled by the components that are attached to them. Unity includes a library of components that you can attach to game objects, but you can also create your own components with scripts. These scripts could conceivably be written in a Unity-specific version of either JavaScript or C#, but Microsoft has chosen to focus on C# for HoloLens development.

For HoloLens development, Visual Studio is used as the development environment (IDE) in which to create the scripts that are then added as components to game objects in Unity. Scripts could be written completely with the MonoDevelop IDE in Unity, but the tools available in Visual Studio make creation there more convenient, and it is currently the only solution endorsed by Microsoft.

# Sensing User Actions with Scripts

The HoloLens device can sense various things about the user who is wearing it. It can sense where that person is looking by sensing head orientation. It can detect select gestures the person makes with her hands. And it can detect voice commands that she makes. The HoloLens can respond to all of these actions if scripts have been written to determine what those responses should be. MonoBehaviour is the default base class from which every script is derived. To help you learn the Unity API, the MonoBehaviour wizard and the Quick MonoBehaviour wizard are provided, and Unity's Help system is also a good resource.

# Unity/Visual Studio Integration

There is tight integration of Visual Studio with Unity, especially with the advent of Visual Studio 2015. Visual Studio Tools for Unity (VSTU) makes a direct connection with the Unity Editor. Common scripting tasks are automated, transferring information from Unity into Visual Studio and sending finished scripts from Visual Studio back to Unity.

Even Unity's scripting documentation is available right in Visual Studio. If VSTU does not find the desired API documentation locally, it will try to find it online. To access Unity documentation from Visual Studio, highlight or place the cursor over the Unity API you want to learn about and press **Ctrl+Alt+M** followed by **Ctrl + H**.

## Unity's MonoBehaviour scripting wizard

In Unity, most scripts are derived from the MonoBehaviour class by overriding some of its methods. With the MonoBehaviour wizard, you can quickly create empty definitions of the MonoBehaviour methods that you want to overload. With this wizard, you can choose one or more methods to overload from the list of available methods. You can also choose where you want to insert those methods in your code and whether to include comments that describe the methods and how they are used.

## The Quick MonoBehaviour scripting wizard

Whereas the MonoBehaviour scripting wizard gives you a lot of information about the methods you may want to override, the Quick MonoBehaviour scripting wizard assumes you already know what you are doing and cuts right to the chase. You start typing the name of the method you want to overload and it displays a list of all methods that start with those same characters. You can pick the one you want from the list and be on your way quickly.

# Debugging Holographic Projects

Creating a holographic application is a fairly involved activity. You must first create a project in Unity, including all its assets, the properties of those assets, user interactions, and the look and feel of the application. Then you must give those assets behaviors using C# coding in Visual Studio. After creating an application and attaching behaviors to the assets of that application, you must deploy the application to a HoloLens device that is paired with your development PC.

Every step along the way is a place where errors can be introduced. Most of these errors will be caused by missteps made by you, the developer. Some may be caused by overreaching the limits of the resources in your development machine, or connection problems between your PC and your HoloLens. Expect the amount of time you spend debugging to exceed the amount of time you spend coding, perhaps by quite a lot, at least until you have climbed up rather high on the learning curve.

## Debugging in Unity

Normally, when we think about debugging, we think about debugging code. However, in HoloLens development, after a pre-build process in Unity, code is not developed in Unity, but rather in Visual Studio. This does not mean that we don't have to worry about the Unity part of the process. It is still possible, quite easy in fact, to mess up a project in the Unity part of the process.

In Unity, you must have all the assets in the proper places in the hierarchy, listed in the Hierarchy panel. Each one of those assets much have the correct attributes in the Inspector panel.

For the Build operation, in the Build Settings dialog box, you must remember to click the Add Open Scenes button to make sure they appear in the Scenes In Build pane. You must also select the proper platform for your app, which in the case of Windows holographic apps is the Windows Store platform. The Player Settings button takes you to the Player Settings panel in the Inspector. You will want to make sure that **Virtual Reality Supported** is checked and that the other settings are what you want.

---

■ **Note**    Sometimes Unity will issue an error message that can be safely ignored, so don't freak out when you get one. Try proceeding to see if the message indicates a real problem. See Figure 9-1 for an example of an ignorable message:

---

ⓘ MissingComponentException: There is no 'Renderer' attached to the "AstroMan" game object, but a script is trying to access it.

*Figure 9-1.*  *An error meseage that did not prevent a successful build*

## Debugging in Visual Studio

Visual Studio is a modern application-development environment that features state of the art tools to help you perfect the applications you write. Error messages for syntax errors are specific and appropriate, enabling you to fix and recompile in rapid order.

When Visual Studio builds an application that incorporates multiple C# scripts, each one doing a specific job, it will display error messages, warnings, and other messages in the Error List panel in the bottom-left corner of the window. In general, warnings (yellow icon) will not cause a build to fail. Error messages (red icon) will usually, but not always, cause a build to fail. Sometimes, as a build progresses, a red icon error message will appear, only to disappear later in the build process.

You can incorporate breakpoints into your scripts and use them to step through an application when running a build with debugging enabled. You can examine the value of expressions in a window on your development machine while the app is running on the HoloLens device.

## Using Intellisense while debugging

Intellisense in C# is a tool that anticipates what you have in mind when you start writing a line of code and suggests an automatic completion of the line. More often than not, its guess of what you intend is correct, so you can save considerable time and typing by accepting its suggestions. This process of saving you time and keystrokes is probably most valuable when you are writing a script for the first time. However, it is also useful when you are debugging existing code.

## Refactoring

Visual Studio enables you to clean up code that may be functional, but not necessarily optimal or easily readable, through refactoring. There are six types of refactoring that you can do:

- Extract Method Refactoring

- Rename Refactoring

- Encapsulate Field Refactoring

- Extract Interface Refactoring

- Remove Parameters Refactoring

- Reorder Parameters Refactoring

These refactoring operations do not change the function of the code being refactored, but they may make it easier to understand. This can be useful if the code is not working properly, making it easier to debug.

## Code Browsing

Code browsing is an analysis technique that you can employ with Visual Studio's Object Browser. The Object Browser is an editor that displays the objects in a project in a hierarchical way. It enables you to select and examine namespaces, classes, methods, and other symbols that you might use in your project. Open the Object Browser by dropping down the View menu and then selecting Object Browser.

Figure 9-2 shows the three panes of the Object Browser as they appear within Visual Studio.

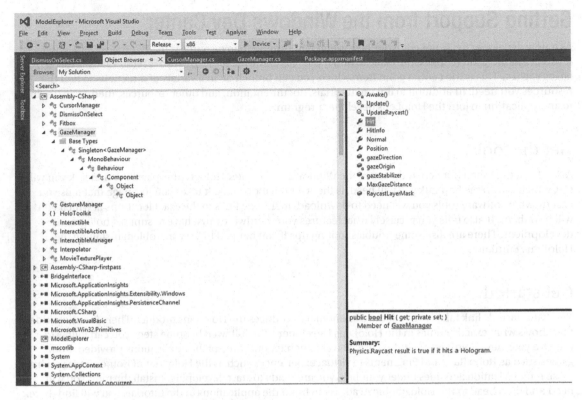

*Figure 9-2.* *Visual Studio's Object Browser*

The Objects pane is on the left, the Members pane is on the upper right, and the Description pane is on the lower right. All the top-level objects are shown in the Objects pane, with the Gaze Manager object expanded to show the levels of hierarchy beneath it. The Members pane shows the members of the selected Gaze Manager object, and the Description pane describes the member selected in the Members pane. In the figure, the Hit member of the Gaze Manager object is described.

With the Object Browser, you can see descriptions of all the members of all the objects, regardless of what level they occupy in the hierarchy. You can limit the scope of the browse to only those objects that are currently of interest. Examining the cascading levels can often bring to mind something that doesn't look right, such as a missing level or a member whose description is not what you thought or intended it to be.

# Visual Studio's Error List

If in a build or deploy operation things don't go exactly as Visual Studio thinks they should, errors or warnings will be posted under the Error List tab in the lower left pane of the Visual Studio development environment. An error, denoted by a red X icon, generally means that the operation you are trying to perform has failed. Be sure that the operation has completed, however. Sometimes errors will appear while a build or deploy is in progress that then disappear later in the process. Warnings, denoted by a yellow triangular icon, on the other hand, may or may not signal a failure. If you see one or more warning indications but no error indications, try to complete the operation. Sometimes you will be able to with no problem.

# Getting Support from the Windows Dev Center

As a new developer for HoloLens, your best friend and number one resource is the Windows Dev Center. If you are in the United States, the place to find it is https://developer.microsoft.com/en-us/windows/holographic. This is the central point from which you can branch off in a variety of directions to find the resources you need. In addition to links to tutorials, documentation, and other resources, there is also a link to an application to join the HoloLens developer program.

## Get the tools

Aside from the menu bar across the top of the Windows Dev Center Holographic page, the first link you will see, which is also the first link you will need, is the "Get the tools" link. It takes you to a page that tells you exactly what software tools you will need to download, including links to the exact locations at which you will find them. It also tells you precisely what features your hardware must have to support holographic development. There are also some troubleshooting tips if you happen to have a problem installing the HoloLens Emulator.

## Get started

The "Get started" link takes you to some content that introduces the HoloLens product. There is a short video that shows what exactly comes in the HoloLens Developer's Kit, followed by some steps you can follow to prepare your new HoloLens for its first use. You can then try out some of the applications provided, from games such as Robo Raid and Fragments to virtual experiences such as the HoloTour of Rome. Once you have these familiarization activities under your belt, you are ready to start developing. Install the tools you will need and then head to the Holographic Academy to build the applications in the tutorials you will find there.

## Academy

In Chapter 5, I gave a brief description of the tutorials found at the Holographic Academy. In Chapter 11, I will walk you through the building and deployment of one of these, Holograms 101. In Chapter 12, I will take you through another, Holograms 240, which allows multiple people to share the same holograms.

Another opportunity is Academy Live. As the name implies, this is a live learning experience that takes place on Microsoft's home turf in Redmond, Washington. It is a six-month program that takes place two days at a time over that six-month period. Over the course of the program, development teams consisting of a developer, a designer, and a technical artist will develop a complete holographic project.

## Documentation

Microsoft, along with Unity, provides you with online documentation, giving you all the information you need to start building holographic applications. At the Windows Dev Center Web site, the Documentation tab leads to an array of topics that covers all the main aspects of holograms, the HoloLens device, and the fundamentals of building holographic applications. This section gives a brief summary of all the major things that are documented.

## Understanding HoloLens

The first thing the Dev Center does in helping you to understand HoloLens is to explain what a hologram is–at least the thing that Microsoft is calling a hologram.

## Holograms

Whereas traditionally a hologram has been considered to be a three-dimensional image in space, when you are wearing a HoloLens, you not only see a three-dimensional image in space, but you hear it too, if it is capable of making sounds. Other people in the room cannot see the hologram unless they are also wearing HoloLens devices. Furthermore, you can affect what the hologram does with gestures and voice commands. It is possible to interact with the holograms in powerful ways. As a developer, you can create holograms that will look, sound, and act the way you want them to.

## Hardware details

Detailed specifications of the physical components of the HoloLens tell you what you need to know in order to understand what tools and capabilities you will have at your disposal as you develop applications. In addition to major components, controls, interfaces, and limitations are explained.

## HoloLens shell overview

The Start menu is the visible component of the shell. It is the main portal through which the user interacts with the mixed-reality world created by the HoloLens. Not only can a person launch apps from the Start menu, but they can also invoke Cortana as well as capture mixed-reality video.

## App views on HoloLens

Although the primary role of a HoloLens is to generate 3D holograms that the user can walk around and view from every angle, it can also generate a 2D image on a virtual slate that mimics what a user would see on a PC, tablet, or smartphone. This means that Universal Windows PC or mobile apps can be ported to HoloLens relatively easily. In 2D mode, up to three apps can be run simultaneously, but in 3D holographic mode, only one app can be run at a time.

## Using mixed-reality capture

You can take both mixed-reality photos and mixed-reality videos with a HoloLens. The photo or video will show what the user is seeing, and in the case of video what she is hearing as well. Photos will be in JPEG format with a resolution of 1408 x 792 pixels. Videos will be in MPEG-4 format with the same resolution, taken at a 30 fps rate.

## Working with accessories

A HoloLens device connects to accessory devices via Bluetooth. Compatible Bluetooth devices that are paired with the HoloLens will provide additional functionality. One Bluetooth device, the HoloLens Clicker, comes with the Development Edition. With it, a user can click and scroll with a minimum of hand motion, replacing the air-tap gesture.

You can use a Bluetooth keyboard with the HoloLens and also a Bluetooth mouse. Other devices may also work as long as they support either the Bluetooth HD or Bluetooth GATT profiles.

# Developing for HoloLens

Holographic apps run on the Universal Windows Platform (UWP). This means that all holographic apps are UWP apps and that all UWP apps can be made to run on HoloLens.

## Basics of holographic development

Holograms are located in space relative to a set of real-world coordinates. The user interacts with them via gaze, gesture, and voice inputs. Spatial sound makes it appear that sounds generated by a hologram are coming from the direction of that hologram. Spatial mapping scans the environment surrounding the user and builds a mesh that tells holograms where things are in their surroundings. This means that if a holographic ball rolls to the edge of a table, it will fall off and hit the floor of the room.

## Tools for developing on HoloLens

Developing 2D apps for HoloLens is essentially the same thing as developing apps for Windows Phone, PC, and tablets. In all cases, it is a Universal Windows app. The difference is that instead of the display being on a screen, it is on a virtual slate floating in the air.

Holographic apps, however, require Windows Holographic APIs. This is easy if you use Unity, which has those APIs "baked in." Rather than using Unity, you can build your own middleware engine if you wish, using DirectX and other Windows APIs. Epic's Unreal Engine could perform in much the same way that Unity does, but Epic has not yet developed a kit to support HoloLens development the way Unity has.

Regardless of what type of application you are building, you will need Visual Studio and the Windows SDK, the Windows Device Portal, and the HoloLens Emulator. All of these, as well as Unity, come in the form of free downloads.

## Getting started

Once you have all your tools lined up, the best way to ease into HoloLens development is to work through the tutorials available at Microsoft's online Holographic Academy. With that experience under your belt, you can develop your first app and then make it available to the world by uploading it to the Windows Store.

## App model

Since Windows Holographic is based on the Universal Windows Platform (UWP), the app model that the HoloLens uses is the same one used by modern Windows apps written for Windows and Windows Mobile. The app model governs how an app is launched, run, suspended, and terminated. Developers building UWP apps for other platforms will find the transition to developing holographic apps to be straightforward.

## Install the tools

This section of the documentation tells you what characteristics your development machine must have as well as the software tools you will have to download and install before you can start developing holographic apps. Follow these guidelines and you will be able to start developing. There is also a brief troubleshooting section to help you when you run into trouble. In these early days, with what is essentially beta software, you can pretty much count on having some obstacles rear up in your path. Patience and persistence will be needed for you to win through to success.

## Using Visual Studio

Visual Studio is the tool you will use to debug and deploy your apps. Assuming you have installed all the needed tools, this section describes how to enable Developer Mode and how to deploy your app to a HoloLens device, both over Wi-Fi and also wired through a USB port. Your HoloLens will need to be paired with your development machine in order for deployment to work. This can be tricky, and you may encounter error messages that don't seem to relate to what you are doing. Once paired, Visual Studio may point out problems caused by errors in the deployment process. You may also encounter error messages even when nothing is wrong. Sometimes just repeating the deployment operation without changing anything will lead to success.

Deploying to the HoloLens Emulator goes through all the same steps as deploying to a HoloLens. Just specify the Emulator as the destination rather than the HoloLens, which is referred to as the *Device* when deploying via USB and as the *Remote Machine* when deploying via Wi-Fi.

The Visual Studio Graphics Diagnostics tools include a graphics debugger that you can use to debug an app that deploys but does not function correctly. This is a powerful tool that is described in detail on MSDN under the title "Visual Studio Graphics Diagnostics." There are also profiling tools that you can use to optimize your application. Information on them can be found on MSDN under the title "Profiling Tools."

## Using the HoloLens Emulator

If you are like me, you have probably found yourself wanting to develop apps for the HoloLens before you actually have one. You can productively use the time that passes while you wait for your HoloLens Development Edition to arrive by coming up to speed on Unity and Visual Studio and building and deploying apps to the HoloLens Emulator. You will be able to create holograms that you can then interact with using your computer's keyboard in place of gestures and voice commands. There are some things you can't do with the Emulator. For example, you can't walk around the emulated hologram and view it from multiple angles. It is confined to your computer's screen. However, you can get a very good idea of your app's function. When you finally do receive your HoloLens, your app will be ready to deploy to it.

## Using the Windows Device Portal

In Chapter 5, I described the Device Portal in detail. There is no point in repeating that here. However, this is the place in the online documentation where you should go if you want to go deeper into the capabilities of the portal than what I covered in Chapter 5.

## Performance recommendations

Developing for the HoloLens is more challenging than many other kinds of software development. A full Windows 10 battery-powered computer with passive cooling, worn lightly on the head, that serves up two dynamic HD images, one for each eye, at a rate of 60 frames per second, represents a major high-dimensional optimization problem. You can only pack so much computer power, memory, and storage in an untethered wearable device. That means that decisions must be made about tradeoffs to give the user the best possible experience.

For different applications, different performance metrics will be more or less important. You must understand what is important for the app you are working on now, and how best to compromise a less important performance metric in order to enhance one that is more important. The documentation in this section gives a large number of possible things you can do that will enhance one metric or another. You have to decide which, if any, of these will improve the overall user experience.

## Testing

Testing is a crucial, but often underestimated, part of the application-development process. Of course, a holographic application must be tested in all the same ways that a PC or mobile app is tested, including for

- functionality,
- interoperability,
- performance,

- security, and

- reliability.

Holographic apps require a great deal of additional testing beyond these traditional areas of concern. One area requiring consideration is user comfort. The user is wearing the HoloLens device on her head. Will your app require unnatural head movements to see the full content? The field of view is a horizontal rectangle. Must the user look up and down too frequently for comfort? Will your app require such a computational load that the HoloLens becomes uncomfortably hot, forcing it to shut down?

Since you can't guarantee the environment that the user will be in when running your app, you will have to test the app in a wide variety of them. Test in all kinds of rooms of all sizes. Even test outside. How does the app react to a user walking down a hallway or ascending a flight of stairs? What about curved walls and domed ceilings?

You need to test in all kinds of lighting conditions. Learn how a wall mirror will affect your app, and what about a glass coffee table? Think of all the weird types of environments that a user might be in while running your app.

There are many other environmental conditions that you will need to consider. The guiding principle is that you have no control over what the environment will be like while your app is running. It needs to be able to adapt to its surroundings, whether cluttered or spare, noisy or quiet. You also don't know whether the user is tall or short, seated or standing. You need to deliver a satisfying experience in all these cases.

## Submitting an app to the Windows Store

For a Windows Holographic app, as with any Windows app for PC or mobile devices, the natural place to make the app available is in the online Windows Store. The procedure for doing this for a holographic app is the same as it is for any Windows Universal app. If you follow the instructions in this section of the documentation, you will be able to make sure your app meets all the requirements for inclusion in the Windows Store and is successfully uploaded to it.

## FAQ

There is a list of several frequently asked questions. Possibly as more HoloLens devices are deployed, more people will ask more questions and this list will be expanded.

## Release notes

This section describes the new features and bug fixes provided by the latest update to the HoloLens software. It also describes any capabilities that have been removed by the latest update.

## Known issues

As is the case with release notes, this section is updated frequently to alert you to known issues that have not been fixed, offering suggestions of workarounds in some cases. It's a good idea to examine this list of known issues carefully before putting a lot of effort into an app-development project. Being aware of an issue may enable you to take a path that avoids it.

# Building blocks of holographic apps

The mixed-reality experience provided by HoloLens is based on six of its features, which are used to add holograms to the real world the user is in and enable her to interact with them.

## World coordinates

Fundamental to mixed-reality apps is the ability to place holograms at specific locations in 3D space and for those holograms to maintain a constant spatial relationship with other holograms and with real, physical objects that share the space with the holograms. This is a more complex problem than the one faced by virtual reality, where there is no need to anchor the virtual world to any point in the real, physical world that the user is inhabiting. This section discusses the different possible ways of treating reference frames and of tracking the location of holographic objects as the user moves around. As a developer, you have some choices to make as to how you locate your holograms in the real world and in relation to the location and movement of the user.

## Gaze input

There are three ways of interacting with holograms: with gaze, gesture, and voice. Of these, gaze is the most fundamental, because it's hard to interact with a hologram that you cannot see. When you look directly at a hologram, a raycast is computed from the direction your head is pointing. If it intersects with a hologram, you can then interact with that hologram with gesture or voice.

A cursor shows where your gaze is pointing at any moment. As developer of an app, you control what that cursor looks like when it is not pointing at a hologram, and you can indicate to the user that they are now targeting a hologram by changing the shape of the cursor. This usually is done by changing the cursor from a dot of light to an open circle. Once the cursor has targeted a holographic object, the user can interact with the object.

## Gesture input

Thanks to tools in the HoloToolkit, when gaze is locked onto a holographic object, that object can be affected by a user's hand gesture. The air-tap gesture is the one most commonly used. It performs a select operation, which causes the holographic object to perform whatever action it has been programmed to perform. Other gestures enable the user to lock onto and hold a holographic object, manipulate the object, or move it.

## Voice input

With voice input, the user can duplicate many of the actions performed by gestures, such as selecting and then activating a hologram or manipulating it in space. The user can also summon Cortana by saying, "Hey, Cortana" followed by some request or question.

## Spatial sound

Spatial sound adds greatly to the immersive quality of HoloLens mixed reality. Sounds emitted by a hologram sound like they are coming from the direction of the hologram, and the sound is louder when the hologram is nearer and fainter when the hologram is farther away.

## Spatial mapping

Spatial mapping is what binds the real world and the virtual world together. The real environment is scanned and mapped so that a mesh representing the real-world objects is stored in memory. You must create your holograms to realistically navigate the space they are in. Characters can walk on the floor. Flower vases can sit on a table. Rubber balls can bounce off the wall. Holograms can occlude real-world objects that are behind them and be occluded by real-world objects that are in front of them. Holograms can respond appropriately to gravity and bounce back when they collide with real-world surfaces.

Spatial mapping can require a high computational load and consume significant amounts of memory. One of your main considerations as a developer is to optimize the way that spatial mapping is done so as to not overload the processor or fill up the memory with meshes of locations that the user has previously scanned but will no longer need.

# Building 2D apps

Since the HoloLens runs on Windows 10, apps that were originally written for desktop, mobile, or Xbox devices can also be run as 2D apps on HoloLens. Just about any app running under Windows Universal can be deployed to the HoloLens after just a few minor tweaks. If your app doesn't run successfully right out of the box, debugging tips in this section of the documentation can help you to zero in on what is causing the problem.

# Building holographic apps with Unity

Unity, built originally as a platform for the development of computer games, works well, after significant modifications, as a platform for developing holographic applications for the HoloLens.

## Unity development overview

Standard Unity game objects, such as the camera, work in exactly the same way for holographic apps. The camera orientation and position are updated automatically as the user turns her head and moves through the world. Aside from the camera, other key building blocks, including gaze, gesture, voice input, world anchor, persistence, spatial sound, and spatial mapping, are implemented in ways consistent with other Unity APIs.

This section of the documentation describes how to configure Unity for holographic development. All the tools are already present in Unity; it is just a matter of selecting the correct configuration for a scene as well as for an entire project. When you install Unity, its scripting reference and manual come along with it, providing any Unity-specific information that you may need.

## Recommended settings for Unity

The default splash screen that will be displayed when your app launches shows the Unity logo for five seconds. If you are selling your app commercially, you probably want to replace that with your own logo. There is a setting that enables you to do that, but only if you are using the Plus version of Unity or greater.

It's possible for the HoloLens to lose track of where it is in the course of running your application. This is called *tracking loss*, and when it happens, Unity will stop rendering holograms. There are several things you can do about this to handle tracking-loss events. There are settings for this eventuality. Use them to give the best user experience when this happens.

## Performance recommendations for Unity

Two opposing forces are in play with the HoloLens. First, melding virtual a 3D hologram with the real world accurately at 60 frames per second is computationally intense. Second, a self-contained device that you wear on your head and that runs on battery power is intrinsically limited in what it can do. These two facts mean that developers of moderately complex applications will need to apply every trick in the book to deliver the performance that is required for a satisfying user experience. This section of the documentation lists a number of suggestions of things you can do to maintain a high frame rate and to minimize glitchiness in the display of holograms due to garbage collection happening at inopportune times.

Suggestion 1: If there are multiple ways to implement a particular function, choose the one that executes the fastest rather than, for example, the one that is easiest to code.

Suggestion 2: Structure your data in a way that minimizes cache misses. Cache misses are far more costly in terms of time than is inefficient code.

## Exporting and building a Unity Visual Studio solution

This section of the documentation describes the steps required in both Unity and Visual Studio to build and deploy an application. It also explains the rationale behind some of those actions. In Chapter 11, I will cover these steps in detail as we work through the building and deployment of the Origami example application.

## Best practices for working with Unity and Visual Studio

In an iterative debugging process, you don't want to be going back and forth between Unity and Visual Studio any more than you have to be. This time waster can be minimized when exporting from Unity by making sure the **Unity C# Projects** checkbox is checked. This causes the same instance of Visual Studio to be used both for writing scripts and for building and deploying your project.

Other things you can do are to download and use Visual Studio Tools for Unity and to use public C# class variables. These actions can make debugging easier and enable you to easily tweak variables in Unity 3D's Inspector pane to tune performance.

If you move to a newer version of either the Windows SDK or Unity, it is a good practice to build a new UWP solution from Unity, rather than expecting the old solution to continue working.

# Adding holographic capabilities to middleware

In all the discussion of holographic application development we have had so far, Unity has served as middleware. It is in the middle between your application and the Windows operating system. Microsoft has worked closely with Unity to provide a platform that is easy for developers to use to create their holographic applications. However, you don't *have* to use Unity. If you wish, you can build your own middleware using DirectX APIs. This will require more work, but could potentially give you more flexibility in what you can produce.

## DirectX development overview

Windows holographic applications use holographic rendering, gaze, gesture, and voice APIs. Unity does a lot of the heavy lifting for you, but if you want to have the maximal level of control, you can use Windows Holographic APIs with DirectX 11. These APIs support apps written in both C++ and C#. If you already have a Windows 10 UWP app that you want to convert to a 2D holographic app for HoloLens, then DirectX 11 is the route you need to take. DirectX 12 does not currently support holographic development at the time of this writing.

## Creating a holographic DirectX project

This section of the documentation describes how to create a simple project using DirectX. It renders a simple cube hologram that spins on an axis. Even this simple application illustrates the higher level of skill required of the developer when using DirectX than what is needed by a developer using Unity.

## Rendering in DirectX

This section goes into detail on the many steps involved with rendering a scene. There are many things that must be updated in each frame, followed by the rendering of that frame. In addition, if the HoloLens loses track of where it is, that situation must be handled gracefully.

# Designing holograms

A major part of designing holograms falls into the domain of 3D computer graphics. This is often accomplished with tools such as Maya and 3ds Max. Just as important, however, is the way you integrate those holograms into the real world. One challenge with this is that black is not a usable color in a hologram. HoloLens interprets black as transparent.

## Designing for mixed reality

Designing holographic apps for HoloLens is similar to developing 3D games for PC or Xbox in many ways, but there are differences that can have a large effect on the user experience. This section of the documentation gives a list of best practices that have been found to work well on the HoloLens. As people gain more experience and send feedback to Microsoft, this list will expand.

## Types of holographic apps

This section of the documentation describes three different types of apps based on the kind of environment they create:

- An *enhanced-environment app* leaves the real world as it is, but adds holographic content to it. This might be a holographic TV screen placed on a wall or a set of cooking instructions placed above the stove in your kitchen. It might put a holographic chess set on the table in your study.

- A *blended-environment app* integrates holographic elements into your real-world environment. It might give your walls a different color or change the color and style of your kitchen cabinets in an interior design app.

- A *virtual-environment app* could cover your real world completely with a virtual world that is entirely different. You would always be able to see the real world with your peripheral vision, but as soon as you turn to face a different direction, the real world would be replaced by the virtual. With this kind of app, you could take a tour through a museum or a famous archeological site.

## Cursors

Just as is true for a 2D screen–based application, the cursor is critical for receiving input from the user. In the HoloLens' case, the cursor is located at the center of the user's gaze when the user is looking straight ahead. Because the cursor is impinging on real and virtual objects in a 3D space, you may want it to change shape and orientation depending on where it is and on what object it might be hitting. This section of the documentation gives tips on how best to use the cursor so as to give the user needed information without being confusing or distracting.

## Gaze targeting

Users select targets by gazing at them. This section gives tips on anticipating what the user intends for a holographic object when their gaze falls upon it or even when it "almost" falls upon it. Sometimes it is a good idea to be forgiving of a close miss. Gaze stabilization can also be helpful for a user whose head shakes or moves around in other ways.

## Gesture design

Gestures are one of the two main ways of providing input to an application. The other is voice. The HoloLens gesture vocabulary is rather limited, so you will have to be mindful of how you use them. The air tap is probably the one you will use most often, but there are also continuous gestures that can scroll through a 2D holographic page or rotate a 3D hologram, or even cause a line to be drawn in space.

## Voice design

Like gesture, voice is a way of sending user input to an application. Many operations can be accomplished by using either gesture or voice, but each method has its own strengths and weaknesses. In some contexts, gesture is preferred over voice, and in others the reverse is true. This section gives you tips on how to select the best voice commands to register so that misunderstandings are minimized and the user can most efficiently elicit the desired behavior from you app.

## Spatial-sound design

If the holograms in your app are generating sounds, you want to use spatial sound so that those sounds appear to be coming from the object that is supposedly generating them. For example, if your application is showing a railroad train moving across the user's field of view from right to left, you want the sound of the engine's horn to appear to be coming from the left, where the engine is, rather than from the midpoint of the train hologram.

## Spatial-mapping design

When a user scans an environment to provide a spatial map to an application, there are a number of things that could cause the resulting map to be less than perfect. Inadequate light levels; differing surface reflectance qualities; things, such as people, that are there one minute and gone the next; and even mirrors on the wall are all things that could interfere with getting a good scan. This section points out these problems and many more and gives you tips on how you can write your app in a way that minimizes the impact of such things on the quality of the user experience while running your app.

## Color design

Holograms are created by adding light to the light coming into the user's eyes from the real world. To have the hologram blend in with the world, attention must be paid to colors. White for example, tends to pop and should be reduced in intensity. Black cannot be rendered at all, since the HoloLens cannot take light away from what is entering the eyes; it can only add light. Any black area of a hologram appears transparent instead, letting the light from the real world come through. The edges of moving holograms may show some color separation, as well as aliasing effects. These are all things to consider when you are designing your app.

## Updating existing universal apps for HoloLens

All apps that run on the Universal Windows Platform (UWP) will run on the HoloLens with minimal adjustment. Thus, migrating a UWP app to HoloLens will be easy, provided you followed the Windows 10 Human Interface Guidelines when you first developed those apps.

## Community

The HoloLens community is growing rapidly as more developers come on board, joining the Micro-softies who are already involved. There are several ways you can interact with the community.

### The Microsoft HoloLens team

On the Dev Center Community page you can find photos and mini-biographies of the members of the HoloLens developer engagement crew. It is their job to help you.

### Follow HoloLens on Twitter for the latest news

The HoloLens Twitter page is where you will find all the latest breaking news about all things HoloLens. The page has over 100,000 followers and continues to grow.

### Interact with other developers on the forums

The HoloLens App Development forum is the place to go when you have a question or when you want to discuss some aspect of holographic development with other developers. Generally, any problem that you are likely to have has already been encountered by either another developer or a Microsoft staffer who monitors this forum. Drop by and join the discussion.

### See what's possible on the HoloLens YouTube channel

The HoloLens YouTube channel is the place where you will find many of the videos that have been produced about the HoloLens. It's a great place to catch a glimpse of the wide variety of experiences that the HoloLens makes possible.

## Support

Two types of support are available on the Windows Dev Center site: developer support and hardware support. You will probably need support in one or the other of these areas sooner or later, if not both.

### Developer support

Developer support helps you with issues you might have in becoming a registered developer, developing a HoloLens app, publishing your app, marketing your app, or getting paid for sales of your app.

### Hardware support

Hardware support helps you with questions or issues you may be having with the HoloLens hardware itself.

# Summary

This has been a long chapter because there is a lot to think about when it comes to developing with Unity and Visual Studio. The combination of the Unity and Visual Studio development tools is described, and the resources available at the Windows Dev Center are summarized. If you run into a problem in the course of developing a holographic app, a clue as to where to turn for answers or help can be found here.

■ ■ ■

# CHAPTER 10

# Using C# with Visual Studio and Unity

If you are going to develop applications with any complexity at all, you will need to do some programming. Holograms are given behaviors via scripts written with either C# or JavaScript if you are using Unity, or with C++ if you are using the DirectX APIs. All of the tools and information on the Windows Dev Center Web site assume you are using C# with Visual Studio. This is also the easiest path to take if you are new to application development. C# is easier to learn than many other development languages and is heavily supported both by Microsoft and by a vast user base.

## The C# Language

C# is a major topic in itself about which many books have been written and many courses are being taught. It is not the purpose of this book to teach C#. Use one of the available books or courses for that. You will be able to create some simple applications with only a cursory knowledge of C#. Start by building some of those using the resources available in Unity. For anything more involved, expect to put in the time and effort needed to gain proficiency in C# programming before you produce the killer app that makes HoloLens a "must have" device for millions of people.

## C# Scripts

Because Unity was originally used as a development platform for computer games, a lot of the names of things in the Unity documentation are game oriented. For example, the components that appear in a scene are called GameObjects. The actions that GameObjects take are called gameplay. Events that occur in the course of the execution of the application are called game events. Unity provides a collection of basic components, and, in addition, you can create your own components and give them behaviors with C# scripts. Rather than your writing a huge program that controls every aspect of your application, each component of the application is controlled by its own C# script. This modularization of the code makes both coding and debugging much easier, as you write and test out the code for each GameObject individually before you have to start thinking about how one GameObject might interact with another. Modular code is also easier to maintain as a software product evolves.

© Allen G. Taylor 2016
A. G. Taylor, *Develop Microsoft HoloLens Apps Now*, DOI 10.1007/978-1-4842-2202-7_10

# Adding Behaviors to Unity Components with C# Scripts

When developers use Unity to create games, they follow the documentation and tutorials provided by Unity to learn how to create and add scripts to the components of their GameObjects. They are instructed to use MonoDevelop as their editor, which is launched from within Unity. This is not the way to develop holographic apps for use with the HoloLens, however.

---

■ **Warning** Don't believe the Unity documentation on creating scripts. The version of Unity that has been modified for holographic development, using Visual Studio as its editor rather than MonoDevelop, requires a different procedure, which I outline next.

---

## Add a script component using Unity's Inspector

Rather than following Unity's documentation for adding a script to a GameObject, select the GameObject in the Hierarchy panel and then click on the Add Component button in the Inspector. This will drop down a dialog box, as shown in Figure 10-1.

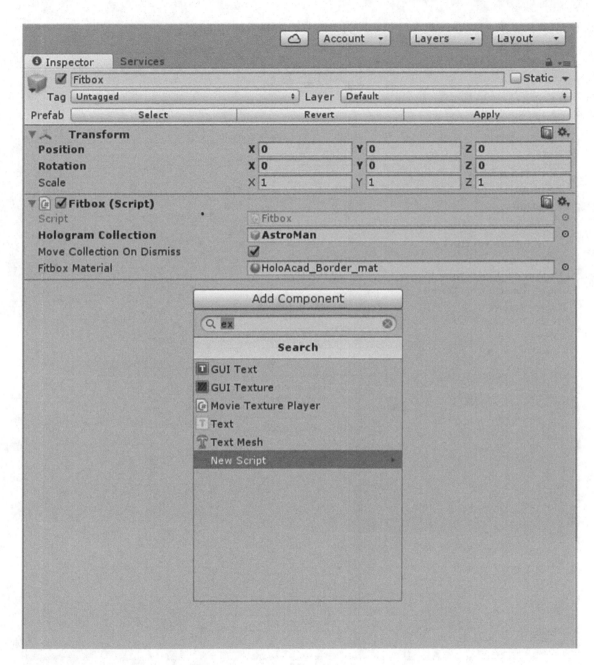

**Figure 10-1.** *Choose **New Script** as the type of component to add*

Click on **New Script**. A dialog box will appear, as shown in Figure 10-2.

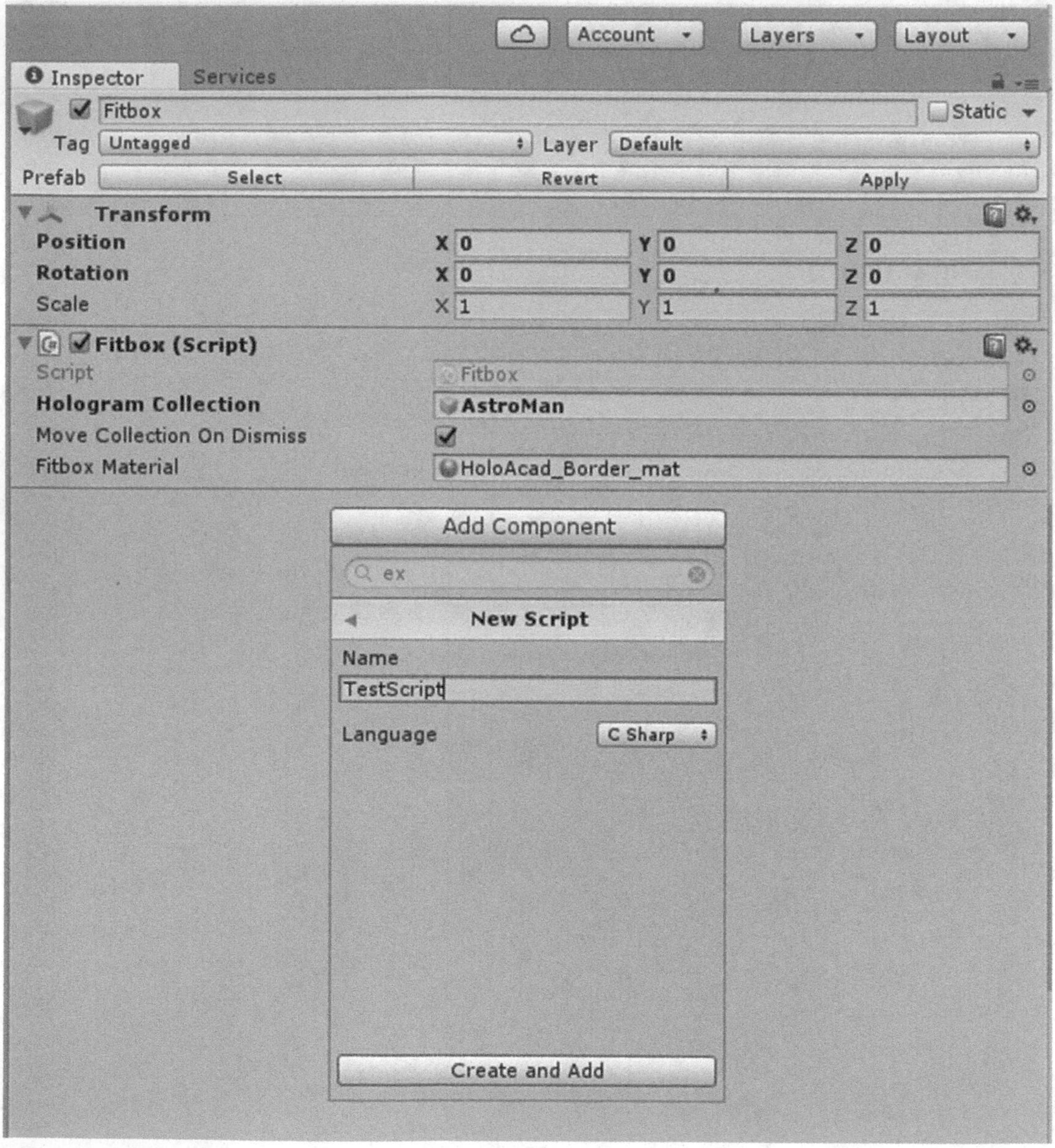

*Figure 10-2.* *Adding a script to a GameObject*

In the Name field, type in the name of the script. One idea is to give the script the same name as the GameObject it is attached to. If the script is usable in more than one context, a name that relates to its function may be better. Make sure that Language is set to **C Sharp**, and then click the Create and Add button. This will add the new script to the Inspector, as shown at the bottom of Figure 10-3.

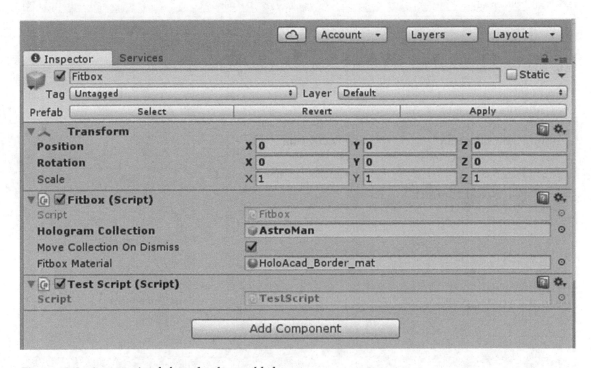

**Figure 10-3.** *A new script skeleton has been added*

To add functionality to the new script, click on the small, gear-shaped icon at the right edge of the script component of your GameObject. This will display a menu like the one shown in Figure 10-4.

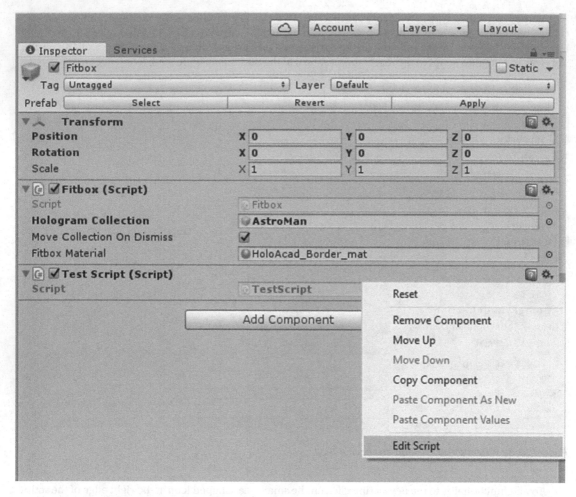

***Figure 10-4.*** *Component settings menu*

Click on **Edit Script**.

# Visual Studio will launch, but MonoDevelop may launch too

Developers are accustomed to working with beta software and with tool chains that have not had a lot of time to become refined. This crops up in HoloLens development too. The default editor for Unity scripts is MonoDevelop. It is a cross-platform editor that works with Linux and Mac OS X as well as with Windows. For that reason, Unity can attract developers with a variety of backgrounds. However, for HoloLens development we are concentrating on the Windows platform, specifically Windows Holographic. We will be using Visual Studio as our editor rather than MonoDevelop.

When you click on the **Edit Script** option, as shown in Figure 10-3, Visual Studio will launch, but sometimes MonoDevelop will launch too. If this happens, just ignore any messages you may receive in MonoDevelop and exit out of it. Visual Studio will display the code skeleton shown in Figure 10-5.

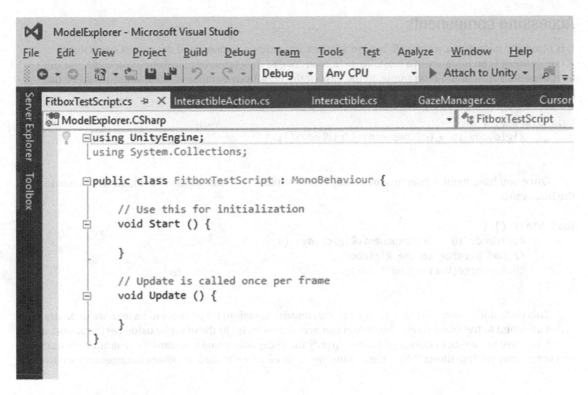

**Figure 10-5.** *Script code skeleton*

## Skeleton of a script file

The bare-bones code skeleton shown in Figure 10-5 is very similar to what MonoDevelop would generate, but the Visual Studio version is compatible with holographic development. MonoDevelop does not take into account the differences between screen-based game development and holographic development.

The Start function is run once at the launch of an application. It is a good place to put initialization code. The Update function is run once every frame. It is where all the frame-by-frame actions of the application take place. There is more information on this available at https://docs.unity3d.com/Manual/ExecutioinOrder.html.

## Controlling GameObjects using components

In Unity, you can make limited changes to a GameObject's component properties using the Inspector. You can change its position by changing values in the Transform component. You can change its color in the Render component, you can change the way it reacts to gravity by changing the mass of the Rigidbody component, and so on. That is all well and good, but you are probably going to want more control over GameObjects than what is offered by the Inspector.

With a script, you can alter the value of a GameObject's properties gradually over time or in response to some action by the user, known to Unity as the Player. The user in a holographic app is very much like the player in a first-person-shooter video game. A holographic app doesn't have to involve shooting, but it can if you want it to.

## Accessing components

It is often the case that a script will need to access some other component of the same GameObject. A component is an instance of a class. To get a reference to the component instance you want, use the GetComponent function. For example, in the case of the Rigidbody component, use something like the following code:

```
Void Start () {
        Rigidbody rb = GetComponent<Rigidbody>();
}
```

Once you have made a reference to a component instance, you can set its value much as you would in the Inspector:

```
Void Start () {
        Rigidbody rb = GetComponent<Rigidbody> ();
        // Add a force to the Rigidbody.
        Rb.AddForce(Vector3.up * 10f);
}
```

This code adds a force of value 10 units in the upward direction. It's possible to have more than one script attached to the same GameObject. You can access one script or the other by using GetComponent as usual. Just use the name of the script class to specify the component type you want. For example, characters in a scene may want to direct their attention toward, or even move toward, another character or the Player.

## Accessing other objects

In many applications, you are going to want a script to be able to track what another GameObject is doing. One way to do that is to add a public GameObject variable to the script:

```
Public class EnemyDrone : Monobehaviour {
        Public GameObject player;

        // Other variables and functions . . .
}
```

Such variables are visible in the Inspector. You can assign this variable to a GameObject by dragging the object onto the variable in the Inspector. The GetComponent function will now work for this object, and component-access variables are also available.

You can now use code like the following:

```
public class EnemyDrone : Monobehaviour {
        public GameObject player;

        void Start() {
                // Start the drone ten units behind and ten units above the player
                Transform.position = player.transform.position - Vector3.forward * 10f -
                Vector3.up * 10f;
        }
}
```

Linking objects together with variables is useful when individual objects have permanent connections. With array variables, you can link several objects of the same type. Those links must be established in Visual Studio rather than a runtime.

## Event functions

Unity applications are event driven rather than executing sequentially, one instruction after another. This means that Unity passes control to a script by calling functions that are contained within it. Once a function has finished executing, control is passed back to the Unity engine. Such functions are called *event functions* since are called by Unity in response to events that occur during the course of the running of the application.

We have already seen the Start and Update event functions, shown in Figure 10-5. There are many more, which are all members of the MonoBehaviour class.

## Update events

A Unity holographic application is much like an animation, where animation frames are generated on the fly. Changes in position, state, and behavior of GameObjects occur just before a frame is rendered.

The physics engine also updates at discrete time intervals, but not necessarily in sync with the frame updates. Physics code should be placed in the FixedUpdate function rather than in the Update function. This is because fixed updates are guaranteed to occur at fixed time intervals. Frame updates have no such guarantee, and may vary depending on the load on the processor.

There is also a LateUpdate function, which becomes active after all objects in the scene and all animations have been calculated.

## Initialization events

Initializations can take place during both the Awake and the Start functions. The Awake function is called for each object in a scene when the scene loads. All Awakes have finished before the first Start is called. Start is called before the first frame or physics update of an object.

## GUI events

When the user performs a Select or some other operation on a hologram, she is performing a GUI event. Code to handle such operations should be placed in an OnGUI function. This function will be called frequently enough so that there is no noticeable delay between the triggering event and the response to that event. Similar functions are OnMouseOver and OnMouseDown, which will trigger actions when a Bluetooth mouse pointer either hovers over or the left mouse button is depressed when the pointer is over a hologram.

## Physics events

The physics engine calls event functions in an object's script when a collision event occurs. When a GameObject contacts another GameObject, assuming a collider has been attached to the GameObject, the OnCollisionEnter function will handle what should be done. If contact is maintained, the OnCollisionStay function comes into play. When contact is finally broken, the OnCollisionExit function is executed.

## Unity scripting resources

Unity's online documentation that deals with scripting is extensive. However, remember that it is written from the point of view of a gaming platform rather than a platform for building holographic apps. It is good to keep that in mind until it is updated to address the unique concerns of HoloLens developers.

# Summary

The combination of the Unity game-development platform and the Visual Studio editor is the recommended tool chain for the development of holographic applications for HoloLens. Unity in particular was not designed for holographic development, but a special beta version of it has been modified to work closely with Visual Studio for the production of holographic apps. As of this writing, the Unity documentation has not caught up with this new use of the Unity Framework. Notwithstanding that, game developers familiar with Unity should be able to transition easily to becoming holographic developers for HoloLens.

■ ■ ■

# CHAPTER 11

# Building the Origami Sample Application

The best way to learn how to create a holographic application is to create a holographic application. Microsoft's Holographic Academy eases you into application creation with a series of tutorials that introduce you to the major features of the tools you will use to develop applications. The tutorials also show you some of the ways to use these tools to create holograms that do interesting things. The first of these is named Origami, which creates a holographic assemblage of paper sculptures that the user can interact with using gaze, gesture, and voice.

Most of the work of creating the application is done for you, but you must make some additions and modifications to the C# code to complete each stage of the project. New functionality is added to the project bit by bit until you have an example of not only gaze, gesture, and voice, but also of spatial sound and spatial mapping.

If you do not yet have a HoloLens device, you can deploy any applications that you build to the HoloLens Emulator. Even if you do have a HoloLens, deploying to the Emulator makes a lot of sense. You can cycle through multiple iterations of your code while debugging without having to download to your device every time.

## Getting Started

To create holographic applications, you must have the correct tools, configured the right way. Requirements for the development PC are quite specific:

- 64-bit Windows 10 Pro, Enterprise, or Education Edition (the Home Edition will not work)

- 64-bit CPU (this is a no-brainer if you are running 64-bit Windows)

- A CPU with at least four cores, or multiple CPUs that add up to at least four cores

- 8 GB of RAM or more

- The PC's BIOS must support:

  - Hardware-assisted virtualization

  - Second Level Address Translation (SLAT)

  - Hardware-based Data Execution Prevention (DEP)

- A GPU that supports DirectX 11.0 or later and WDDM 1.2 driver or later

© Allen G. Taylor 2016
A. G. Taylor, *Develop Microsoft HoloLens Apps Now*, DOI 10.1007/978-1-4842-2202-7_11

In addition to the preceding requirements, make sure that Hyper-V is enabled on your system. You can reach this from Control Panel ➤ Programs ➤ Programs and Features ➤ Turn Windows Features on or off. The Emulator will not install successfully without Hyper-V support.

## Install the tools you will need

There are three software tools that you will need. All three may be downloaded for free. The needed tools are:

- Visual Studio 2015 Update 2 or later. The Community Edition is a free download from Microsoft and supports holographic development.

- HoloLens Emulator. This also is a free download from Microsoft.

- Unity 5.4.0f3-HTP or later. This is a free download from Microsoft or Unity. Until Unity comes out with a major release that supports it, be sure you use a version with the HTP suffix, which is specifically for HoloLens.

## Download the Origami project files

The files for the Origami project can be downloaded from a link under the Origami project within Microsoft's Holographic Academy, or directly from Github.com. The files are archived in a zip file. Unarchive them to a convenient location, leaving the file name as Origami.

# Setting the Stage

In Chapter 8, we built the simplest possible hologram, a featureless cylinder that just hovered in space. In this chapter, we will use some pre-existing assets to create a more complex scene with several different holographic objects (called GameObjects) that have properties such as color and complex shapes, as well as behaviors.

## Opening the Origami project in Unity

Follow these steps to get started:

1. Start Unity and select **Open**, since you want to open an existing project (Origami) rather than start a new project.

2. Enter the location of the Origami folder that you unarchived after downloading it from either the Holographic Academy or GitHub.

3. Select **Origami** and then click the Select Folder button, as shown at the bottom of Figure 11-1. It will take some time to load the project into Unity. Be patient. A prompt may appear, saying that the files you are importing were created using a different version of Unity. You can safely ignore this.

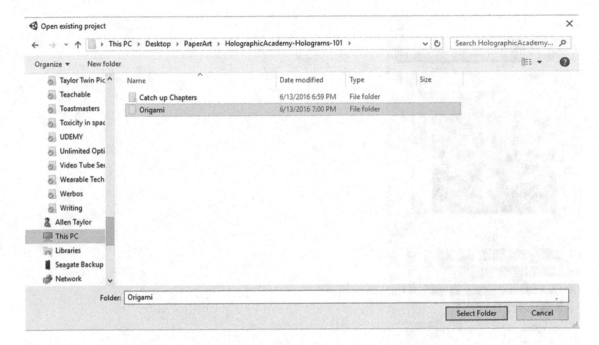

***Figure 11-1.*** *Connecting with the Origami project files*

Create a new _Scenes directory and then save the new scene into it, going to File ➤ Save Scene As in the menu at the top left of the Unity screen. In the Save Scene dialog box that appears, give the scene a file name of Origami and then click the Save button.

## Setting up the main camera

The main camera establishes the point of view of the person wearing the HoloLens. The main camera is located where the HoloLens user is located, and it sees what the HoloLens user sees. To be optimized for holographic mixed reality, the main camera must be set up as follows:

1. In the Hierarchy panel at the upper left, select **Main Camera**.

   In the Inspector panel, set the camera's transform position to 0,0,0.

2. Find the Clear Flags property in the Inspector, and in the dropdown menu, change Skybox to **Solid color**.

3. Click on the Background field to display the color picker shown in Figure 11-2.

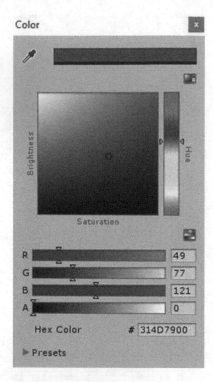

*Figure 11-2. Color picker*

4. Set the RGBA values all to zero. You can do this either by dragging the circle in the center of the Saturation/Brightness panel to the lower right-hand corner, or by entering 0 in each of the four RGBA fields, or by entering #00000000 as the Hex Color.

## Creating a scene

Once you have set up the main camera, the next task is to create a scene, as follows:

1. In the Hierarchy panel, click on **Create**, and from the menu that drops down, select **Create Empty**. This causes a new GameObject to appear.

2. Right-click on the new GameObject, and from the menu that appears, select **Rename**.

3. Rename the object OrigamiCollection.

4. In the Project panel, under Assets, click to open the Holograms folder.

5. Drag the **Stage** hologram into the Hierarchy panel as a child of OrigamiCollection.

6. Drag the **Sphere1** hologram into the Hierarchy panel as a child of OrigamiCollection.

7. Drag the **Sphere2** hologram into the Hierarchy panel as a child of OrigamiCollection.

8. Right-click the **Directional Light** object in the Hierarchy panel and delete it.

9. Drag the **Lights** hologram into the root level of the Hierarchy panel.

10. In the Hierarchy panel, select **OrigamiCollection**.

11. In the Inspector, set the transform position to 0, -0.5, and 2.0. This establishes the location of the OrigamiCollection relative to the position of the main camera, which is the position of the HoloLens user.

12. Press the Play button ( ▶ ) at the top center of the Unity window. This shows what the scene looks like from the point of view of the main camera. The center panel should have turned black, with the stage in the center, including some origami cubes, paper airplanes, and two spheres, as shown in Figure 11-3.

*Figure 11-3. OrigamiCollection as seen in Unity*

If you do not see the stage in the center of the field of view, press Play again to exit Play mode and check the position coordinates for both the main camera and the stage. Make sure they are right. If you do see the stage in the center, after viewing the hologram, press Play again to exit Play mode.

## Exporting the project to Visual Studio

Now that your hologram is complete, you will need to export it to Visual Studio so that it can be deployed to the HoloLens Emulator. To start the process, do the following:

1. In Unity, go to File ➤ Build Settings.

2. Select **Windows Store** in the Platform list and click the Switch Platform button.

3. Set SDK to **Universal 10** and Build Type to **D3D**.

4. Check the **Unity C# Projects** box.

5. Click the Add Open Scenes button to add the current scene to what will be built. The Build Settings window should now look like Figure 11-4.

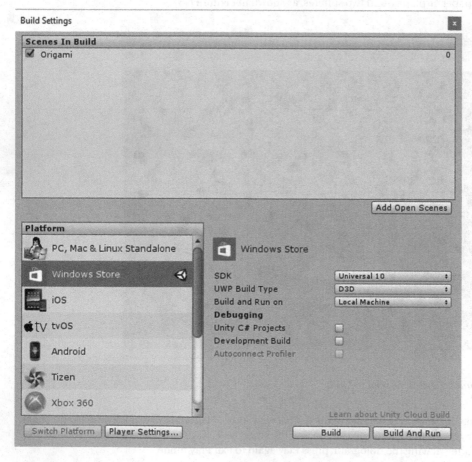

***Figure 11-4.*** *Build Settings window after proper choices for holograms have been made but before C# Projects box has been checked*

We now transition from the Build Settings dialog box to the Inspector panel. Do the following:

1. Click the Player Settings. . . button.

2. In the Inspector, select the small green Windows Store logo.

3. Scroll down to the bottom of the panel and select **Publishing Settings**.

4. In the Capabilities section at the bottom of the panel, make sure that the **Microphone** and **Spatial Perception** capabilities are checked.

5. Back in the Build Settings window, click the Build button. The Build Windows Store dialog box will appear, showing the contents of the Origami folder.

6. Right-click in the open area, and from the menu that appears select **New** and then create a new folder named App.

7. Single-click the App folder to select it.

8. Click on the Select Folder button in the lower right of the Build Windows Store dialog box. Unity will start building your project. When it is finished, a File Explorer window will appear.

9. Double-click the App folder to enter it.

10. Open the Origami Visual Studio Solution named Origami.sln by double-clicking on it. Visual Studio will launch, and your project will be loaded.

At the bottom of the Visual Studio screen, you may see something disheartening, such as the Error List shown in Figure 11-5.

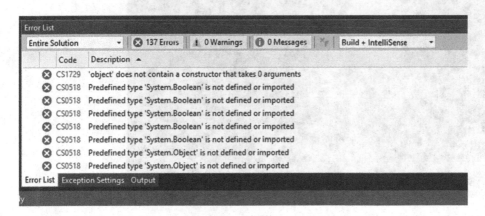

***Figure 11-5.*** *Error List upon export to Visual Studio*

Don't panic! Even though it says there are 137 errors, you are probably fine if you carefully followed directions up to this point. Go ahead and deploy the project to the HoloLens Emulator anyway.

# Deploying the project to the HoloLens Emulator

Once the project has been built in your development machine, you want to deploy it to your target device. In this case, that will be the HoloLens Emulator, which runs under a virtual machine on your development machine. Perform these steps:

1. In Visual Studio's top toolbar, change the target from Debug to **Release** and from ARM to **X86**.

2. Click on the little down-pointing arrow next to the Device button to drop a menu of possible targets.

3. Select **HoloLens Emulator** from the menu. There may be several versions of this. If so, select the latest one.

4. From the main menu, go to Debug ➤ Start Without debugging. **Ctrl + F5** will do the same thing, which is to deploy your project to the HoloLens Emulator.

   If the deploy operation has succeeded, after a period of time the HoloLens Start menu will appear in the Emulator window, as shown in Figure 11-6.

*Figure 11-6. Emulator view of HoloLens Start menu*

After a while, the Emulator screen will go blank, and after another while, the Unity logo will appear. After a third while, your hologram will appear. It may look something like Figure 11-7.

**Figure 11-7.** *Not exactly the hologram you wanted to see*

The main camera is not quite perfectly aimed at the OrigamiCollection hologram. You can fix this by clicking on the Human Input button in the vertical menu at the upper-right corner of the Emulator display and then depressing the right mouse button to move the view down. The result should look like Figure 11-8.

**Figure 11-8.** *Looking at the OrigamiCollection straight on*

Congratulations! You have created a holographic project with multiple elements. Now, let's add some functionality to that project with a C# script.

# Adding Gaze Functionality

Since the HoloLens is self-contained and untethered, the user is free to roam. This means she is not sitting at a desk with a keyboard under one hand and a mouse under the other. Although the HoloLens works fine with a Bluetooth keyboard and Bluetooth mouse, using such input devices restricts what a person can do with a holographic app. What is needed is a way of interacting with the app that does not tie the user down to any specific location. This interaction is enabled by the user's gaze.

On the HoloLens, there is a camera that is pointed straight ahead. This means that the camera sees whatever the user sees, as long as she is looking straight ahead. Because the HoloLens "knows" where all the holograms are that it has created, it also knows whether the user's gaze is falling on a particular hologram at any given moment. This provides a means for the user to interact directly with the target hologram, either by a gesture, which is also visible to the HoloLens, or by a voice command. We can add the ability to target a hologram with gaze by adding a script to the Origami project.

## Adding a script to the project

Here's a step-by-step set of instructions for adding gaze capability to your project:

1. Return to your Unity project and close the Build Settings window if it is still open.

2. Open the Holograms folder under Assets in the Project panel.

3. Drag the **Cursor** object into the root level of the Hierarchy panel.

4. Double-click on the **Cursor** object in the Hierarchy panel. This displays the Cursor object as a red ring at the origin of the coordinate system in the Scene panel. Figure 11-9 shows what it looks like.

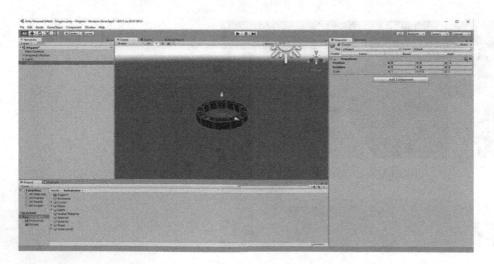

***Figure 11-9.*** *Cursor hologram*

5. Right-click on the Scripts folder in the Project panel.

6. In the menu that appears (Figure 11-10), select **Create**.

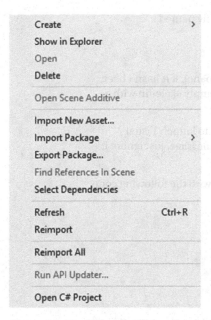

**Figure 11-10.** *Menu that drops down after right-clicking on the Scripts folder*

7. From the Create submenu (Figure 11-11), select **C# Script**.

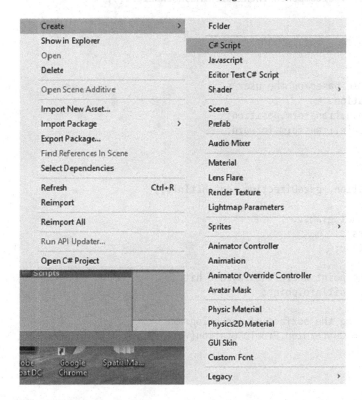

**Figure 11-11.** *Create submenu*

8. In the Assets area, a new script has been added, temporarily named NewBehaviourScript. Rename it WorldCursor.

9. Select the **Cursor** object in the Hierarchy panel.

10. Drag and drop the WorldCursor script into the Inspector panel, if it hasn't been placed there automatically. At this point, the script is an empty skeleton with a Start function and an Update function.

11. Double-click the **WorldCursor** script in the Project panel to launch Visual Studio. If MonoDevelop launches and gives you an error message, just ignore it and exit MonoDevelop.

12. Overwrite the script skeleton that is now in Visual Studio with the following code:

```
using UnityEngine;

public class WorldCursor : MonoBehaviour
{
    private MeshRenderer meshRenderer;

    // Use this for initialization
    void Start()
    {
        // Grab the mesh renderer that's on the same object as this script.
        meshRenderer = this.gameObject.GetComponentInChildren<MeshRenderer>();
    }

    // Update is called once per frame
    void Update()
    {
        // Do a raycast into the world based on the user's
        // head position and orientation.
        var headPosition = Camera.main.transform.position;
        var gazeDirection = Camera.main.transform.forward;

        RaycastHit hitInfo;

        if (Physics.Raycast(headPosition, gazeDirection, out hitInfo))
        {
            // If the raycast hit a hologram...
            // Display the cursor mesh.
            meshRenderer.enabled = true;

            // Move the cursor to the point where the raycast hit.
            this.transform.position = hitInfo.point;

            // Rotate the cursor to hug the surface of the hologram.
            this.transform.rotation = Quaternion.FromToRotation(Vector3.up, hitInfo.normal);
        }
        else
        {
```

```
        // If the raycast did not hit a hologram, hide the cursor mesh.
        meshRenderer.enabled = false;
    }
  }
}
```

■ **Note**   If you have an electronic copy of this book, doing a copy and paste will be much easier than retyping this code.

From the File menu, select **Save All**.

## Rebuild and reload

Back in Unity, rebuild the project with File ➤ Build Settings. The choices you made previously should still be there. The new WorldCursor code has replaced the skeleton code in the Inspector. Click on the Build button.

## Redeploy to the Emulator

After the Unity build operation completes, perform the following steps to deploy what you have built:

1. In the Build Windows Store dialog box, select App and click on the Select Folder button.

2. After the build completes, in the dialog box that pops up, double-click on the App folder to open it.

3. Double-click on **Origami.sln**.

4. Make sure Visual Studio is set to Debug, X86, and HoloLens Emulator.

5. From the menu, go to Debug ➤ Start Without Debugging

6. You may get a warning in the Error window partway through the deploy process. Just ignore it.

If all went well, the Emulator will appear, show a brief triangle mesh scan, show the Unity logo, and then show the OrigamiCollection hologram. If you have an Xbox controller, you can use it to look around the scene and see how the cursor interacts with the objects in the Collection. Lacking an Xbox controller, you can use the keyboard and mouse to move the position of the user as it relates to the hologram.

If all is almost well, but not quite, try Debug ➤ Start Without Debugging again. Sometimes it will work the second time but not the first.

■ **Tip**   Documentation at the online HoloLens Academy suggests leaving the Emulator active between runs, as it takes a while to reload. That may not be a good idea. Something might have been left in an anomalous state on the previous run. If you are not experiencing a successful deployment, try exiting the Emulator before attempting to deploy again.

# Adding Gesture Functionality

I suppose it's great to see a cursor hitting one of your holograms, and thereby know what you are looking at. However, the excitement soon wears off. If you want your holograms to actually do something, such as respond to an action of the user, you will have to add some more functionality. This is where gestures come in.

The most frequently used gesture is the air tap, which normally initiates a Select operation, but can alternatively mean anything that the developer wants it to mean in the context of a given application. Often a user will sweep her gaze over a holographic object without wanting to do anything to it. At other times, she *will* want to do something. On those occasions, there needs to be a way for her to select the object. The air tap fills the bill. With your hand in the field of view, raise the index finger vertical, then tap it briefly against the thumb. HoloLens recognizes that gesture as an air tap and, if the proper script is available, executes an operation of some sort. The meaning of that operation will depend on the contents of the script that senses the air tap and performs the operation.

In the Origami application, we want holographic objects to take some action when they are the object of the user's gaze and have been activated by an air tap gesture. To accomplish that, we will add two new scripts to the application. First, we will add a script to manage the user's gaze and gesture, and then we will add a script to manage what a holographic object does when it is being looked at and an air tap is performed.

## Create a script to manage gaze and gesture

Follow these steps:

1. In Unity, right-click on the Scripts folder in the Project panel, then select **Create** and **C# Script** from the menus that appear.

2. Name the new script GazeGestureManager.

3. Drag the GazeGestureManager script onto the OrigamiCollection in the Hierarchy panel.

4. Double-click the **GazeGestureManager** script to open it in Visual Studio. Once again, if MonoDevelop launches, exit it. You will not be using it. After removing MonoDevelop, you may have to double-click on GazeGestureManager again to cause the skeleton code for it to appear in Visual Studio.

5. Replace the skeleton code with the following:

```
using UnityEngine;
using UnityEngine.VR.WSA.Input;

public class GazeGestureManager : MonoBehaviour
{
    public static GazeGestureManager Instance { get; private set; }

    // Represents the hologram that is currently being gazed at.
    public GameObject FocusedObject { get; private set; }

    GestureRecognizer recognizer;

    // Use this for initialization
    void Start()
    {
        Instance = this;
```

```
    // Set up a GestureRecognizer to detect Select gestures.
    recognizer = new GestureRecognizer();
    recognizer.TappedEvent += (source, tapCount, ray) =>
    {
        // Send an OnSelect message to the focused object and its ancestors.
        if (FocusedObject != null)
        {
            FocusedObject.SendMessageUpwards("OnSelect");
        }
    };
    recognizer.StartCapturingGestures();
}

// Update is called once per frame
void Update()
{
    // Figure out which hologram is focused this frame.
    GameObject oldFocusObject = FocusedObject;

    // Do a raycast into the world based on the user's
    // head position and orientation.
    var headPosition = Camera.main.transform.position;
    var gazeDirection = Camera.main.transform.forward;

    RaycastHit hitInfo;
    if (Physics.Raycast(headPosition, gazeDirection, out hitInfo))
    {
        // If the raycast hit a hologram, use that as the focused object.
        FocusedObject = hitInfo.collider.gameObject;
    }
    else
    {
        // If the raycast did not hit a hologram, clear the focused object.
        FocusedObject = null;
    }

    // If the focused object changed this frame,
    // start detecting fresh gestures again.
    if (FocusedObject != oldFocusObject)
    {
        recognizer.CancelGestures();
        recognizer.StartCapturingGestures();
    }
}
}
```

## Create a script to manage the Origami spheres

Now it is time to create a script for the folded paper spheres, each of which is a separate holographic object:

1. Create a new script in the Scripts folder in Unity's Project panel and name it SphereCommands.

2. Expand the **OrigamiCollection** object in the Hierarchy view if it is not already expanded.

3. Drag the **SphereCommands** script onto the **Sphere1** object in the Hierarchy panel.

4. Drag the **SphereCommands** script onto the **Sphere2** object in the Hierarchy panel.

5. Replace the SphereCommands skeleton script with the following code:

```
using UnityEngine;

public class SphereCommands : MonoBehaviour
{
    // Called by GazeGestureManager when the user performs a Select gesture
    void OnSelect()
    {
        // If the sphere has no Rigidbody component, add one to enable physics.
        if (!this.GetComponent<Rigidbody>())
        {
            var rigidbody = this.gameObject.AddComponent<Rigidbody>();
            rigidbody.collisionDetectionMode = CollisionDetectionMode.Continuous;
        }
    }
}
```

On the File menu, choose **Save All**. Now, export, build, and redeploy the project:

1. Back in Unity, do a Build operation.

2. Send the solution file (Origami.sln) in the App folder to Visual Studio.

3. With Visual Studio's icon bar set to Debug, x86, HoloLens Emulator, go to Debug ➤ Start Without Debugging to commence the deployment of the app to the Emulator.

---

■ **Warning** Don't be surprised by behavior that is inconsistent from one deployment to the next, with no changes made in between. Earlier, I suggested exiting the emulator before making a new deployment of an existing app. When you do that, you may get an error message such as that shown in Figure 11-12. Often after receiving a message such as this, trying again without changing anything and without exiting the Emulator will lead to success. Go figure.

---

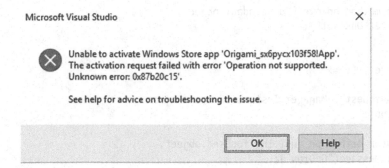

*Figure 11-12. Error message similar to one you might receive when deploying an app*

If things have worked well, placing the cursor on a sphere and then doing an air tap will suddenly make the sphere subject to the law of gravity and it will fall down onto the paper airplane and from there to the stage and finally off and out of sight.

# Enabling Voice Input

The other way to affect a holographic object besides gesture is with a voice command. This is also accomplished by adding a C# script to the app. We can upgrade the Origami app by making the spheres sensitive to voice commands as well as to gestures. The behavior of the spheres is to fall under the influence of gravity when they are activated. We can add a script that enables voice input. In addition, we can add a script that specifically applies to the spheres. We want to be able to command the spheres to fall, and we also want to be able to restore them to their original position so that we can have the fun of dropping them repeatedly.

Create a script to manage speech input:

1.  Back in the Unity Scripts folder, create a new script named SpeechManager.

2.  Drag the **SpeechManager** script onto the **OrigamiCollection** object in the Hierarchy panel.

3.  Open the **SpeechManager** script in Visual Studio.

4.  Replace the skeleton code in SpeechManager with the following:

```
using System.Collections.Generic;
using System.Linq;
using UnityEngine;
using UnityEngine.Windows.Speech;

public class SpeechManager : MonoBehaviour
{
    KeywordRecognizer keywordRecognizer = null;
    Dictionary<string, System.Action> keywords = new Dictionary<string, System.Action>();

    // Use this for initialization
    void Start()
    {
        keywords.Add("Reset world", () =>
        {
```

```
        // Call the OnReset method on every descendant object.
        this.BroadcastMessage("OnReset");
    });

    keywords.Add("Drop Sphere", () =>
    {
        var focusObject = GazeGestureManager.Instance.FocusedObject;
        if (focusObject != null)
        {
            // Call the OnDrop method on just the focused object.
            focusObject.SendMessage("OnDrop");
        }
    });

    // Tell the KeywordRecognizer about our keywords.
    keywordRecognizer = new KeywordRecognizer(keywords.Keys.ToArray());

    // Register a callback for the KeywordRecognizer and start recognizing!
    keywordRecognizer.OnPhraseRecognized += KeywordRecognizer_OnPhraseRecognized;
    keywordRecognizer.Start();
}

private void KeywordRecognizer_OnPhraseRecognized(PhraseRecognizedEventArgs args)
{
    System.Action keywordAction;
    if (keywords.TryGetValue(args.text, out keywordAction))
    {
        keywordAction.Invoke();
    }
}
}
```

That takes care of the general procedure for getting a holographic object to respond to a spoken command. Now, to generate the specific commands we want to use with the paper spheres.

Edit the sphere-management script to manage the spheres' response to speech commands:

1.  Open the **SphereCommands** script in Visual Studio.

2.  Replace the script skeleton with the following:

```
using UnityEngine;

public class SphereCommands : MonoBehaviour
{
    Vector3 originalPosition;

    // Use this for initialization
    void Start()
    {
        // Grab the original local position of the sphere when the app starts.
        originalPosition = this.transform.localPosition;
    }
```

```
// Called by GazeGestureManager when the user performs a Select gesture
void OnSelect()
{
    // If the sphere has no Rigidbody component, add one to enable physics.
    if (!this.GetComponent<Rigidbody>())
    {
        var rigidbody = this.gameObject.AddComponent<Rigidbody>();
        rigidbody.collisionDetectionMode = CollisionDetectionMode.Continuous;
    }
}

// Called by SpeechManager when the user says the "Reset world" command
void OnReset()
{
    // If the sphere has a Rigidbody component, remove it to disable physics.
    var rigidbody = this.GetComponent<Rigidbody>();
    if (rigidbody != null)
    {
        DestroyImmediate(rigidbody);
    }

    // Put the sphere back into its original local position.
    this.transform.localPosition = originalPosition;
}

// Called by SpeechManager when the user says the "Drop sphere" command
void OnDrop()
{
    // Just do the same logic as a Select gesture.
    OnSelect();
}
}
```

## Export, build, and redeploy

As before, build Origami in Unity, export to Visual Studio, and deploy to the HoloLens Emulator. Then, assuming you have a microphone on your development machine, practice placing the world cursor on a ball and saying "Drop sphere." After you have dropped both spheres, restore them to their original position by saying "Reset World."

# Giving Holograms Spatial Sound

One of the features that helps to sell the illusion that the holographic objects that the HoloLens generates are really there is spatial sound. Unlike stereophonic sound, which tells you whether a sound is coming from the left or the right or somewhere in between, spatial sound tells you precisely where a sound is coming from, whether in front of you, in back of you, or coming in from any given angle. It also gives you a sense of how far away a hologram is by how loud the sound is that it makes. Spatial sounds can be assigned to the objects in the Origami project. All it takes is a script. First, though, there needs to be some setup.

The following are the steps to set up spatial sound for the project:

1.  In Unity, from the top menu, go to Edit ➤ Project Settings ➤ Audio.

2.  In the Inspector panel, set the Spatializer Plugin to **MS HRTF Spatializer**.

3.  Drag the **Ambience** object from the Holograms folder in the Project panel onto the **OrigamiCollection** object in the Hierarchy panel.

4.  Select **OrigamiCollection** in the Hierarchy panel and then locate the Audio Source component in the Inspector panel. Change the following properties of the Audio Source:

    •   Check the **Spatialize** property.

    •   Check the **Play On Awake** property.

    •   Change Spatial Blend to **3D** by dragging the slider all the way to the right.

    •   Check the **Loop** property.

    •   Expand 3D Sound Settings and enter 0.1 for Doppler Level.

    •   Set Volume Rolloff to **Custom Rolloff**.

5.  In the Scripts folder in the Project panel, create a script named SphereSounds.

6.  Drag and drop the **SphereSounds** script onto both the **Sphere1** and **Sphere2** objects in the Hierarchy panel.

Now, add the SphereSounds script to the project:

1.  Double-click on the **SphereSounds** script in the Project panel to open it in Visual Studio. If MonoDevelop launches, exit it and wait for Visual Studio to finish loading.

2.  Navigate to the **SphereSounds.cs** script in Visual Studio if it is not already displayed in the script panel.

3.  Replace the skeleton code for SphereSounds.cs with the following:

```
using UnityEngine;

public class SphereSounds : MonoBehaviour
{
    AudioSource audioSource = null;
    AudioClip impactClip = null;
    AudioClip rollingClip = null;

    bool rolling = false;

    void Start()
    {
        // Add an AudioSource component and set up some defaults
        audioSource = gameObject.AddComponent<AudioSource>();
        audioSource.playOnAwake = false;
        audioSource.spatialize = true;
        audioSource.spatialBlend = 1.0f;
```

```
        audioSource.dopplerLevel = 0.0f;
        audioSource.rolloffMode = AudioRolloffMode.Custom;

        // Load the Sphere sounds from the Resources folder
        impactClip = Resources.Load<AudioClip>("Impact");
        rollingClip = Resources.Load<AudioClip>("Rolling");
    }

    // Occurs when this object starts colliding with another object
    void OnCollisionEnter(Collision collision)
    {
        // Play an impact sound if the sphere impacts strongly enough.
        if (collision.relativeVelocity.magnitude >= 0.1f)
        {
            audioSource.clip = impactClip;
            audioSource.Play();
        }
    }

    // Occurs each frame that this object continues to collide with another object
    void OnCollisionStay(Collision collision)
    {
        Rigidbody rigid = this.gameObject.GetComponent<Rigidbody>();

        // Play a rolling sound if the sphere is rolling fast enough.
        if (!rolling && rigid.velocity.magnitude >= 0.01f)
        {
            rolling = true;
            audioSource.clip = rollingClip;
            audioSource.Play();
        }
        // Stop the rolling sound if rolling slows down.
        else if (rolling && rigid.velocity.magnitude < 0.01f)
        {
            rolling = false;
            audioSource.Stop();
        }
    }

    // Occurs when this object stops colliding with another object
    void OnCollisionExit(Collision collision)
    {
        // Stop the rolling sound if the object falls off and stops colliding.
        if (rolling)
        {
            rolling = false;
            audioSource.Stop();
        }
    }
}
```

Now, save the SphereSounds script and return to Unity.

Now you are ready to export, build, and redeploy:

1. Select **Build Settings** from the File menu.

2. Click on the Build button in the Build Settings dialog box.

3. In the Build Windows Store dialog box, select **App** and then click on the Select Folder button.

4. When the build is complete, double-click on **App** in the Origami folder that appears.

5. Double-click on the **Origami.sln** file to launch Visual Studio.

6. Deploy to the Emulator as usual.

If things have gone well, some pleasant Japanese-sounding music will accompany the hologram. An emulated "movement" closer to the hologram will make the sound louder, and an emulated move away will make the sound quieter.

# Establishing Context with Spatial Mapping

You will want to place your holograms in locations that make sense in your real-world surroundings. To do that, your HoloLens must have a map of its surroundings. That map is drawn based on the spatial-mapping operation. We can add that capability to our Origami application with some adjustments and a new script.

The next task is to set up spatial mapping for this project:

1. In Unity, click on the Holograms folder in the Project panel.

2. Drag the **Spatial Mapping** asset into the root level of the Hierarchy panel.

3. Click on the **Spatial Mapping** object in the Hierarchy panel to select it.

4. In the Inspector panel, make the following changes:

   • Check the **Draw Visual Meshes** box.

   • Locate Draw Material and click on the circle on the right. A menu of drawing materials will appear. Scroll down and then click on **Wireframe**, then close the window. This should set the value for Draw Material to Wireframe in the Inspector.

5. Build, export, and deploy Origami as you have done before.

   a. When the app runs, a mesh of a previously scanned real-world living room will be rendered in wireframe.

6. Command a sphere to drop and watch how it rolls off the stage and onto the floor.

## Move the OrigamiCollection to a new location

   • In Unity's scripts folder, create a new script named TapToPlaceParent.

   • In the Hierarchy panel, expand the OrigamiCollection and select the **Stage** object.

- Drag the **TapToPlaceParent** script onto the Stage object.

- Open the **TapToPlaceParent** script in Visual Studio and replace the script skeleton with the following:

```
using UnityEngine;

public class TapToPlaceParent : MonoBehaviour
{
    bool placing = false;

    // Called by GazeGestureManager when the user performs a Select gesture
    void OnSelect()
    {
        // On each Select gesture, toggle whether the user is in placing mode.
        placing = !placing;

        // If the user is in placing mode, display the spatial-mapping mesh.
        if (placing)
        {
            SpatialMapping.Instance.DrawVisualMeshes = true;
        }
        // If the user is not in placing mode, hide the spatial-mapping mesh.
        else
        {
            SpatialMapping.Instance.DrawVisualMeshes = false;
        }
    }

    // Update is called once per frame
    void Update()
    {
        // If the user is in placing mode,
        // update the placement to match the user's gaze.

        if (placing)
        {
            // Do a raycast into the world that will only hit the spatial-mapping mesh.
            var headPosition = Camera.main.transform.position;
            var gazeDirection = Camera.main.transform.forward;

            RaycastHit hitInfo;
            if (Physics.Raycast(headPosition, gazeDirection, out hitInfo,
                30.0f, SpatialMapping.PhysicsRaycastMask))
            {
                // Move this object's parent object to
                // where the raycast hit the spatial-mapping mesh.
                this.transform.parent.position = hitInfo.point;
```

```
            // Rotate this object's parent object to face the user.
            Quaternion toQuat = Camera.main.transform.localRotation;
            toQuat.x = 0;
            toQuat.z = 0;
            this.transform.parent.rotation = toQuat;
        }
    }
  }
}
```

From the file menu, select **Save All**.

## Export, build, and deploy

Export, build, and deploy to the Emulator as before. If everything worked as it should, you will be able to place the stage at a specific location and then freeze it there with a Select gesture (either the letter A or the spacebar when running the Emulator). Move your gaze to a new location and use the Select gesture again to move it to a new location.

# Shifting from the Emulator to the HoloLens Device

Everything you have done in building Origami and deploying it to the HoloLens Emulator will work equally well when deploying to the HoloLens device. Assuming your HoloLens is properly paired with your development machine, the procedure is exactly the same except for the deployment target. Whereas in this chapter we have always deployed to Debug, x86, HoloLens Emulator, when deploying over USB cable the corresponding destination is Debug, x86, Device. When deploying to the HoloLens device over Wi-Fi, the corresponding destination is Debug, x86, Remote Machine.

# Summary

This chapter, by walking you through the Origami sample application, introduces you to the procedure for building an application in Unity, exporting it to Visual Studio, adding scripts for functionality, and finally deploying the app to the HoloLens Emulator. Once you have deployed to the Emulator, deploying to a HoloLens device will give you a much cooler experience. There are more advanced tutorials on the Holographic Academy Web site, but this one gives you all the basics.

## CHAPTER 12

■ ■ ■

# Building the Holograms 240 Shared Application

Amazing as the HoloLens mixed-reality experience can be when you are experiencing it by yourself, it reaches a whole new level when you can share that experience with other people. HoloLens technology supports multiple people, all wearing HoloLens devices, sharing the same mixed reality. They can all see, hear, and interact with the same holographic objects. This capability is directly applicable to learning and training applications, whether they be in a college class; an industrial, commercial, or military setting; or even in a brainstorming session. Of course, multiplayer games are also an obvious application.

## Getting Started

As with the Holograms 101E tutorial covered in Chapter 11, to create holographic applications you must have the correct tools, configured the right way. Requirements for the development PC are quite specific. If you have successfully worked through Chapter 11, then you already have all of the following:

- 64-bit Windows 10 Pro, Enterprise, or Education Edition (the Home Edition will not work)

- 64-bit CPU with at least four cores, or multiple CPUs that add up to at least four cores

- 8 GB of RAM or more

- The PC's BIOS must support:

    - Hardware-assisted virtualization

    - Second Level Address Translation (SLAT)

    - Hardware-based Data Execution Prevention (DEP)

    - A GPU that supports DirectX 11.0 or later and WDDM 1.2 driver or later

In addition to all of this, make sure that Hyper-V is enabled on your system. You can reach this from Control Panel ➤ Programs ➤ Programs and Features ➤ Turn Windows Features on or off. The Emulator will not install successfully without Hyper-V support.

## Install the tools you will need

There are three software tools that you will need. All three may be downloaded for free:

- Visual Studio 2015 Update 3. The Community Edition is a free download from Microsoft and supports holographic development.

- HoloLens Emulator. This also is a free download from Microsoft

- Unity version 5.4.0f3-HTP or later. Unless a major new release beyond Unity version 5.4 has been released, be sure to use the one with the HTP suffix. It is specifically designed for HoloLens.

## Download the Sharing Holograms project files

The files for the Sharing Holograms project can be downloaded from a link under the Holograms 240 Sharing Holograms project in Microsoft's Holographic Academy. The files are archived in a zip file. Unarchive them to a convenient location, leaving the file name as SharedHolograms.

# Building the App

In Chapter 11, we built the Origami application. The procedure here will be similar, but it is important to get every step exactly right. Just about any slight deviation from the steps involved will lead to failure. If you do crash and burn and cannot tell why, starting from absolute scratch is often the best route to success.

## Opening the Shared Holograms project in Unity

- Start Unity and select **Open**, since you want to open an existing project rather than start a new project.

- Enter the location of the SharedHolograms folder that you unarchived after downloading it from either the Holographic Academy or Github.

- Select **SharedHolograms** and then click the Select Folder button, as shown at the bottom of Figure 12-1. It will take some time to load the project into Unity. Be patient. You may see a warning that the project was created with a different version of Unity than the one you are using. As long as the version you are using is later than the one under which the project was created, this is not a problem. Just ignore the warning.

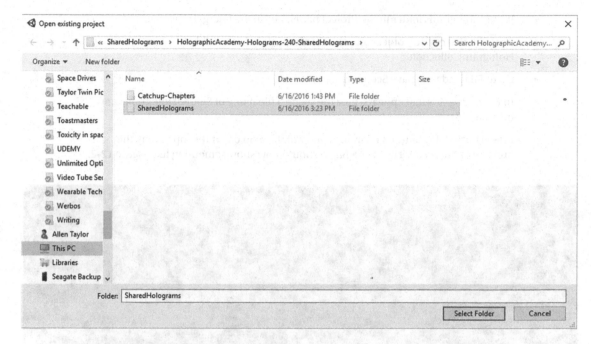

***Figure 12-1.*** *Connecting with the SharedHolograms project files*

- Save the new scene, going to File ➤ Save Scene As in the menu at the top left of the Unity screen.

- In the Save Scene dialog box that appears, give the scene a file name of SharedHolograms and then click the Save button.

## Populate the Hierarchy panel with assets

Rather than using the default main camera, we will use a prefab that contains a customized main camera, as follows:

- In the Hierarchy panel, right-click on **Main Camera** and select **Delete** from the menu that appears.

- In the HoloToolkit folder under Assets in the Project panel, select **Prefabs** and then **Camera**.

- From the Camera folder, drag the **Main Camera** prefab into the Hierarchy root level and drop it there.

- In the Hierarchy panel, click on the Create button and then on the Create Empty button. This will put a GameObect into the Hierarchy panel.

- Right-click on the GameObject and select **Rename** from the menu that appears.

- Rename the GameObject to HologramCollection.

- Select the **HologramCollection** object.

- In the Inspector, set the Transform Position to X: 0, Y: -0.25, Z: 2.

- In the Holograms folder in the Project panel, locate the EnergyHub asset.

- Drag the **EnergyHub** object into the Hierarchy panel as a child of HologramCollection.

- Go to File and then Save Scene As . . .

- In the dialog box that appears, give the scene a file name of SharedHolograms and then click Save.

- Press Unity's Play button ( ▶ ) in the center of the icon bar at the top to play the preview of the scene. The Scene panel should now show something like Figure 12-2.

***Figure 12-2.*** *Preview of the HologramCollection scene*

- Press Play again to stop the preview of the scene.

## Export the project to Visual Studio

- In Unity, go to File ➤ Build Settings in the main menu.

- In the Build Settings dialog box, click on the Add Open Scenes button to add the scene you have just created to the build.

- Select **Windows Store** from the Platform list and click the Switch Platform button.

- Set SDK to **Universal 10** and UWP Build Type to **D3D**.

- Check the **Unity C# Projects** box.

- Click the Build button.

- In the File Explorer window that appears, create a new folder named App.

- Single-click the App folder and then click the Select Folder button.

- Unity will start building the project. When it is finished, a File Explorer window will appear.

- In the File Explorer window, open the App folder.

- Double-click on **SharedHolograms.sln** to launch Visual Studio.

You may see some warnings in the Error List in the bottom panel. Often such warnings are of no consequence. Proceed with the deployment.

## Deploying the project to the HoloLens Emulator

- In Visual Studio, set the destination to Release, x86, HoloLens Emulator.

- From the menu, go to Debug ➤ Start Without Debugging. The deployment to the Emulator will commence.

If all has gone well, the HoloLens Emulator will appear and, after displaying the Unity logo, will show the Energy Hub and play some accompanying music. Figure 12-3 shows what this looks like. If, by chance, the app works in the editor but does not successfully deploy to the Emulator, try exiting the Emulator and then redeploying. Sometimes the Emulator is not left in the proper state after a previous use, causing deployment to fail.

*Figure 12-3. Energy Hub as seen in the HoloLens Emulator*

## Deploying the project to the HoloLens device

Assuming your HoloLens is properly connected either by USB or Wi-Fi to your development PC, you can now easily deploy the SharedHolograms project to your device.

In Visual Studio:

- In the icon bar, change Release, x86, HoloLens Emulator to Release, x86, Remote Machine.

- If you are asked for the network address of the HoloLens device, you can find it from the Start Pins menu at Settings ➤ Network & Internet, Wi-Fi, Proxy ➤ Advanced Options. The address you want is the IPv4 address.

---

■ **Warning**    Sometimes the IPv4 address of your device will be changed without notifying you. If you find that deploying to the HoloLens suddenly fails where it was working before, check your IPv4 address. If it has changed, you will have to inform Visual Studio of the new address.

---

- Assuming your device has been successfully paired with your development machine, from the Visual Studio menu, select Debug ➤ Start Without Debugging. After displaying the Unity logo, the Energy Hub will pulsate in all its 3D, holographic glory, and music will play in your ears.

# Interacting with the Hologram

It's fun for a while to watch an active, animated object such as the Energy Hub do its thing. However, that starts to get old after it keeps doing the same thing time after time. Much more satisfying is to be able to affect the Energy Hub directly. To do that you need to be able to select it, and in order to do that you must create a raycast with your gaze and then follow up with a gesture. Let's add gaze recognition.

## Adding gaze functionality

Gaze is what determines where the cursor is located, and cursor location determines whether a hologram is being targeted. To add gaze functionality, do the following:

- In Unity's Hierarchy panel, select the **HologramCollection** object.

- In the Inspector panel, click the Add Component button.

- In the menu search box, type "Gaze Manager" and select the corresponding search result.

- Note that a Gaze Manager script has been added to the Inspector panel.

- In the HoloToolkit ➤ Prefabs ➤ Input folder, find the Cursor asset.

- Drag the **Cursor** asset onto the root level of the Hierarchy panel and drop it there.

## Adding gesture functionality

To add gesture functionality, do the following:

- In the Hierarchy panel, select the **HologramCollection** object.

- Click the Add Component button and type "Gesture Manager" into the Search field.

- Select the corresponding search result.

- Note that a Gesture Manager script has been added to the Inspector panel.

- In the Hierarchy panel, expand HologramCollection to show its child objects.

- Select the **Energy Hub** child object.

- In the Inspector panel, scroll down and click the Add Component button.

- In the menu that drops down, type "Hologram Placement" in the Search box and select the corresponding search result.

- Note that a Hologram Placement script has been added to the Inspector panel.

- Save the scene by going to File ➤ Save Scene.

- Build the project and deploy it to the HoloLens as you did in the preceding section.

---

■ **Note**    If you get a deployment error, don't necessarily believe it. Deploy again without changing anything. It might work. There is sometimes some initialization flakiness that gets corrected the second time through.

---

- Launch the app on your HoloLens and observe what the Energy Hub does as you move your head.

- Note the appearance of the cursor when it is hitting a hologram and when it is not.

- With your gaze, move the Energy Hub to a location you choose and then use an air tap to place it there.

# Establishing Shared Coordinates

In order for two or more people to share the same holographic experience, they have to agree on where the holograms are located. This means that they must see the holograms in relation to the same coordinate system. To do this, all devices involved must be members of the same network and must agree on a common reference point. HoloLens devices may be paired with different PCs, as long as all PCs are members of the network. To establish the shared coordinate system, do the following:

- In Unity's Project panel, navigate to the HoloToolkit ➤ Prefabs ➤ Sharing folder.

- Drag the **Sharing Prefab** object into the root level of the Hierarchy panel.

- Click on the **HoloToolkit** menu tab.

- Select **Launch Sharing Service** from the dropdown menu.

- Click on the **Allow access from the Windows Security Alert firewall** dialog box.

- Note the IPv4 address displayed in the Sharing Service console window. This is the address of the machine running the sharing service. Several addresses could be displayed. If so, use the one with either an address of 192.168.10.X or 10.0.0.X. You can always try the others if this one does not work.

Do the following on ALL of the PCs that will be engaged in the sharing experience:

- In the Hierarchy panel, select the **Sharing** object.

- In the Inspector panel, on the Sharing Stage component, set the Server Address to the IPv4 address that you just copied from the SharingService.exe console window of the server PC.

- In the Hierarchy panel, select the **HologramCollection** object.

- In the Inspector panel, click on the Add Component button.

- In the Search box that appears below the Add Component button, type "Import Export Anchor Manager." Select the search result.

- In the Project panel, navigate to and open the Scripts folder.

- Double-click the **HologramPlacement** script to open it in Visual Studio.

- Replace the contents of the HologramPlacement script with the following code:

```
using UnityEngine;
using System.Collections.Generic;
using UnityEngine.Windows.Speech;
using HoloToolkit.Unity;
using HoloToolkit.Sharing;

public class HologramPlacement : Singleton<HologramPlacement>
{
    /// <summary>
    /// Tracks if we have been sent a transform for the anchor model.
    /// The anchor model is rendered relative to the actual anchor.
    /// </summary>
    public bool GotTransform { get; private set; }

    private bool animationPlayed = false;

    void Start()
    {
        // We care about getting updates for the anchor transform.
        CustomMessages.Instance.MessageHandlers[CustomMessages.TestMessageID.StageTransform]
        = this.OnStageTransfrom;

        // And when a new user joins we will send the anchor transform we have.
        SharingSessionTracker.Instance.SessionJoined += Instance_SessionJoined;
    }

    /// <summary>
    /// When a new user joins we want to send them the relative transform for the anchor if
    we have it.
```

```
/// </summary>
/// <param name="sender"></param>
/// <param name="e"></param>
private void Instance_SessionJoined(object sender, SharingSessionTracker.
SessionJoinedEventArgs e)
{
    if (GotTransform)
    {
        CustomMessages.Instance.SendStageTransform(transform.localPosition, transform.
        localRotation);
    }
}

void Update()
{
    if (GotTransform)
    {
        if (ImportExportAnchorManager.Instance.AnchorEstablished &&
            animationPlayed == false)
        {
            // This triggers the animation sequence for the anchor model and
            // puts the cool materials on the model.
            GetComponent<EnergyHubBase>().SendMessage("OnSelect");
            animationPlayed = true;
        }
    }
    else
    {
        transform.position = Vector3.Lerp(transform.position,
        ProposeTransformPosition(), 0.2f);
    }
}

Vector3 ProposeTransformPosition()
{
    // Put the anchor 2m in front of the user.
    Vector3 retval = Camera.main.transform.position + Camera.main.transform.forward * 2;

    return retval;
}

public void OnSelect()
{
    // Note that we have a transform.
    GotTransform = true;

    // And send it to our friends.
    CustomMessages.Instance.SendStageTransform(transform.localPosition, transform.
    localRotation);
}
```

```
/// <summary>
/// When a remote system has a transform for us, we'll get it here.
/// </summary>
/// <param name="msg"></param>
void OnStageTransfrom(NetworkInMessage msg)
{
    // We read the user ID but we don't use it here.
    msg.ReadInt64();

    transform.localPosition = CustomMessages.Instance.ReadVector3(msg);
    transform.localRotation = CustomMessages.Instance.ReadQuaternion(msg);

    // The first time, we'll want to send the message to the anchor to do its animation and
    // swap its materials.
    if (GotTransform == false)
    {
        GetComponent<EnergyHubBase>().SendMessage("OnSelect");
    }

    GotTransform = true;
}

public void ResetStage()
{
    // We'll use this later.
}
}
```

If MonoDevelop opens along with Visual Studio, just exit it and display the existing **HologramPlacement.cs** file in Visual Studio:

- Go to File ➤ Save All.

- Back in Unity, select **HologramCollection** in the Hierarchy panel.

- In the Inspector panel, click the Add Component button.

- In the Search box, type "App State Manager." Select the result.

- Now build the project and deploy it to your HoloLens device.

Once again, you may get an error message on deployment. Try deploying again without changing anything. This usually works for me.

Verify that everyone participating is seeing the Energy Hub in the same place and that it is oriented the same way for all of them.

# Seeing Others as Avatars

Now that you can all see the Energy Hub, let's add code to enable you all to see each other, at least as avatars, if not in the flesh. Do the following:

- In the Project panel, open the Holograms folder.

- Drag the **PlayerAvatarStore** object into the root level of the Hierarchy.

- In the Project panel, open the Scripts folder.

- Double-click the **AvatarSelector** script to open it in Visual Studio.

- Replace the contents of the AvatarSelector script with the following code:

```
using UnityEngine;
using HoloToolkit.Unity;

/// <summary>
/// Script to handle the user selecting the avatar.
/// </summary>
public class AvatarSelector : MonoBehaviour
{
    /// <summary>
    /// This is the index set by the PlayerAvatarStore for the avatar.
    /// </summary>
    public int AvatarIndex { get; set; }

    /// <summary>
    /// Called when the user is gazing at this avatar and air taps it.
    /// This sends the user's selection to the rest of the devices in the experience.
    /// </summary>
    void OnSelect()
    {
        PlayerAvatarStore.Instance.DismissAvatarPicker();

        LocalPlayerManager.Instance.SetUserAvatar(AvatarIndex);
    }

    void Start()
    {
        // Add Billboard component so the avatar always faces the user.
        Billboard billboard = gameObject.GetComponent<Billboard>();
        if (billboard == null)
        {
            billboard = gameObject.AddComponent<Billboard>();
        }

        // Lock rotation along the Y axis.
        billboard.PivotAxis = PivotAxis.Y;
    }
}
```

- Go to File ➤ Save All.

- In the Hierarchy panel, select the **HologramCollection** object.

- In the Inspector panel, click the Add Component button.

- In the Search box, type "Local Player Manager." Select the search result.

- In the Hierarchy panel, select the **HologramCollection** object.

- In the Inspector panel, click on the Add Component button.

- In the Search box, type "Remote Player Manager." Select the search result.

- Open the **HologramPlacement** script in Visual Studio.

- Replace the contents of the script with the following code:

```
using UnityEngine;
using System.Collections.Generic;
using UnityEngine.Windows.Speech;
using HoloToolkit.Unity;
using HoloToolkit.Sharing;

public class HologramPlacement : Singleton<HologramPlacement>
{
    /// <summary>
    /// Tracks if we have been sent a transform for the model.
    /// The model is rendered relative to the actual anchor.
    /// </summary>
    public bool GotTransform { get; private set; }

    /// <summary>
    /// When the experience starts, we disable all of the rendering of the model.
    /// </summary>
    List<MeshRenderer> disabledRenderers = new List<MeshRenderer>();

    void Start()
    {
        // When we first start, we need to disable the model to avoid its obstructing the
        // user picking a hat.
        DisableModel();

        // We care about getting updates for the model transform.
        CustomMessages.Instance.MessageHandlers[CustomMessages.TestMessageID.StageTransform]
        = this.OnStageTransfrom;

        // And when a new user joins we will send the model transform we have.
        SharingSessionTracker.Instance.SessionJoined += Instance_SessionJoined;
    }

    /// <summary>
    /// When a new user joins we want to send them the relative transform for the model if
    /// we have it.
    /// </summary>
    /// <param name="sender"></param>
    /// <param name="e"></param>
    private void Instance_SessionJoined(object sender, SharingSessionTracker.
    SessionJoinedEventArgs e)
    {
        if (GotTransform)
        {
```

```
        CustomMessages.Instance.SendStageTransform(transform.localPosition, transform.
        localRotation);
    }
}

/// <summary>
/// Turns off all renderers for the model.
/// </summary>
void DisableModel()
{
    foreach (MeshRenderer renderer in gameObject.GetComponentsInChildren<MeshRenderer>())
    {
        if (renderer.enabled)
        {
            renderer.enabled = false;
            disabledRenderers.Add(renderer);
        }
    }

    foreach (MeshCollider collider in gameObject.GetComponentsInChildren<MeshCollider>())
    {
        collider.enabled = false;
    }
}

/// <summary>
/// Turns on all renderers that were disabled.
/// </summary>
void EnableModel()
{
    foreach (MeshRenderer renderer in disabledRenderers)
    {
        renderer.enabled = true;
    }

    foreach (MeshCollider collider in gameObject.GetComponentsInChildren<MeshCollider>())
    {
        collider.enabled = true;
    }

    disabledRenderers.Clear();
}

void Update()
{
    // Wait till users pick an avatar to enable renderers.
    if (disabledRenderers.Count > 0)
    {
        if (!PlayerAvatarStore.Instance.PickerActive &&
        ImportExportAnchorManager.Instance.AnchorEstablished)
```

```
            {
                // After which we want to start rendering.
                EnableModel();

                // And if we've already been sent the relative transform, we will use it.
                if (GotTransform)
                {
                    // This triggers the animation sequence for the model and
                    // puts the cool materials on the model.
                    GetComponent<EnergyHubBase>().SendMessage("OnSelect");
                }
            }
        }
        else if (GotTransform == false)
        {
            transform.position = Vector3.Lerp(transform.position, ProposeTransformPosition(), 0.2f);
        }
}

Vector3 ProposeTransformPosition()
{
    // Put the model 2m in front of the user.
    Vector3 retval = Camera.main.transform.position + Camera.main.transform.forward * 2;

    return retval;
}

public void OnSelect()
{
    // Note that we have a transform.
    GotTransform = true;

    // And send it to our friends.
    CustomMessages.Instance.SendStageTransform(transform.localPosition, transform.
    localRotation);
}

/// <summary>
/// When a remote system has a transform for us, we'll get it here.
/// </summary>
/// <param name="msg"></param>
void OnStageTransfrom(NetworkInMessage msg)
{
    // We read the user ID, but we don't use it here.
    msg.ReadInt64();

    transform.localPosition = CustomMessages.Instance.ReadVector3(msg);
    transform.localRotation = CustomMessages.Instance.ReadQuaternion(msg);

    // The first time, we'll want to send the message to the model to do its animation and
    // swap its materials.
```

```
        if (disabledRenderers.Count == 0 && GotTransform == false)
        {
            GetComponent<EnergyHubBase>().SendMessage("OnSelect");
        }

        GotTransform = true;
    }

    public void ResetStage()
    {
        // We'll use this later.
    }
}
```

- Go to File ➤ Save All.

- Open the **AppStateManager** script in Visual Studio.

- Replace the contents of the script with the following:

```
using UnityEngine;
using HoloToolkit.Unity;

/// <summary>
/// Keeps track of the current state of the experience.
/// </summary>
public class AppStateManager : Singleton<AppStateManager>
{
    /// <summary>
    /// Enum to track progress through the experience.
    /// </summary>
    public enum AppState
    {
        Starting = 0,
        WaitingForAnchor,
        WaitingForStageTransform,
        PickingAvatar,
        Ready
    }

    /// <summary>
    /// Tracks the current state in the experience.
    /// </summary>
    public AppState CurrentAppState { get; set; }

    void Start()
    {
        // We start in the 'picking avatar' mode.
        CurrentAppState = AppState.PickingAvatar;

        // We start by showing the avatar picker.
        PlayerAvatarStore.Instance.SpawnAvatarPicker();
    }
```

```
    void Update()
    {
        switch (CurrentAppState)
        {
            case AppState.PickingAvatar:
                // Avatar picking is done when the avatar picker has been dismissed.
                if (PlayerAvatarStore.Instance.PickerActive == false)
                {
                    CurrentAppState = AppState.WaitingForAnchor;
                }
                break;
            case AppState.WaitingForAnchor:
                if (ImportExportAnchorManager.Instance.AnchorEstablished)
                {
                    CurrentAppState = AppState.WaitingForStageTransform;
                    GestureManager.Instance.OverrideFocusedObject = HologramPlacement.
                    Instance.gameObject;
                }
                break;
            case AppState.WaitingForStageTransform:
                // Now if we have the stage transform we are ready to go.
                if (HologramPlacement.Instance.GotTransform)
                {
                    CurrentAppState = AppState.Ready;
                    GestureManager.Instance.OverrideFocusedObject = null;
                }
                break;
        }
    }
}
```

- Go to File ➤ Save All.

- Build and deploy the project to your HoloLens devices.

- When you hear a ping sound, find the avatar selection menu and select an avatar with an air tap gesture.

- Look at the other people participating. You should see an avatar next to each of their heads.

# Anchoring a Hologram to a Position in Space

When multiple people are all experiencing the same hologram, it is probably best to locate the hologram in the middle of the group. The following additions to the SharedHolograms project will place the Energy Hub in the center of the participants, who are arrayed in a circle:

- Navigate to the Holograms folder in the Project panel.

- Drag the **CustomSpatialMapping** prefab onto the root level of the Hierarchy.

- In the Projects panel, navigate to the Scripts folder.

- Double-click on the **AppStateManager** script to open it in Visual Studio.

- Replace the contents of the script with the following:

```
using UnityEngine;
using HoloToolkit.Unity;

/// <summary>
/// Keeps track of the current state of the experience.
/// </summary>
public class AppStateManager : Singleton<AppStateManager>
{
    /// <summary>
    /// Enum to track progress through the experience.
    /// </summary>
    public enum AppState
    {
        Starting = 0,
        PickingAvatar,
        WaitingForAnchor,
        WaitingForStageTransform,
        Ready
    }

    // The object to call to make a projectile.
    GameObject shootHandler = null;

    /// <summary>
    /// Tracks the current state in the experience.
    /// </summary>
    public AppState CurrentAppState { get; set; }

    void Start()
    {
        // The shootHandler shoots projectiles.
        if (GetComponent<ProjectileLauncher>() != null)
        {
            shootHandler = GetComponent<ProjectileLauncher>().gameObject;
        }

        // We start in the 'picking avatar' mode.
        CurrentAppState = AppState.PickingAvatar;

        // Spatial mapping should be disabled when we start up so as not
        // to distract from the avatar picking.
        SpatialMappingManager.Instance.StopObserver();
        SpatialMappingManager.Instance.gameObject.SetActive(false);

        // On device we start by showing the avatar picker.
        PlayerAvatarStore.Instance.SpawnAvatarPicker();
    }
```

```csharp
    public void ResetStage()
    {
        // If we fall back to waiting for anchor, everything needed to
        // get us into setting the target transform state will be set up.
        if (CurrentAppState != AppState.PickingAvatar)
        {
            CurrentAppState = AppState.WaitingForAnchor;
        }

        // Reset the underworld.
        if (UnderworldBase.Instance)
        {
            UnderworldBase.Instance.ResetUnderworld();
        }
    }

    void Update()
    {
        switch (CurrentAppState)
        {
            case AppState.PickingAvatar:
                // Avatar picking is done when the avatar picker has been dismissed.
                if (PlayerAvatarStore.Instance.PickerActive == false)
                {
                    CurrentAppState = AppState.WaitingForAnchor;
                }
                break;
            case AppState.WaitingForAnchor:
                // Once the anchor is established we need to run spatial mapping for a
                // little while to build up some meshes.
                if (ImportExportAnchorManager.Instance.AnchorEstablished)
                {
                    CurrentAppState = AppState.WaitingForStageTransform;
                    GestureManager.Instance.OverrideFocusedObject = HologramPlacement.
                    Instance.gameObject;

                    SpatialMappingManager.Instance.gameObject.SetActive(true);
                    SpatialMappingManager.Instance.DrawVisualMeshes = true;
                    SpatialMappingDeformation.Instance.ResetGlobalRendering();
                    SpatialMappingManager.Instance.StartObserver();
                }
                break;
            case AppState.WaitingForStageTransform:
                // Now if we have the stage transform we are ready to go.
                if (HologramPlacement.Instance.GotTransform)
                {
                    CurrentAppState = AppState.Ready;
                    GestureManager.Instance.OverrideFocusedObject = shootHandler;
                }
                break;
        }
    }
}
```

- Go to File ➤ Save All.

- In the Projects panel, navigate to the Scripts folder.

- Double-click on the **HologramPlacement** script to open it in Visual Studio.

- Replace the contents of the script with the following:

```
using UnityEngine;
using System.Collections.Generic;
using UnityEngine.Windows.Speech;
using HoloToolkit.Unity;
using HoloToolkit.Sharing;

public class HologramPlacement : Singleton<HologramPlacement>
{
    /// <summary>
    /// Tracks if we have been sent a transform for the model.
    /// The model is rendered relative to the actual anchor.
    /// </summary>
    public bool GotTransform { get; private set; }

    /// <summary>
    /// When the experience starts, we disable all of the rendering of the model.
    /// </summary>
    List<MeshRenderer> disabledRenderers = new List<MeshRenderer>();

    /// <summary>
    /// We use a voice command to enable moving the target.
    /// </summary>
    KeywordRecognizer keywordRecognizer;

    void Start()
    {
        // When we first start, we need to disable the model to avoid its obstructing the
        user picking a hat.
        DisableModel();

        // We care about getting updates for the model transform.
        CustomMessages.Instance.MessageHandlers[CustomMessages.TestMessageID.StageTransform]
        = this.OnStageTransfrom;

        // And when a new user joins we will send the model transform we have.
        SharingSessionTracker.Instance.SessionJoined += Instance_SessionJoined;

        // And if the users want to reset the stage transform.
        CustomMessages.Instance.MessageHandlers[CustomMessages.TestMessageID.ResetStage] =
        this.OnResetStage;

        // Set up a keyword recognizer to enable resetting the target location.
        List<string> keywords = new List<string>();
        keywords.Add("Reset Target");
        keywordRecognizer = new KeywordRecognizer(keywords.ToArray());
```

```
    keywordRecognizer.OnPhraseRecognized += KeywordRecognizer_OnPhraseRecognized;
    keywordRecognizer.Start();
}


/// <summary>
/// When the keyword recognizer hears a command, this will be called.
/// In this case we only have one keyword, which will re-enable moving the
/// target.
/// </summary>
/// <param name="args">information to help route the voice command.</param>
private void KeywordRecognizer_OnPhraseRecognized(PhraseRecognizedEventArgs args)
{
    ResetStage();
}


/// <summary>
/// Resets the stage transform, so users can place the target again.
/// </summary>
public void ResetStage()
{
    GotTransform = false;

    // AppStateManager needs to know about this so that
    // the right objects get input routed to them.
    AppStateManager.Instance.ResetStage();

    // Other devices in the experience need to know about this as well.
    CustomMessages.Instance.SendResetStage();

    // And we need to reset the object to its start animation state.
    GetComponent<EnergyHubBase>().ResetAnimation();
}


/// <summary>
/// When a new user joins we want to send them the relative transform for the model if
we have it.
/// </summary>
/// <param name="sender"></param>
/// <param name="e"></param>
private void Instance_SessionJoined(object sender, SharingSessionTracker.
SessionJoinedEventArgs e)
{
    if (GotTransform)
    {
        CustomMessages.Instance.SendStageTransform(transform.localPosition, transform.
        localRotation);
    }
}


/// <summary>
/// Turns off all renderers for the model.
```

```
/// </summary>
void DisableModel()
{
    foreach (MeshRenderer renderer in gameObject.GetComponentsInChildren<MeshRenderer>())
    {
        if (renderer.enabled)
        {
            renderer.enabled = false;
            disabledRenderers.Add(renderer);
        }
    }

    foreach (MeshCollider collider in gameObject.GetComponentsInChildren<MeshCollider>())
    {
        collider.enabled = false;
    }
}

/// <summary>
/// Turns on all renderers that were disabled.
/// </summary>
void EnableModel()
{
    foreach (MeshRenderer renderer in disabledRenderers)
    {
        renderer.enabled = true;
    }

    foreach (MeshCollider collider in gameObject.GetComponentsInChildren<MeshCollider>())
    {
        collider.enabled = true;
    }

    disabledRenderers.Clear();
}

void Update()
{
    // Wait till users pick an avatar to enable renderers.
    if (disabledRenderers.Count > 0)
    {
        if (!PlayerAvatarStore.Instance.PickerActive &&
        ImportExportAnchorManager.Instance.AnchorEstablished)
        {
            // After which we want to start rendering.
            EnableModel();

            // And if we've already been sent the relative transform, we will use it.
            if (GotTransform)
            {
                // This triggers the animation sequence for the model and
                // puts the cool materials on the model.
```

```csharp
                GetComponent<EnergyHubBase>().SendMessage("OnSelect");
            }
        }
    }
    else if (GotTransform == false)
    {
        transform.position = Vector3.Lerp(transform.position,
        ProposeTransformPosition(), 0.2f);
    }
}

Vector3 ProposeTransformPosition()
{
    Vector3 retval;
    // We need to know how many users are in the experience with good transforms.
    Vector3 cumulatedPosition = Camera.main.transform.position;
    int playerCount = 1;
    foreach (RemotePlayerManager.RemoteHeadInfo remoteHead in RemotePlayerManager.
    Instance.remoteHeadInfos)
    {
        if (remoteHead.Anchored && remoteHead.Active)
        {
            playerCount++;
            cumulatedPosition += remoteHead.HeadObject.transform.position;
        }
    }

    // If we have more than one player ...
    if (playerCount > 1)
    {
        // Put the transform in between the players.
        retval = cumulatedPosition / playerCount;
        RaycastHit hitInfo;

        // And try to put the transform on a surface below the midpoint of the players.
        if (Physics.Raycast(retval, Vector3.down, out hitInfo, 5, SpatialMappingManager.
        Instance.LayerMask))
        {
            retval = hitInfo.point;
        }
    }
    // If we are the only player, have the model act as the 'cursor' ...
    else
    {
        // We prefer to put the model on a real-world surface.
        RaycastHit hitInfo;

        if (Physics.Raycast(Camera.main.transform.position, Camera.main.transform.
        forward, out hitInfo, 30, SpatialMappingManager.Instance.LayerMask))
        {
            retval = hitInfo.point;
        }
```

```
            else
            {
                // But if we don't have a ray that intersects the real world, just put the
                model 2m in
                // front of the user.
                retval = Camera.main.transform.position + Camera.main.transform.forward * 2;
            }
        }
        return retval;
    }

    public void OnSelect()
    {
        // Note that we have a transform.
        GotTransform = true;

        // And send it to our friends.
        CustomMessages.Instance.SendStageTransform(transform.localPosition, transform.
        localRotation);
    }

    /// <summary>
    /// When a remote system has a transform for us, we'll get it here.
    /// </summary>
    /// <param name="msg"></param>
    void OnStageTransfrom(NetworkInMessage msg)
    {
        // We read the user ID but we don't use it here.
        msg.ReadInt64();

        transform.localPosition = CustomMessages.Instance.ReadVector3(msg);
        transform.localRotation = CustomMessages.Instance.ReadQuaternion(msg);

        // The first time, we'll want to send the message to the model to do its animation and
        // swap its materials.
        if (disabledRenderers.Count == 0 && GotTransform == false)
        {
            GetComponent<EnergyHubBase>().SendMessage("OnSelect");
        }

        GotTransform = true;
    }

    /// <summary>
    /// When a remote system has a transform for us, we'll get it here.
    /// </summary>
    void OnResetStage(NetworkInMessage msg)
    {
        GotTransform = false;

        GetComponent<EnergyHubBase>().ResetAnimation();
        AppStateManager.Instance.ResetStage();
    }
}
```

- Go to File ➤ Save All.

- Build and deploy the project to your HoloLens devices.

- When the app is ready, stand in a circle and notice that the Energy Hub appears in the center of everyone. If there is only one participant, it will appear in front of you.

- Perform an air tap to fix the Energy Hub in place.

- Try the "Reset Target" voice command to release the fixed placement of the Energy Hub, move it, and try placing it again.

# Turning on Physics

By turning on physics, we can get the holograms to act like real objects. When they collide with other holograms, they bounce off each other. To add this functionality, do the following:

- In the Hierarchy panel, select the **HologramCollection** object.

- In the Inspector panel, click the Add Component button.

- In the Search box, type "Projectile Launcher." Select the search result.

- Build and deploy the project to the HoloLens devices.

- When the app is running on all the devices, perform an air tap to launch a projectile at a real-world surface.

# Unlock a New World through Collaboration

In this final section, we will see how people can work together to accomplish something that none of them could achieve working alone. Make the following changes to the project:

- In the Project panel, navigate to the Holograms folder.

- Drag the **Underworld** asset onto the HologramCollection in the Hierarchy folder.

- With **HologramCollection** selected, click the Add Component button in the Inspector panel.

- In the Search box, type "Explode Target." Select the search result.

- With the **HologramCollection** selected, drag the **EnergyHub** object from the Hierarchy to the Target field in the Inspector panel.

- With the **HologramCollection** selected, drag the **Underworld** object from the Hierarchy to the Underworld field in the Inspector panel.

- Build the project and deploy it to your HoloLens devices.

- After the app is launched and activated, everyone start launching projectiles at the Energy Hub as rapidly as possible.

- When the Energy Hub explodes and the Underworld appears, launch projectiles at the evil Underworld robots. See what happens when you hit them multiple times.

# Summary

This project reinforces what you have learned in previous chapters by giving you practice at using gaze, gesture, and voice to interact with holograms. More important, it shows how to configure a setup where multiple people wearing HoloLens devices can interact with holograms and with each other. This may be the biggest benefit of HoloLens technology–the fact that people can collaborate while sharing and interacting with holographic objects or even holographic environments.

# Deep Dive into HoloLens

# CHAPTER 13

# HoloLens Hardware

The HoloLens is a breakthrough device that opens up a whole new, more intimate way for humans to interact with technology, but it is not in itself a new technology. Rather, it is a new way of bringing together a number of existing technologies, and in so doing creates massive new opportunities for creativity and communication.

The individual components that make up the hardware part of the HoloLens, although based on existing technology, have been miniaturized and optimized so that the entire device is light enough to be worn comfortably on the head without any wire to external power or an external computational resource. Kudos go to the packaging engineers and designers as much as to those who developed the holographic functionality. Figure 13-1 shows the elegant, clean design of the HoloLens Development Edition device.

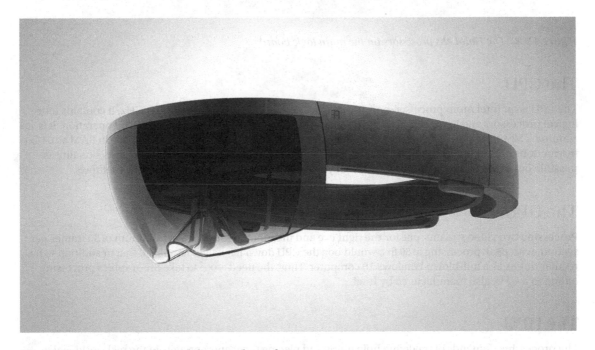

***Figure 13-1.*** *Breakthrough capability in a classic design*

Every component included in the HoloLens is state of the art, but, beyond that, those components come together as a cohesive system that gives the user an immersive and engaging experience. In the following sections, I describe the components that form the HoloLens, but the whole is indeed greater than the sum of its parts. All the parts fit together beautifully to create a truly elegant as well as functional device.

© Allen G. Taylor 2016

A. G. Taylor, *Develop Microsoft HoloLens Apps Now*, DOI 10.1007/978-1-4842-2202-7_13

# The Processors

The core of any computing device is the processing unit. In the case of the HoloLens, there are three processor chips, each assigned a different segment of the overall processing task. In addition to the central processing unit (CPU), there is a graphics processing unit (GPU) as well as a holographic processing unit (HPU). Figure 13-2 shows the processors and their support chips in a breakout view from the HoloLens device.

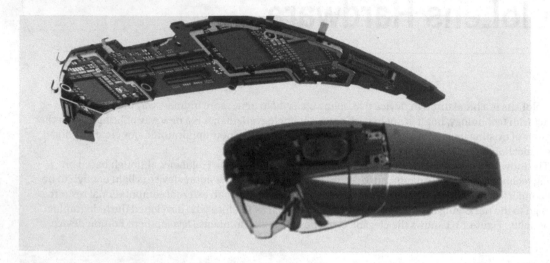

***Figure 13-2.*** *The HoloLens processors on the main logic board*

## The CPU

The CPU is an Intel Atom processor–specifically, the Atom x5-Z8100–running at 1.04 GHz. It contains four logical processors and is capable of 64-bit operation. Although the CPU is capable of 64-bit operation, it is running a 32-bit version of Windows 10. 32-bit instructions take up only half as much space in RAM as 64-bit instructions do, and for a computer that you wear on your head, you want to get as much functionality as possible out of the limited amount of RAM that you can reasonably carry just above your eyebrows.

## The GPU

Processing two video streams, one for the right eye and the other for the left, at a minimum of 30 frames per second, with peak processing at 60 fps, would bog the CPU down if it had to handle all that in addition to its regular duties as a full-blown Windows 10 computer. Thus, the need arose to take the graphics processing offline to a GPU, also manufactured by Intel.

## The HPU

The processing demands of rendering holograms and placing them appropriately in the real world make it necessary for a specialized processor built specifically for holographic processing to be included in the HoloLens. This is a custom chip, designed and built specifically for the HoloLens.

# Memory Limits

If you have to wear all your electronics on a visor that sticks out from your forehead, there is not a lot of room for memory, RAM or otherwise. However, the HoloLens has quite a bit, considering the space restrictions. There is 2 GB of RAM and 64 GB of Flash SSD. Of the 64 GB of Flash, 54 GB is available for use. Of the 2 GB of RAM, 980 MB are reserved for shared system memory, 114 MB are dedicated video memory, and 900 MB are available for applications to use.

# The Head Band

The head band that secures the HoloLens firmly to your head is separate from the visor that holds all the functional parts of the device. Its main function is to support the HoloLens as comfortably as possible. As Figure 13-3 shows, the head band is adjustable by the turning of a wheel located at the back, which either shortens or lengthens the head band's diameter. The range of sizes accommodates just about any adult head size likely to be encountered. Microsoft specifically states that the HoloLens is not for children. Their head sizes would be too small for the head band to adjust to. The lesson here is that the apps you create initially should be targeted at adults rather than children. Perhaps by the time the commercial version of the HoloLens arrives, it will be able to work for children too.

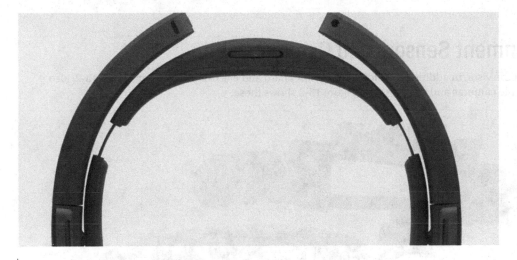

*Figure 13-3.* *Adjustable head band*

# The Visor

The visor, which is connected to the head band, but is not aligned with it, as shown in Figure 13-4, contains all the sensors, speakers, and microphones that enable the user to interact with the holographic constructs in her environment.

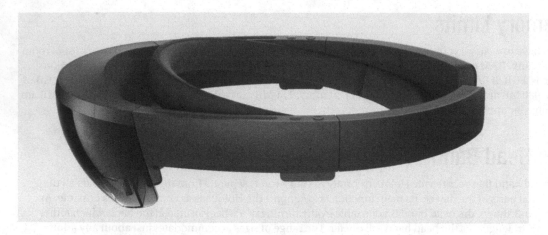

***Figure 13-4.*** *The visor is not aligned with the head band*

Whereas the head band is positioned so as to give the most comfortable fit on the user's head, the visor is positioned so as to give the user the best view through the lenses and to have the cameras track with the user's eyes.

# Environment Sensors and Cameras

The front of the visor, in addition to holding the circuit board and electronics shown in Figure 13-2, also holds multiple cameras and a light sensor. Figure 13-5 shows these.

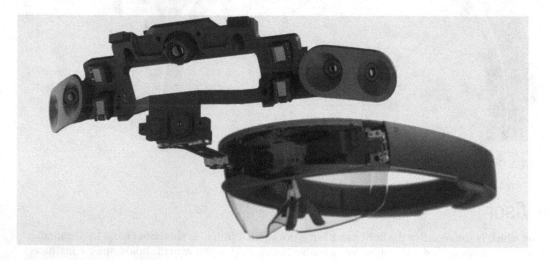

***Figure 13-5.*** *Cameras and light sensor*

At the center top of the sensor fixture is the depth camera. An infrared flash is sent out, and the time it takes for a reflection to return tells the distance to the real-world object that the user is looking at. This is important in order for holographic objects to interact properly with the environment. If you want one of your holographic characters to sit on a couch in the room, you will need to know how far away from the user the couch is.

Two cameras are located on the left side of the fixture, and two more are located on the right side. These give the HoloLens awareness of the environment outside of where the user is looking at the moment.

Suspended from the bottom of the fixture, closest to the position of the user's eyes, is a 2.4 megapixel camera/HD video camera. This enables the user to make either still or video recordings of exactly what she sees, including both real and holographic content. When taking still photos, the camera takes a 2.4 megapixel picture in a 2048 x 1152 format. When taking video, it delivers 1.1 megapixel frames in a 1408 x 792 format, at a speed of 30 frames per second.

Off to the right of the 2.4 MP camera is an ambient light sensor. The HoloLens must know what the ambient light level is in the room in order to project the holograms with an appropriate level of brightness. If the room is very bright, then the holograms must be bright as well in order to be seen properly in context.

## The Light Engines and Lenses

The HoloLens creates holograms in the user's field of view with a light engine for each eye that takes the 3D images created by your application and processes them into lines of light that are then projected into the user's eyes from grooves in the lenses that the user looks through. The grooves are so fine that they are invisible to the naked eye. Each light engine shoots out holographic images at a minimum rate of 30 frames per second, which is the same rate that video from DVDs is sent to TVs. Figure 13-6 shows the lenses and the IMU.

*Figure 13-6.* *Lenses, light engines, and IMU*

The light engines, found at the bottom of the fixture holding the lenses, deliver a 16 x 9 HD image to each eye. The IMU (inertial measurement unit) measures the movement and rotation of the user's head. This enables your app to respond to the movements that the user makes.

## Sound Generation

Just as a hologram can have visible attributes, such as color, shape, and depth, it can have an audible attribute too. Sound files can be incorporated into a hologram, and they will play when the hologram is instantiated. If a user is too far away from a hologram to see it, she will probably be too far away to hear it. As she moves closer, the audio signal–whether music, speech, or just noise–will get progressively louder. The sound emerges from two red but otherwise unobtrusive speakers that are attached to the visor just above the ears. Figure 13-7 shows a closeup view of one of them.

*Figure 13-7. Speaker*

By adjusting the phase of the sound sent to each ear, it can appear to the user that the sound coming from a hologram is actually coming from the location of the hologram in space, regardless of whether the hologram is to the left, right, or behind the user. This feature, called spatial sound, greatly enhances the immersiveness of the user's experience.

There is a pair of buttons above each speaker. The pair above the speaker on the right controls the sound volume. The concave button decreases the volume coming out of both speakers, and the convex button increases it. Figure 13-8 shows the buttons above the speaker on the right.

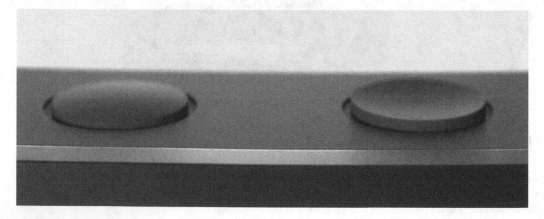

*Figure 13-8. Volume controls*

On the left side, above the speaker for the left ear, there are two buttons that are identical to the ones on the right, but in this case they control the brightness of the holograms. Press the convex button to make the hologram brighter and the concave button to make it dimmer.

Whereas the Micro USB 2.0 connector on the back end of the left wing of the visor provides access to the Device Portal of your PC and power to recharge the HoloLens battery, there is a 3.5mm audio mini-jack on the back end of the right wing of the visor.

# The Microphones

The HoloLens includes four microphones so the user can issue voice commands. They are integrated into the visor in such a way as to be invisible.

# Battery Capacity and Recharging

The HoloLens is untethered and self-contained. That means that, with no external power source, it must depend on battery power. Its battery has a 16,500 mWh capacity, which translates to about 2.5 hours of continuous usage before needing a recharge. It can be recharged through the same USB cable that is used to connect it to your development PC when you are uploading your apps to the HoloLens via the Device Portal. There are five LEDs on the visor near the micro-USB connector that give you an indication of the state of charge of the battery.

# Bluetooth

HoloLens supports Bluetooth 4.1 LE and can be used with Bluetooth keyboards, mice, and other Bluetooth peripheral devices.

# Wi-Fi

HoloLens connects to its paired PC as well as it does to the world in general through Wi-Fi 802.11ac. You can access the Internet using the Edge browser on the HoloLens Start Pins menu, and you can also make Skype calls directly from your HoloLens.

# Cortana

Cortana is available to assist you, just as she is on your PC. She is listening all the time, so when you say "Hey, Cortana" she will ask you how she can help you. You can also reach her from the Start Pins menu. Select the top tile with an air tap, and she will be at your service.

# Summary

This chapter gives a complete rundown of the hardware that is included in the HoloLens device. A tremendous amount of optical, computational, and auditory capability is packed into an elegant, self-contained, wearable package that is easy and comfortable to wear in a wide variety of situations.

## CHAPTER 14

■ ■ ■

# Creating Holographic Objects

The first part of developing a holographic app is to decide on the audience for the app and what you want the app to accomplish with that audience. What does that audience need, and what will engage their interest? After you have planned out what you want the app to do, it is time to get down to the nitty gritty of actually building it. This is where designing a holographic app differs in important ways from designing an app to be run on a device with a flat screen. Unlike flat-screen apps, holographic apps incorporate awareness of the physical space that the user is embedded in. The holograms you create must take into account where the user is, what she does, and how she relates to her surroundings.

In previous chapters, we covered the mechanics of creating holograms using the Unity/Visual Studio/ HoloLens Emulator tool chain. In one sense, that is the way to create holograms. But, in another sense, that is only a superficial way of looking at the task. To create truly engaging holographic content, we must dig deeper into what makes a good holographic design. That is the subject of this chapter.

## The Interaction Model (Gaze, Gesture, and Voice)

The mixed-reality characteristic of holographic applications is just the latest aspect of a trend toward ever more participatory media. A hundred years ago, the dominant medium was radio, which you could hear but not see. That was followed by television, which you could see but not interact with, unless you call changing the channel an interaction. Computer games added a level of interaction in that you could control the actions of Mario and Luigi to a relatively limited extent by pressing buttons on a console. The Nintendo Wii and later the Microsoft Kinect technology added gestures to the ways you could affect what happened in the game you were running.

The HoloLens takes the next step in interactivity by combining what you are looking at (your gaze) with how you want to affect what the app is doing (your gestures and voice commands). In an app that generates multiple holograms, the user can select which one she wants to activate or affect in some other way merely by looking at it. Once the user has locked her gaze on a specific target, she can cause it to enter an animated sequence with a gesture, or grow bigger or shrink smaller with a voice command. You, as an app developer, can give a hologram a variety of behaviors and enable the user to invoke them with corresponding voice commands.

The number of gestures available is fairly limited. There are three: the air tap, the tap and hold, and the bloom. In the context of the operating system, these gestures have specific meanings. The air tap generally means the same thing as the "Select" voice command. It activates the hologram in some way. The tap and hold gesture may display some information about the hologram your gaze is fixed upon, or it may enable you to scroll content into the field of view that is not initially visible. The bloom gesture takes you from wherever you are in an app back to the Start menu.

Once the user is in an app that you have written, you can reassign what these gestures do to new functions. For example, you might make the air tap fire a projectile at an enemy spaceship rather than perform the Select function. You could give new functions to the tap and hold and the bloom gestures too.

© Allen G. Taylor 2016
A. G. Taylor, *Develop Microsoft HoloLens Apps Now*, DOI 10.1007/978-1-4842-2202-7_14

You have more flexibility with voice commands than you do with gestures, since you can program a hologram to respond in many different ways to many different voice commands. The only restriction is that you want to make sure that the voice commands that you use are distinct enough that the speech recognizer can understand what was said rather than becoming confused by similar-sounding utterances. Commands made up of short, one-syllable words work best.

## Spatial Sound

Just as a 3D hologram that you can walk around and view from any angle is a step beyond a 2D image on a screen in terms of visual realism, spatial sound, which seems to be coming from anywhere in a 360 degree circle around the user, is a step beyond stereo sound, which comes from one stereo speaker on the user's left and another on the user's right, in terms of auditory realism. If the app that you develop can make use of a sound component, you are going to want the sound supposedly being emitted by a hologram to actually seem to be coming from the direction of that hologram, and the volume of the sound to be louder the closer the user is to it. You don't have to do anything special to make this happen. The sound asset that you assign to a hologram will share the location of that hologram. The HoloLens holographic processor chip will compute where each hologram is in space relative to the user and alter the phasing and volume of the sound coming out of the speakers above the user's ears to make the sound appear to come from the hologram.

One effective, but often neglected, use of spatial sound is to direct the user's attention to the area in which you want her to be looking. If an important GameObject is behind her, when she hears the sound it is emitting, she will turn around to look for the source of the sound.

## Spatial Mapping and Location Awareness

In order to place holographic objects appropriately in the user's environment, the HoloLens must be aware of where it is located relative to its surroundings. This means that, assuming it is in a room or series of connected spaces, it must know where the walls and the floor are, as well as all the furniture and other obstacles. To gain this information, it does a scan of wherever the user is looking and builds up a map of its surroundings.

Some applications ask the user to look around or even walk around, looking all over while doing so in order to build up a map of the space. This map is then used while the app is running so that the holographic objects interact realistically with the real-world objects they encounter. If a holographic ball drops onto a real table, you don't want it to pass right through. You want it to roll off the edge and fall to the floor, where it eventually will come to a stop. The accuracy of such behavior depends heavily on the accuracy of the spatial map produced by the initial scan of the room. Scans continue to be done while the app is running so as to refine the map and also to modify it as objects such as tables and chairs are moved to new locations or are taken out of the room completely.

## Designing a Mixed-Reality App

When you are designing a mixed-reality app, there are several things you must be mindful of. One is the design of the holograms that the app will contain, and others have to do with putting those holograms in the context of the real-world environment in which the app will execute. Each one of these concerns is important, and thus requires advance thought.

# Design

The design of the holograms can be a collaborative effort, but the job of actually creating them should fall to the graphic designer on your team. This person should be adept at using modern 3D modeling software tools to produce holographic assets with a high level of quality using as little in the way of computational resources as is possible. Execution speed depends on the complexity of a scene. You want your holograms to be detailed and realistic, but also simple enough so as not to bog down the HPU.

There are several software tools that are specifically designed for the creation of three-dimensional assets. These could be items that appear in screen-bound 3D games or models to be used with a 3D printer to create an actual physical artifact, or they could be holograms that will become visible to the user of a HoloLens.

Maya from Autodesk is one of the most popular of the computer graphics design tools. The latest version is HoloLens-aware. This means that as you make modifications to a design on your screen in Maya, they are reflected immediately on the hologram that corresponds to the design. It's possible to make changes using your keyboard and mouse that appear both on screen and on hologram. You can even activate hologram menu controls with your mouse, causing your hologram to rotate, change size, or do whatever you want.

If you are more familiar with other CG tools, such as Autodesk's 3ds Max or the open-source Blender package, you can use them instead to create the 3D models that you can then transfer to Unity, and from there turn into holograms.

# Placement

The designer of a virtual-reality app has complete control over where elements are placed in the VR world. A mixed-reality designer has a more complex problem, because the holographic elements of an app must mesh seamlessly with the room the user happens to be in, as well as with any furniture or other objects that might occupy space in the room. The user's position in the room when the app launches, as well as the direction she is facing, can affect the placement of holograms, which can, in turn, affect the user experience.

While prototyping your app, you will want to run it in as many different environments as you can imagine your user inhabiting. You may find some problems that you might not have otherwise considered, which only show up in some rooms or in a room with furniture arranged in a certain way.

# Lighting

One of the areas in which it is most difficult to make holograms seem to be a part of the real landscape is lighting. You may know the layout of the room due to a scan that is done before your app starts executing, but that does not tell you how the room is lit, which may vary with the time of day or even with the weather.

In Unity, you can place light sources where you want them in a scene, but in most cases you will not have advance knowledge of what the light environment will be in the room where the app will be run. Furthermore, holograms cannot cast shadows, which represent the absence of light. Holograms are made by adding light to a scene, not subtracting it.

---

■ **Tip** One hack that you can use to simulate a shadow is to add an aura of light around a holographic object and then subtract out that light from where a shadow would normally be.

---

One thing that *can* be controlled is the intensity of the light coming from a hologram. An ambient light sensor on the HoloLens gives an ambient light level, which you can use to help set the brightness level of your hologram. If the ambient light is very bright, you will want to increase the brightness of your hologram so that it is not washed out by the real-world lighting conditions.

# Size

Consideration of the size of a mixed-reality hologram is more involved than it is in VR. In virtual reality, the developer has control over the entire "world" and so can ensure that everything is the right size relative to everything else. With mixed reality, holographic objects must be adjusted to be the same size that they would be in the real world, because they must fit in with the real-world objects in the room. If a holographic representation of a real object is not the right size relative to its surroundings, the illusion of reality is lost. This means that you must pay attention to the scale of the holograms you create. Not only must the holograms in a scene all be proportionally sized to each other, but also they must be appropriately sized for their real-world surroundings.

# Animation

3D animation is a well-established discipline in the video game field. The tools and techniques that game developers use are directly applicable to the design of animated holograms. In addition to visible movement, an animated hologram can also emit audible sounds, including speech, that go along with the movement. This is an area where skills you may have acquired in the process of developing games carries over essentially intact to developing for the HoloLens.

# Connecting the Holographic World with the Real

In a virtual-reality experience or a 3D video game, once you designate where things are relative to each other, there is no question about where they will be at any point in the future. Any movement that an object makes will be calculated, and can be reversed at any time to bring the object back to its original position if that is what is desired. This is because the field of play will be laid out according to a coordinate system. The position of any object in 3D space can be defined relative to three mutually perpendicular axes, normally labeled X, Y, and Z.

## Coordinate systems

Coordinate systems based on three mutually perpendicular coordinate systems are called Cartesian coordinate systems after French mathematician Rene Descartes, who originated the idea. Unity uses a particular form of Cartesian coordinate system called a spatial coordinate system. One unit of distance in Unity's spatial coordinate system corresponds to one meter of distance in the real world. When dealing with mixed reality, if you want your holographic objects to interact appropriately with your real-world surroundings, the coordinate system you use for your holograms must accurately locate the real objects in the user's environment. This is not as easy as you might think.

When you first place a holographic object into the world, you establish a stationary frame of reference based on the location of that object. As the user, and thus the HoloLens on her head, moves around the environment, the object remains fixed at that location. This system keeps the positions of holographic objects near the user as stable as possible. An app will typically establish one stationary frame of reference at startup and maintain it throughout the app's lifetime. Any content located relative to that stationary frame of reference is called world-locked content.

The HoloLens' mapping of a user's environment is an ongoing activity, constantly refining and adjusting the locations of real-world objects while your app is running. This can lead to offsets in the positions of your holograms as time goes on, particularly as the user moves farther way from the origin of the reference frame.

## Spatial anchors

If the elements in a scene extend beyond a distance of about nine meters, distortions in the locations of these elements may start to appear. In trying to maintain their positions relative to each other, holographic objects may drift away from their initial position in the real world. Usually, you will not want that to happen. To address this issue, you can place a hologram using a spatial anchor. A spatial anchor fixes the position of an object in the real world. If adjustments are needed, they will be made with respect to the distant holographic objects rather than with the real-world anchor point.

A good approach to this issue is to drop a spatial anchor every time you place a holographic object. If the distance between a nearby object and a faraway object changes a little, that will be a lot less noticeable to the user than would be an offset of the nearby object from its real-world context.

Spatial anchors can be persisted from one running of an app to another in the app's spatial anchor store. When you save or load an anchor, provide a string key that your app recognizes and will use to identify the anchor later. You can associate other data with the anchor, such as the hologram that is located at that spot, by saving it to local storage and associating it with the key that you chose.

## Attached frame of reference

In contrast to the stationary frame of reference just discussed, some holograms are designed to move with the user, floating at a chosen position with respect to the user. These holograms are located in an attached frame of reference, which moves with the user as she walks around. The user can comfortably look at the holograms while walking from one place to another. Content that follows the user in this way is called body-locked content because its position is locked relative to the position of the user's body.

## Head-locked content

Head-locked content stays in the same position relative to the user's gaze in the same way that a heads-up display stays in front of a fighter pilot's view of the world. This is what the Start menu does after you invoke it with the bloom gesture. It appears right in front of you, and when you move your head it moves to stay in the center of your vision. This may be fine for the Start menu, but it is a bad idea for any app that you might write. It's not natural and quickly becomes annoying, as it gets in the way of other things that you might want to do.

# Types of Holographic Objects

Holographic objects could potentially come in a variety of shapes and sizes. One way of characterizing them is by how they interact with the real world. Some objects are most appropriately located in one kind of environment and others in a different kind of environment.

## Table top

As the name implies, small holograms designed to be viewed close up are best located on a flat surface such as a table or desk. A classic example of this was the holographic chess game between R2-D2 and Chewbacca in *Star Wars: A New Hope*, where C-3PO wisely counseled R2-D2 to let the wookie win.

## Surface-locked

Surface-locked objects are fixed in place on a surface, such as a wall. An Edge browser window or a Calendar screen are two examples of 2D apps that would be easy to use if locked to a wall or other flat surface.

## Floating

A floating object just hangs suspended in mid-air. This is fine for anything that does not require a direct connection with the real world. A Skype screen could possibly work as a floating object, but, depending on the situation, surface-locked might be better. The holograms you can invoke from the Start menu are examples of floating objects. Once you invoke one, you can fix it where you want in space, and it will remain there.

## Companion

A companion object would be one that moves along with the user. A companion object would be body-locked to the user by an attached frame of reference.

## Immersive

In immersive holographic environment is one that puts you into another world. NASA's *Destination: Mars* puts you in the middle of a Martian landscape with Buzz Aldrin as your guide (Figure 14-1).

***Figure 14-1.*** *HoloLens view of a holographic Buzz Aldrin on a holographic Mars (Courtesy of NASA)*

That is an immersive application.

# Sharing and Collaboration

In many applications, you will want your app to be shared by multiple people, enabling them to collaborate in ways that would be impossible otherwise. As we saw with the Holograms 240 app in Chapter 12, it is quite possible to not only share a holographic experience with multiple people, but also for those people to act collaboratively to achieve what none of them could do alone. One user must launch the sharing service on one PC on the network. Other users select the Sharing object in Unity's Hierarchy panel and connect to the IPv4 address of the PC upon which the sharing service is running. Once communication is established, serious work can begin.

# Importing an Object Definition

Sometimes you don't have to create a holographic object, because the object already exists. Any 3D object created in a computer graphics package such as Maya or 3ds Max can be uploaded to a HoloLens as a hologram and then be given behaviors with scripts, if appropriate. Considering the flexibility, power, and resources of products such as Maya, using such tools will probably be the preferred method of creating holographic assets.

# Creating an Object with HoloStudio

Whereas creating a holographic object with professional tools such as Maya or 3ds Max requires quite a bit of knowledge of the tools as well as experience using them, Microsoft offers a free hologram-creation app named HoloStudio to get you started in holographic app development. When you download HoloStudio from the Windows Store and launch it, you are taken through a tutorial that walks you through the hologram-creation process.

HoloStudio includes a toolbox that contains a number of holographic objects that you can combine to make more complex objects. It also includes tools that enable you to alter the holograms so as to transform them into the shapes, colors, and sizes that you want. If you leave the tutorial mid-lesson for any reason, when you return you will find yourself right where you left off.

# Summary

This chapter discusses many of the considerations that you must deal with when creating a mixed-reality application. Meshing the virtual with the real adds a number of complications beyond what you would need to think about when designing a purely virtual app. There are a variety of ways in which the virtual relates to the real, including spatially, aurally, and in terms of lighting. Holographic scenes made up of multiple holographic elements must be carefully arranged in order to maintain the illusion that the virtual objects are a part of the real world. That's what we will discuss in the next chapter.

# CHAPTER 15

■ ■ ■

# Manipulating Holographic Objects

In Chapter 14, we discussed creating virtual objects. Once an object has been created, it must be located somewhere in the space surrounding the user, and if it is an active object it must have behaviors of some kind, either in response to user actions or things that it does regardless of user actions. For example, in the RoboRaid first-person shooter game that comes with the Developer's Kit, the alien robotic scorpion enemies break through the walls and maneuver independent of user actions. However, when the user shoots at one and scores a direct hit, the scorpion explodes in a satisfying manner in response. These actions are programmed by scripts that the developer has written.

There are a number of behaviors that you can assign to an object, either in response to some action by the user or in response to some other event, such as a collision with another hologram or with a surface in the real environment, such as a wall or table.

## Creating a Holographic Object

There are several ways to create a holographic object, but the easiest is to use the Unity/Visual Studio/ Emulator tool chain described in several of the earlier chapters in this book. That is the method most heavily supported by Microsoft and the developer community that has grown up around the HoloLens. Once you have created a 3D object and it is resident in Unity, you can start working on locating the object relative to the user who will be running your app while wearing the HoloLens. Beyond that, you can add behaviors to the object with C# scripts.

You can either create a 3D object in Unity using the tools it includes for creating GameObjects, or you can import 3D objects that you have created externally with tools such as Maya, 3dsMax, and Blender. The external tools, since they are specifically designed for the creation of 3D objects rather than for the creation of games, are capable of highly detailed representations of objects both real and fanciful.

Creating a simple 3D object in Unity is easy. From the GameObject menu, select **3D Object** and then choose one of the submenu options as a starting point. Cubes, spheres, and cylinders are examples of things you can choose. Once you have chosen one, you can change its size or shape. You can make it bigger or smaller along each of the X, Y, or Z directions, effectively stretching it or squashing it along one or more of those directions. You could, for example, create a cylinder and then squash it into a disk of minimal thickness.

## Establishing the Location of a Holographic Object

As the app developer, you establish the initial location of all the objects in a scene. That location will be relative to the initial location of the user. In most cases, it's a good idea to place the most significant object directly in front of the user. You can give the user audible or visual cues as to where to look if she is looking away from where she should be in order for the app to carry forward.

© Allen G. Taylor 2016

A. G. Taylor, *Develop Microsoft HoloLens Apps Now*, DOI 10.1007/978-1-4842-2202-7_15

You can set the initial position of an object in Unity's Inspector panel, as shown in Figure 15-1. The user is located where you have placed the main camera, and the initial hologram is located where you have placed it in the Cartesian X, Y, Z coordinate system.

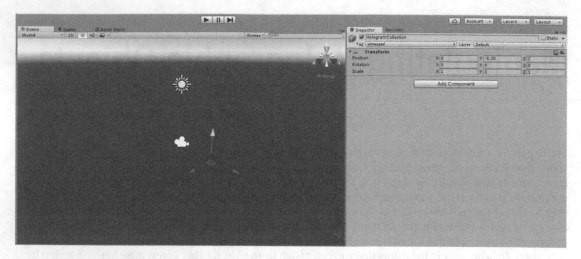

**Figure 15-1.** *Inspector panel's Transform section shows offsets from origin in X, Y, and Z directions*

Once the user has seen your initial hologram, you may give her the ability to move the holograms in the scene or manipulate them in some other way.

# Programming the Behavior of a Holographic Object

There are a variety of behaviors that you can give to a holographic object. Here are some examples:

- You can give it the ability to move appropriately through the environment.
- You can make it move in response to the user's gaze.
- You can make it respond in some way to a user's gesture.
- You can make it respond to a user's voice command.
- You can enable the user to affix it to a real-world surface.
- You can enable it to play music or emit other sounds.
- You can animate it.
- You can cause an animation to loop continuously.

In summary, you have a lot of control over what the user sees and hears. You can use that control to create an engaging experience for the user.

# Moving a holographic object around in space

Gaze, gesture, and voice are the three main tools you have at your disposal to affect the position of a holographic object. When you look directly at a holographic object, a raycast from the HoloLens hits the point in space where the object is apparently located. The HoloLens recognizes that the hologram is being targeted and changes the gaze-following cursor from a point of light to a small annulus or ring. This alerts the user to the fact that an air tap or voice command is directed to the targeted hologram rather than to any other.

## Locking a holographic object to the user's gaze and then giving it a fixed location

One way of moving a holographic object is to have it move such that it remains centered in the user's field of view. In this way, the user can move it to a desired location and then fix it there with either an air tap gesture or a voice command. It can be pretty annoying to have a hologram always centered in your field of view no matter where you are looking. But if you materialize a hologram in front of you and then move it to where you want it placed just by looking at your chosen destination for it and making an air tap gesture, you can fix it there and then move around it to view it from any angle.

Let's consider the example of a simple cube. With a simple series of operations, we can create a holographic cube, materialize it in front of and facing the user, and then with an air tap gesture place it at a desired spot in the world. It will persist in that spot even if we turn off the HoloLens and then launch the project again at a later time.

To create a cube hologram from scratch, follow these steps:

1. Start a new Unity project named Scratch.

2. Select **Main Camera** in the Hierarchy, and in the Inspector give it a Transform of X=0, Y=0, Z=0.

3. Set Clear Flags to **Solid Color** and Background to **0,0,0,0**. The Inspector panel should look like Figure 15-2.

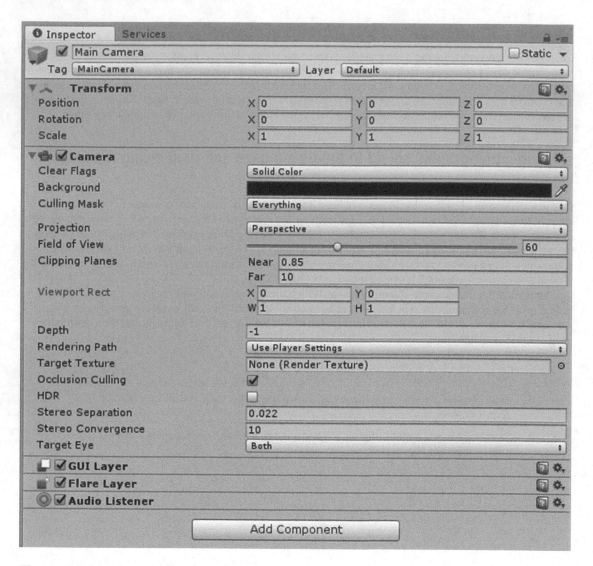

*Figure 15-2.* *Inspector panel for the main camera*

4.  From the GameObject menu, go to 3D Object ➤ Cube.

5.  Select **Cube** and set its Transform to X=0, Y=0, Z=3. Set its Scale to x=0.25, Y=0.25, Z=0.25. The Inspector panel should look like Figure 15-3.

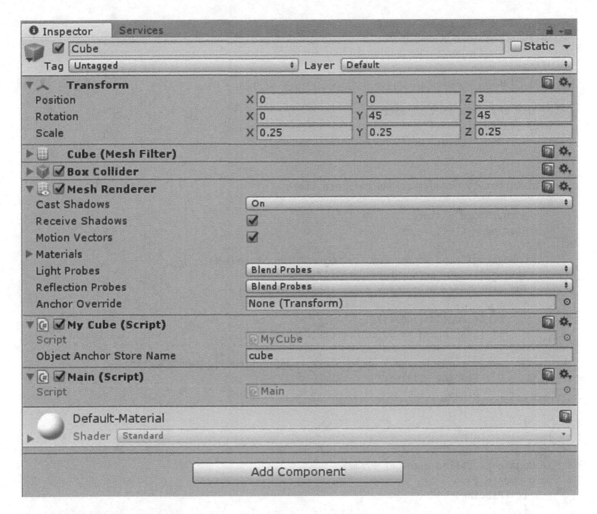

*Figure 15-3. Inspector panel for a cube*

6. Add the **MyCube.cs** C# script to the Assets folder of your project, then drag it onto the cube's Inspector panel. This script and the Main.cs script seen later use functions available in the HoloToolkit, which can be found at https://github.com/Microsoft/HoloToolkit-Unity:

```
using UnityEngine;
using System.Collections;

using UnityEngine.VR.WSA.Persistence;
using UnityEngine.VR.WSA;

public class MyCube : MonoBehaviour {

    //unique id for the cube
    public string ObjectAnchorStoreName;
```

```
//persistant location storage
WorldAnchorStore anchorStore;

//state
bool Placing = false;

// Use this for initialization
void Start () {
    WorldAnchorStore.GetAsync(AnchorStoreReady);
}

void AnchorStoreReady(WorldAnchorStore store)
{
    anchorStore = store;
    Placing = true;

    Debug.Log("Find Anchor for " + ObjectAnchorStoreName);
    string[] ids = anchorStore.GetAllIds();
    for (int index = 0; index < ids.Length; index++)
    {
        Debug.Log(ids[index]);
        if (ids[index] == ObjectAnchorStoreName)
        {
            WorldAnchor wa = anchorStore.Load(ids[index], gameObject);
            Placing = false;
            break;
        }
    }
}


// Update is called once per frame
void Update () {
    if (Placing)
    {
        //look at the user while placing, follow the gaze
        gameObject.transform.position = Camera.main.transform.position + Camera.main.
        transform.forward * 2;
        gameObject.transform.LookAt(Camera.main.transform);
    }
}

public void Place()
{
    Debug.Log("Place");

    if (anchorStore == null)
    {
        return;
    }

    if (Placing)
    {
```

```
        WorldAnchor attachingAnchor = gameObject.AddComponent<WorldAnchor>();
        if (attachingAnchor.isLocated)
        {
            Debug.Log("Saving persisted position immediately");
            bool saved = anchorStore.Save(ObjectAnchorStoreName, attachingAnchor);
            Debug.Log("saved: " + saved);
        }
        else
        {
            attachingAnchor.OnTrackingChanged += AttachingAnchor_OnTrackingChanged;
        }
    }
    else
    {
        WorldAnchor anchor = gameObject.GetComponent<WorldAnchor>();

        //delete any previous state
        if (anchor != null)
        {
            DestroyImmediate(anchor);
        }

        string[] ids = anchorStore.GetAllIds();
        for (int index = 0; index < ids.Length; index++)
        {
            Debug.Log(ids[index]);
            if (ids[index] == ObjectAnchorStoreName)
            {
                bool deleted = anchorStore.Delete(ids[index]);
                Debug.Log("deleted: " + deleted);
                break;
            }
        }
    }

    Placing = !Placing;
}

private void AttachingAnchor_OnTrackingChanged(WorldAnchor self, bool located)
{
    if (located)
    {
        Debug.Log("Saving persisted position in callback");
        bool saved = anchorStore.Save(ObjectAnchorStoreName, self);
        Debug.Log("saved: " + saved);
        self.OnTrackingChanged -= AttachingAnchor_OnTrackingChanged;
    }
}
}
```

The MyCube.cs script locates the hologram relative to the user's gaze. The following Main.cs script recognizes the user's air tap gesture and sends a message back to MyCube.cs that fixes the cube in its current position. With **Cube** selected in the Hierarchy, drag **Main.cs** from the Assets section of the Project window onto a blank area of the Inspector panel. Here's the code for Main.cs:

```
using UnityEngine;
using System.Collections;

using UnityEngine.VR.WSA.Persistence;
using UnityEngine.VR.WSA.Input;
using UnityEngine.VR.WSA;

public class Main : MonoBehaviour {

    GestureRecognizer recognizer;

    // Use this for initialization
    void Awake()
    {

        recognizer = new GestureRecognizer();
        recognizer.SetRecognizableGestures(GestureSettings.Tap);
        recognizer.TappedEvent += Recognizer_TappedEvent;

        recognizer.StartCapturingGestures();
    }

    private void Recognizer_TappedEvent(InteractionSourceKind source, int tapCount, Ray headRay)
    {
        Debug.Log("tapped");

        // Figure out which hologram is the focus of this frame.
        GameObject focusedObject;

        // Do a raycast into the world based on the user's
        // head position and orientation.
        var headPosition = Camera.main.transform.position;
        var gazeDirection = Camera.main.transform.forward;

        RaycastHit hitInfo;
        if (Physics.Raycast(headPosition, gazeDirection, out hitInfo))
```

```
    {
        // If the raycast hits a hologram, use that as the focused object.
        focusedObject = hitInfo.collider.gameObject;
        MyCube cube = focusedObject.GetComponent<MyCube>();
         if (cube != null)
        {
            cube.Place();
            Debug.Log("focusedObject is" + cube.ObjectAnchorStoreName);
        }

    }
    else
    {
        // If the raycast did not hit a hologram, clear the focused object.
        focusedObject = null;
        Debug.Log("focusedObject is null");
    }
}

}
```

7. Save the scene.

8. Go to File ➤ Build Settings.

9. In the Build Settings window, do the following:

   a. Click the Add Open Scenes button.

   b. Switch Platform to **Windows Store**.

   c. Switch SDK to **Universal 10**.

   d. Switch UWP Build Type to **D3D**.

10. Check the **Unity C# Projects** box. The Build Settings window should look like Figure 15-4.

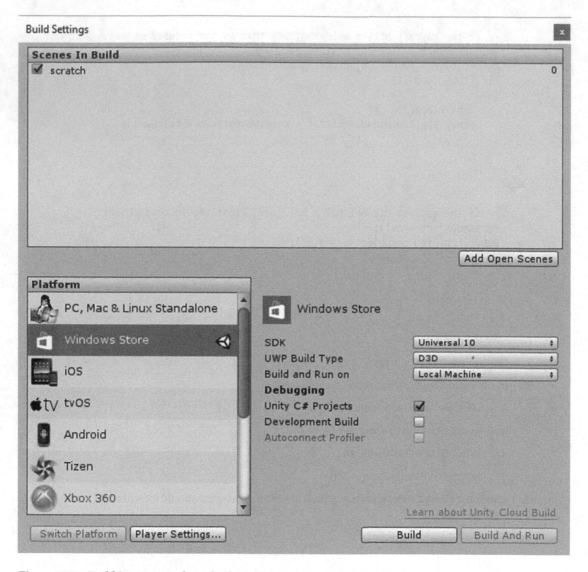

*Figure 15-4.* *Build Settings window after being configured correctly*

11. Click the Build button. Unity build operation will commence.

12. After a wait, the Scratch directory will appear, containing a number of subfolders created by the build operation. Create a new folder named App and select it.

13. Click the Select Folder button. This builds the project and puts it into the new App folder.

14. The directory will reappear. Double-click on the **App** folder to enter it.

15. Double-click on **scratch.sln**, the solution file, to launch Visual Studio.

16. When Visual Studio appears, set the parameters in the icon row to Debug, x86, and Remote Machine, as shown in Figure 15-5.

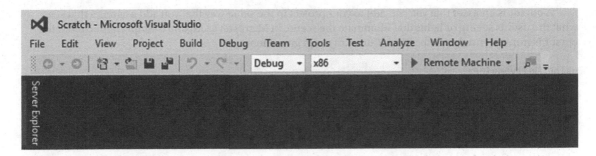

***Figure 15-5.*** *Settings for deployment of application to HoloLens*

17. Put on your HoloLens and turn it on.

18. Go to Debug ➤ Start Without Debugging. A build and deploy operation will commence.

19. After Visual Studio goes through its operations, with luck the "Made with Unity" logo will appear, followed by a white square right in front of your face. The square is the closest face of your cube.

20. Look around and see how the square follows your gaze.

21. Decide where you want to place the cube, move it there with your gaze, and give it an air tap to fix it in place.

22. Move around it to see that it is indeed a three-dimensional cube and not just a 2D square in the center of your vision.

## Hologram movement can be scripted

Another way to cause a holographic object to move is to add a script to it that choreographs its movement in light of real-world furniture and other environmental features that were mapped by a previous room scan. In the Young Conker game, Conker can jump onto tables and climb up walls based on the scan. This feature also enables characters in the Fragments mystery game to sit on a real couch in the room.

## Hologram movement can be controlled by physics

You can also move a holographic object by turning on the Physics option, which makes the object respond as if it were influenced by gravity, causing it to fall out of the air or roll down hills, finally coming to rest due to "friction" on the floor. This is showcased in the Origami sample application in the HoloLens tutorials.

## Creating a cursor that follows the user's gaze

In order for a HoloLens user to affect a hologram in some way, she must first designate which hologram she means to affect. This can be done with a cursor, and the cursor can designate a spot in space by following the user's gaze. A raycast shooting out from the HoloLens will follow the user's gaze as long as she is looking straight ahead. The processor in the HoloLens knows where the user is looking and also knows where all the holograms in the room are located. Thus, it knows if one of them is being targeted by the cursor, and if one is, it knows which hologram to affect if the user performs an air tap or issues a voice command.

A cursor is an asset that you can add to your project in the same way that you add a camera that sees what the user is seeing or lights that illuminate the scene. In Microsoft's Origami example application, the cursor is implemented with the WorldCursor.cs script given here:

```
using UnityEngine;

public class WorldCursor : MonoBehaviour
{
    private MeshRenderer meshRenderer;

    // Use this for initialization
    void Start()
    {
        // Grab the mesh renderer that's on the same object as this script.
        meshRenderer = this.gameObject.GetComponentInChildren<MeshRenderer>();
    }

    // Update is called once per frame
    void Update()
    {
        // Do a raycast into the world based on the user's
        // head position and orientation.
        var headPosition = Camera.main.transform.position;
        var gazeDirection = Camera.main.transform.forward;

        RaycastHit hitInfo;
        if (Physics.Raycast(headPosition, gazeDirection, out hitInfo))
        {
            // If the raycast hit a hologram...

            // Display the cursor mesh.
            meshRenderer.enabled = true;
            // Move the cursor to the point where the raycast hit.
            this.transform.position = hitInfo.point;
            // Rotate the cursor to hug the surface of the hologram.
            this.transform.rotation =
                Quaternion.FromToRotation(Vector3.up, hitInfo.normal);
        }
        else
        {
            // If the raycast did not hit a hologram, hide the cursor mesh.
            meshRenderer.enabled = false;
        }
    }
}
```

The default cursor is a doughnut-shaped marker that moves with the user's gaze and hugs the surface of whatever hologram it contacts. This means that if the cursor is on a vertical surface, the user sees it face on. If it is on a horizontal surface, the user sees it edge on. If the surface is sloping, the cursor appears slanted. In the last statement of the preceding code, we see that if the cursor does not hit a hologram, it becomes invisible.

# Changing a cursor when it hits a hologram

Often, you do not want a cursor to be invisible when it is not impinging on a hologram. The user wants to know where the cursor is so that she can move her head in a manner that will move the cursor onto a hologram. This is hard to do if you don't know where the cursor is to begin with. Thus, many applications have a cursor with two different appearances: one when it is hitting a hologram and the other when it is not. A common convention is to use the doughnut shape when the cursor is hitting a hologram and just a dot of light when it is not.

# Activating a targeted hologram with an air tap

As we saw with the preceding MyCube.cs example, you can write a script that does something to a targeted hologram when an air tap gesture is performed. In that example, the action was to fix the hologram in its current position. However, any action that you would like to perform when the air tap gesture is made can be done, as long as you can code it into a script.

# Activating a targeted hologram with a voice command

Just as you can affect a hologram with a gesture, you can affect it with a voice command. Voice command is even more powerful than gesture in that there are a lot more recognized commands than there are recognized gestures. While you can count the number of recognized gestures on the fingers of one hand, the number of voice commands available is virtually infinite. It's good if a voice command is short and not similar to other voice commands that it might be confused with, but beyond that there are more possibilities than you are ever likely to need. (W3C has a formal grammar definition for speech recognition called the Speech Recognition Grammar Specification. It is available here: www.w3.org/TR/speech-gramar/.) The code for voice commands in the Origami sample application is given here:

```
using System.Collections.Generic;
using System.Linq;
using UnityEngine;
using UnityEngine.Windows.Speech;

public class SpeechManager : MonoBehaviour
{
    KeywordRecognizer keywordRecognizer = null;
    Dictionary<string, System.Action> keywords = new Dictionary<string, System.Action>();

    // Use this for initialization
    void Start()
    {
        keywords.Add("Reset world", () =>
        {
            // Call the OnReset method on every descendant object.
            this.BroadcastMessage("OnReset");
        });

        keywords.Add("Drop Sphere", () =>
        {
            var focusObject = GazeGestureManager.Instance.FocusedObject;
            if (focusObject != null)
            {
```

```
                // Call the OnDrop method on just the focused object.
                focusObject.SendMessage("OnDrop");
            }
        });

        // Tell the KeywordRecognizer about our keywords.
        keywordRecognizer = new KeywordRecognizer(keywords.Keys.ToArray());

        // Register a callback for the KeywordRecognizer and start recognizing!
        keywordRecognizer.OnPhraseRecognized += KeywordRecognizer_OnPhraseRecognized;
        keywordRecognizer.Start();
    }

    private void KeywordRecognizer_OnPhraseRecognized(PhraseRecognizedEventArgs args)
    {
        System.Action keywordAction;
        if (keywords.TryGetValue(args.text, out keywordAction))
        {
            keywordAction.Invoke();
        }
    }
}
```

As you can see, to add a keyword just add it to the dictionary with a statement like the following:

```
    {
        keywords.Add("Reset world", () =>
        {
            // Call the OnReset method on every descendant object.
            this.BroadcastMessage("OnReset");
        });
```

# Summary

In this chapter we have seen how to create holographic objects, give them behaviors, and control how they respond to actions taken by the user. We have seen how to perform the basic operations of hitting a target hologram with a cursor, affecting it with a gesture, and affecting it with a voice command. Now that we can do all these things, in the next chapter we will look at a practical use of HoloLens holography in an educational context.

**PART V**

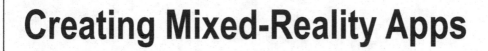

# Creating Mixed-Reality Apps

■ ■ ■

# CHAPTER 16

# Creating a Holographic Teaching Tool

HoloLens technology could be profitably applied in a wide variety of contexts, but there are several for which it is particularly valuable. One that stands to benefit the most is the field of education. Education is one of the oldest professions that humans have engaged in, right after hunting and gathering. In prehistoric times, skilled hunters and gatherers had to pass on their expertise to the next generation before the end of their short lives. In those days, education was one to one and very hands-on. Later, as the student-teacher ratio increased, the connection between teacher and student became weaker.

## The Limitations of Traditional Education

The education model that has come down to us over the past few centuries has a single teacher in a room with a large number of students, perhaps aided by a blackboard and a piece of chalk. Numerous studies have shown that this model is not particularly effective at transferring knowledge from the teacher to the students. Recently, technological advances have changed this picture somewhat, but we still largely have a teacher/ instructor/professor standing up in front of a class and lecturing. For some subjects, this arrangement works reasonably well, provided the instructor is not only knowledgeable about the subject matter, but also is an excellent communicator. For other subject areas, this method does not work very well at all. Happily, technological advances are improving the situation.

## How Education Is Changing

In many schools and other educational venues, computer-hosted PowerPoint slideshows have replaced blackboards and chalk. Photos and graphs enhance the text to provide students with a more visually engaging experience. Video and sound may augment the presentation. The instructor still has to know how to use these tools wisely, but, in general, more time is spent in the actual transmission of information and less in scribbling on a blackboard. The PowerPoint can be distributed to the students after class, so they don't have to take extensive notes during class. They can concentrate on the lesson being taught and only take notes on points not covered in the slides. This may seem to be an advantage, but in reality it makes the student less of a participant and more of being merely an observer.

Now, with the HoloLens being employed in an educational context, rather than the student being talked at and viewing a distant screen, she can become an active participant in the learning experience. An instructor can point out different parts of a hologram and comment on them. A student can move closer–or rather, left, right, or completely around the hologram–to get a more holistic idea of it than is possible on a screen or a page in a book.

© Allen G. Taylor 2016
A. G. Taylor, *Develop Microsoft HoloLens Apps Now*, DOI 10.1007/978-1-4842-2202-7_16

# Seeing the Unseen: Inside the Human Body

Some of the hardest subjects to teach are those that have a lot of internal complexity that is not visible from the outside. Consider human anatomy. There is a lot going on under the skin, and medical students need to understand how it all works. Machines that need to be diagnosed and repaired represent a similar problem. How do you teach human anatomy or auto mechanics to students in a way that they understand in depth? How can they see how the digestive system fits in with the circulatory system, the nervous system, and the skeletal system? How can they see the way the gears of an automatic transmission mesh and turn depending on which clutches are applied? If you take apart a human or an automatic transmission in order to see its parts, you miss out on seeing those parts in operation.

Figure 16-1 shows a professor explaining details of the human skeleton to a small group of medical students, all wearing HoloLenses.

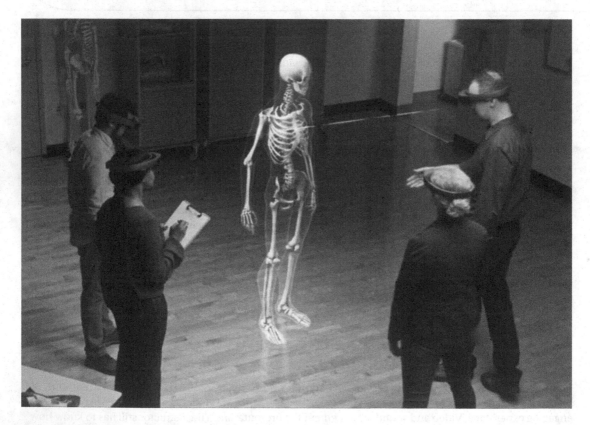

*Figure 16-1.* *HoloLens-aided anatomy class*

The medical school at Carnegie-Mellon University is using HoloLens in this way. They are pioneering use cases that many other educational institutions are bound to follow. Once you see what has always been unseeable, you will never want to go back to color slides, videos, or transparent overlays in books.

## Mixed reality home study

A student with a HoloLens can carry on the learning experience at home. Once you have a hologram resident on the device, you can call it up anywhere that is convenient and take all the time you want to study it in detail. Figure 16-2 shows the digestive system as seen from the back of the anatomical model, with the pancreas located and labeled.

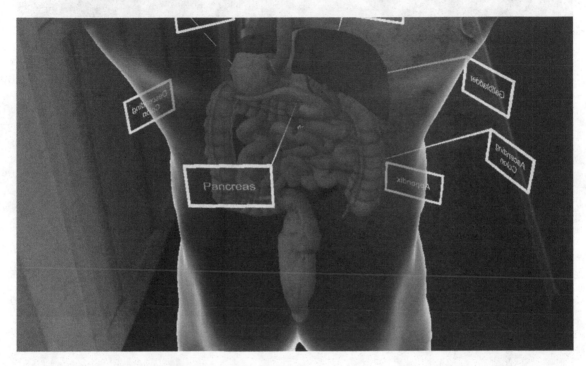

*Figure 16-2.* *Transparent anatomical model showing digestive system and highlighting the pancreas. Taken with a HoloLens in a dimly lit hallway*

Even models of the brain can be viewed in full three dimensionality, with brain regions identified and differentiated by color. Figure 16-3 shows such a model.

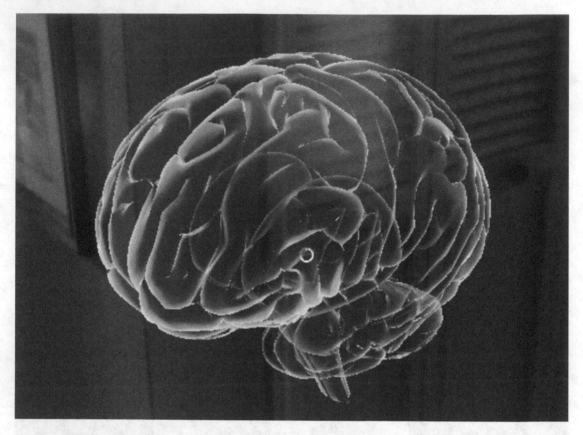

*Figure 16-3.* *Model of brain with frontal lobe highlighted*

Internal neural networks, shown differentiated by color, control different body and mental functions. Seeing, for example, the location of a tumor relative to these networks will indicate which impairments a patient is likely to start experiencing. Figure 16-4 shows a tumor in red impinging on a network in light blue. Yellow, red, and dark blue networks are not affected.

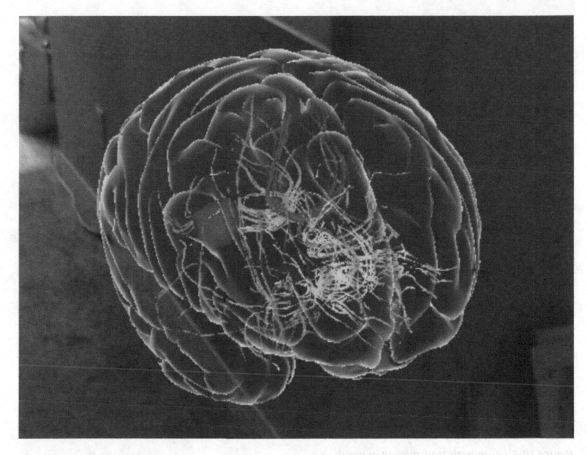

*Figure 16-4. Brain showing tumor discovered by an MRI scan of an actual patient*

# Seeing the Unseen: Inside an Automotive Automatic Transmission

Automotive repair is much like the practice of medicine. In both cases, the practitioner diagnoses a problem and then decides on a course of action to fix it. Automotive technicians are like doctors for cars. As such, they need a comprehensive education, just as medical doctors do. There are hundreds of millions of cars on the road in the United States alone, and the overwhelming majority of them have automatic transmissions. Transmission repair, along with engine repair and repair of other major subsystems, is taught at community colleges and trade schools around the country as well as at training centers owned by car manufacturers.

## How does it all fit together?

For complex mechanisms such as automatic transmissions, being able to see how all the many parts not only fit together, but also work together, is one of the key advantages that holographic learning can provide. In a relatively simple transmission, a sun gear, a set of planetary gears, and a ring gear all either rotate or not depending on the condition of a set of clutches. It's hard to imagine how this works just from looking at the disassembled parts. Figure 16-5 shows the main components of a disassembled automatic transmission.

***Figure 16-5.*** *Automatic transmission in pieces*

When a student mechanic takes apart a transmission in the shop, this is the result. She may be able to put it back together again correctly, but that does not tell her much about how it works. This is where HoloLens instruction can really add to the learning experience.

## Hands-on experience will always be needed, but . . .

Having an active holographic representation of either a human body or an automatic transmission does not mean that hands-on experience in the dissection lab or the shop is no longer necessary. Future practitioners need to know how tissues feel and how heavy gears and casings are. The holographic representations supplement current learning practices and give a deeper appreciation of what is being operated on. As a result, they become better diagnosticians and can solve more problems quickly and efficiently.

As is the case with human anatomy, it's impossible to see what all the gears and clutches in a transmission are doing while the transmission is operating. That makes it difficult to gain a true understanding of what is going on. With a HoloLens, student mechanics can see through the case of a model transmission and see the operation of all the parts. By issuing voice commands, for example, an instructor can have the transmission run through the gears while he describes which clutches are engaged and which gears are rotating with the shaft. Descriptions of gear ratios and the corresponding speed of rotation of the drive shaft can accompany the animation of the action. Figure 16-6 shows a hologram of an automatic transmission used in a transmission repair course at Clackamas Community College in Oregon City, Oregon. Clackamas Community College and nearby Portland Community College are leaders in applying holographic technology to automotive repair courses.

***Figure 16-6.*** *Photo of hologram of exploded view of an automatic transmission, taken in the author's messy office*    [AU5]

By actually being able to see the clutches engage and the change in the speed of the gears, students are much better able to grasp how the mechanism works. Figure 16-7 shows the same hologram from a different angle.

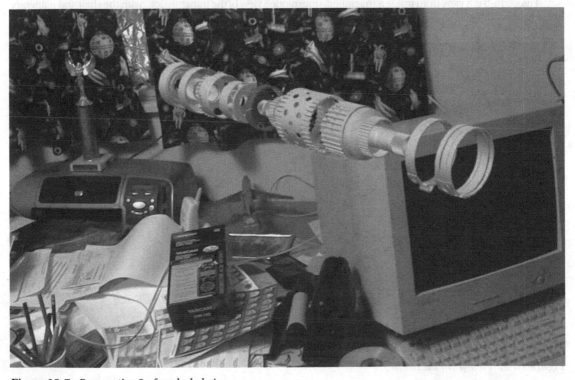

***Figure 16-7.*** *Perspective 2 of exploded view*

Figure 16-8 shows a closer view with more detail of the planetary gears.

***Figure 16-8.*** *Closer view of transmission*

Figure 16-9 is a view from inside a magnified, unexploded view of the transmission, with the shaft and planetary gears removed. You can actually walk through the entire transmission, examining how the parts fit together.

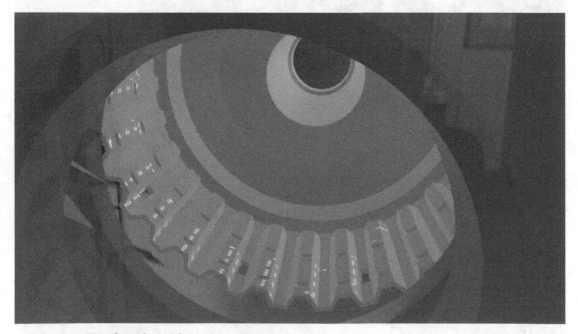

***Figure 16-9.*** *View from the inside*

# Instructor-driven Animation

One of the cool things about the type of holography that HoloLens produces is the fact that you can array students all around a hologram or even inside it. What better way to see the internals of something than from inside it? Since you can scale a hologram any way you want, you could put students inside a large hologram while describing what is happening, as in Figure 16-9.

The hologram can be animated, with voice commands from the instructor starting and stopping the animation as she describes what's happening to the students. This type of instruction could be even more effective in an architecture class, for example, than in one about anatomy or auto mechanics. You could put students inside a holographic building so they could see what it would be like for people to live in the real thing.

# Making the Student an Active Participant

The instructor isn't the only one who could affect the hologram in a class situation. In addition to moving around and viewing the hologram from any desired position, students could also affect it with air taps and voice commands. The instructor may want to set rules about what students may do. In addition, the app should probably have a "Reset" command that puts everything back in its original condition, to be used if student interactions change the hologram in a way that does not contribute to learning.

# Creating a Compelling Educational App

Creating an app that teaches human anatomy, transmission repair, or any equally complex topic is not a job for the lone developer. A team with diverse areas of expertise is required. First of all, you need a domain expert who is highly knowledgeable about the subject matter. You also need an experienced teacher who knows how to communicate ideas in an easily understandable way. You need a computer graphics guru who is a master with tools such as Maya, 3ds Max, or Blender, and a wizard with Unity and Visual Studio development tools. Just as important, you need a tester or quality assurance person who is adept at finding the weaknesses and bugs that infest any and all complex applications. To get involved in HoloLens development, find and get involved with people whose skills and interests complement your own. You will need them, and they will need you.

# Summary

There is broad agreement that feeding students facts through lectures and having them regurgitate the information back on tests and exams is not the best way to promote learning. Recent advances in presentation using computer-facilitated media has improved this situation somewhat. The HoloLens technology has the potential to transform education in a much more profound way. It has the potential to put the student right in the middle of the subject matter by mixing the student's environment with the environment of what is being studied in such a way that makes the subject matter real to the student, unlike what they experience through listening to a lecture, reading a book, or viewing a 2D video presentation. Finally, find those people whose talents complement yours. Find some simple projects that you can work on together, and in the process forge a working relationship that works for everyone.

I mentioned that your team needs a specialist in testing and quality assurance. Many times developers give little thought to this. However, if you want to deliver a quality product that will build your reputation rather than destroy it, you need to give quality assurance the attention it deserves. It is not unusual for more time and effort to be spent on the quality assurance of a complex application than is spent on coding it in the first place. In the next chapter, we will talk about Microsoft's HoloToolkit, which makes application development much easier than it otherwise would be. In the chapter after that, we will delve into the many important aspects of software quality assurance.

■ ■ ■

# CHAPTER 17

# Creating Your App Using HoloToolkit

In Chapter 5, we got a first look at creating holographic applications by working through the tutorials at Microsoft's online Holographic Academy. From the Holograms 101 Origami tutorial through to the Holograms 240 Shared Holograms tutorial, we were able to see the features and interactivity of some real, although simple, holographic applications. This was fine as far as it went, but it didn't give a real feel for what it would be like to actually develop an application ourselves, because the holographic objects in the tutorials were already created and the scripts that gave them active capabilities were already written. This is a far cry from developing a non-trivial application from scratch.

Developing a holographic application from scratch is pretty challenging. You need a top-notch computer graphics designer to create the 3D assets that will be turned into holograms. You need a Unity wizard who is adept at putting those holograms into the context of an environment, and you need a C# coding guru who can give those holograms the functionality that they need. It is rare to find a single person who can perform all of these functions at a top level. Microsoft knows this, and to help out has produced the HoloToolkit.

## What is HoloToolkit?

The HoloToolkit is a collection of scripts and components that will make it easier for you to create applications that target Windows Holographic. It makes it possible to build holographic apps without using Unity. You can find information about how to do that at https://github.com/Microsoft/HoloToolkit. If you are using Unity, as I describe in this book, a targeted subset of the HoloToolkit is available at https://github.com/microsoft/HoloToolkit-Unity. The Unity version of HoloToolkit contains prebuilt assets and scripts that you will be able to apply in a wide variety of situations in your applications. They will save you from having to build assets and code scripts from absolute scratch so that you can concentrate on those aspects of your application that are unique rather than having to spend a lot of time on the boilerplate that underlies all applications.

After downloading the zipped HoloToolkit from GitHub, create a new project in Unity or open an existing one. From there, navigate to the package you just downloaded via:

Assets ➤ Import Package ➤ Custom Package (package you downloaded)

Once you have done this, a HoloToolkit menu item should appear in your main menu.

Regardless of what holographic app you are developing, you should delete the default camera that appears in Unity when you create a new project and replace it with the **Main Camera** prefab that was added to your assets from the Toolkit. This main camera is specifically designed for holographic applications. If you add the **ManualCameraControl.cs** script to the Main Camera prefab, you will be able to manually control the camera when in Unity player mode. This will let you see what things look like without having to build and deploy the project to either the HoloLens Emulator or the HoloLens device.

© Allen G. Taylor 2016

A. G. Taylor, *Develop Microsoft HoloLens Apps Now*, DOI 10.1007/978-1-4842-2202-7_17

Before building and deploying a project, it is also a good idea to make the following selections:
HoloToolkit ➤ Configure ➤ Apply HoloLens Scene Settings
HoloToolkit ➤ Configure ➤ Apply HoloLens Project Settings

# Toolkit Contents

The assets in the Toolkit fall into six major categories:

1. Input

2. Sharing

3. Spatial Mapping

4. Spatial Sound

5. Utilities

6. Build

The assets include prefabs and scripts that are useful in a wide variety of situations. Also included are tests of the capabilities provided by these assets to help you learn how to use them effectively.

# Input Assets

A hologram's interactivity with the user is one of the most dynamic aspects of its presence. How it responds to a user's gaze, gesture, and voice is controlled by assets in the Toolkit that you can incorporate into your apps. The Input folder contains several subfolders, each containing a different category of asset that you might want to use in your scene. The assets contained in these subfolders will probably grow over time as new features are added.

## Materials

The hand_up material is an image of a hand with the index finger pointing up. You might want to use this as a cursor when the user is gazing at something that will respond to an air tap. The ring_shadow material is a dark ring with fuzzy edges that you might want to use as a cursor shadow.

## Models

There are models of several different cursors in this folder.

## Prefabs

The prefabs in this folder are all variations of the cursor. There are cursors for when the user's gaze is on a hologram (a ring) and when it is off (a dot). There is also a cursor shaped like a hand to indicate that the user's hand is in the field of view.

- BasicCursor.prefab is a torus-shaped cursor that follows the user's gaze around.

- Cursor.prefab is a torus-shaped cursor when the user is gazing at a hologram (CursorOnHolograms) and a point of light when the user's gaze is not impinging on any holograms (CursorOffHolograms).

- CursorWithFeedback.prefab is a torus-shaped cursor that follows the user's gaze and gives the user feedback when a hand is detected in the ready state (index finger pointing up).

- FocusedObjectKeywordManager.prefab is a keyword manager that sends messages to the object currently being focused upon by the FocusedObjectMessageSender component.

- SelectedObjectKeywordManager.prefab is a keyword manager that sends messages to the currently selected object via the SelectedObjectMessageSender component.

# Scripts

Scripts are associated with various GameObjects and give them functionality. You can pretty much tell which GameObjects the scripts relate to by the following brief descriptions.

- BasicCursor.cs does three things. It
  1. decides where to display the cursor;
  2. positions the cursor at the gazed-at hit location; and
  3. rotates the cursor to match the hologram normals so that it seems to be hugging the surface of the hologram.

- CursorFeedback.cs gives the user feedback if a hand is detected when a GameObject is being hit by the cursor.

- CursorManager.cs does three things. It
  1. shows the appropriate cursor when a hologram is hit;
  2. places the appropriate cursor at the hit position; and
  3. matches the cursor normal to that of the hit surface.

  You must provide GameObjects for the CursorOnHologram and CursorOffHologram public fields. CursorOnHologram is the cursor object to display when the user is gazing at a hologram. CursorOffHologram is the cursor object to display when the user is not gazing at a hologram.

  DistanceFromCollision is the distance in meters to offset the cursor from a collision with a hologram in the scene. This prevents the cursor from being occluded by a hologram.

- FocusedObjectMessageSender.cs sends a Unity message to the object currently focused on by the Gaze Manager.

- GazeManager.cs performs a Physics Raycast in the direction of the user's gaze to get the position and normal of any collision.

  The MaxGazeDistance is the maximum distance to raycast. Any holograms beyond this distance will not be raycasted to.

  The RaycastLayerMask declares the Unity layers that will be raycasted against. If you have holograms that should not be raycasted against, such as a cursor, do not include their layers in this mask.

- GazeStabilizer.cs stabilizes the user's gaze to account for head jitter. Multiple samples are taken and the average of all of them is used to define the gaze direction.

- StoredStabilitySamples is the number of samples that you want to use. A larger number will correspond to more stability, but less performance. It's a tradeoff.

  PositionDropOffRadius is the position-based distance away from the gravity well.

  DirectionDropOffDistance is the direction-based distance away from the gravity well.

  PositionStrength is the position lerp (linear interpolation) factor.

  DirectionStrength is the direction lerp factor.

  StabilityAverageDistanceWeight is the stability average weight multiplier factor.

  StabilityVarianceWeight is the stability variance weight multiplier factor.

- GestureManager.cs creates a gesture recognizer and looks for an air tap gesture. When one is detected, it uses GazeManager to find the target object and then sends a message to that object. GestureManager also has an OverrideFocusedObject function that lets you send a message to a specific object by overriding the gaze.

- HandGuidance.cs displays a GameObject when the user's hand is close to leaving the camera's view. This script requires a cursor and a HandGuidanceIndicator public field. The HandGuidanceIndicator will be rendered around the cursor and will be displayed when the user's hand is about to lose tracking. The HandGuidanceThreshold determines when to start showing the HandGuidanceIndicator.

- HandsManager.cs tracks when the user's hand has been detected in the ready position.

- KeywordManager.cs enables you to specify keywords and methods in the Unity Inspector rather than including them in code. For this to work, microphone capability must be enabled in Unity. Find it under Edit ➤ Project Settings ➤ Player ➤ Settings for Windows Store ➤ Publishing Settings ➤ Capabilities.

  Use KeywordsAndResponses to set the size of the number of keywords you want to listen for, then specify the keywords and method responses to complete the array.

  Set RecognizerStart to determine whether the keyword recognizer will start immediately or wait for your code to tell it to start.

- SelectedObjectMessageSender.cs sends a Unity message to the currently selected object. Object selection is controlled by OnSelectObject and OnClearSelection events. Because messages can be triggered by voice commands, keyword responses must be registered in the KeywordManager.

## Shaders

There is a cursor shader that has a sprite texture.

## Tests

The tests included in the Input folder of the HoloToolkit are simple scenes that test basic functionality of input.

- BasicCursor creates a target sphere and a cursor. The sphere is fixed in space, while the cursor is torus-shaped when the user's gaze is on the sphere and disappears when the user's gaze moves off the sphere.

- Cursor creates a target sphere and a cursor. The sphere is fixed in space, while the cursor is torus-shaped and hugs the surface of the sphere when the user's gaze is on the sphere. The cursor changes to a diffuse point of light when the user's gaze moves off the sphere.

- CursorWithFeedback creates a target sphere and cursor as in the preceding Cursor test. In addition, when the user's hand comes into view in the ready position, the cursor changes from a torus to a hand-with-upraised-index-finger icon.

- FocusedObjectKeywords tests the ability to send keyword messages. When the cursor is on the focused object, saying "Make Bigger" will make the object bigger and saying "Make Smaller" will make the object smaller.

- SelectedObjectKeywords tests the selecting of a gaze-targeted object with a "Select Object" voice command. The selection persists even after gaze is removed from the object. Further voice commands, such as "Make Bigger" or "Make Smaller," continue to affect the selected object regardless of cursor position. Finally, the "Clear Selection" command deselects the object.

# Sharing

For many applications, and most especially educational ones, the ability for multiple people to share a mixed-reality experience is crucial. The HoloToolkit supports this requirement with plugins, prefabs, and scripts. In the Toolkit Sharing folder there are five subfolders.

## Editor

The Editor folder contains the Sharing Menu script. It exposes the HoloToolkit menu option, which launches the sharing service, among other functions.

## Plugins

This folder contains compiled architecture-specific binaries for Sharingclient.dll, which are needed for access to sharing APIs.

## Prefabs

The Sharing prefab enables sharing and networking in a Unity application and enables communication between a Windows and a non-Windows device.

In the prefab, SharingStage.cs allows you to be a Primary Client. Server Address is the IP address of the machine running the HoloToolkit ➤ Launch Sharing Service program. Server Port displays the port being used for communicating.

SharingSessionTracker.cs keeps track of clients joining and leaving a shared session.

AutoJoinSession.cs creates a shared session with Session Name "Default." It joins a new client to that session if it already exists.

## Scripts

This folder contains scripts that relate to the sharing and networking features of a project. One folder contains the Sharing SDK, which holds a large number of scripts. The Utilities folder contains several scripts, including the AutoJoinSession script just mentioned in the Prefabs section. Also included here are the SharingStage and SharingSessionTracker scripts.

## Tests

To test the sharing features:

- Navigate to the Tests folder under Sharing in the HoloToolkit.

- Drag the Sharing project from the Project folder into the root level of the Hierarchy panel.

- Go to File ➤ Build Settings to display the Build Settings window.

- Click the Add Open Scenes button to add the Sharing project to Scenes to Build.

- Uncheck any other projects that are already in Scenes to Build.

- Make sure Platform is **Windows Store**, SDK is **Universal 10**, and UWP Build Type is **D3D**.

- Check the **Unity C# Projects** box.

- Click the Build button.

- Create an App folder.

- When the compile is finished, open the .sln solution.

- Build and deploy with Visual Studio.

The Sharing project demonstrates how to use the Sharing prefabs for networking and sharing custom messages with client HoloLens devices. It also demonstrates how to share world anchors between clients to establish a shared space.

To run the tests:

- Ensure the sharing service is launched, using HoloToolkit ➤ Launch Sharing Service.

- Enter the IP address displayed in the console window into the Server Address of the Sharing object.

- CustomMessages.cs shows how to communicate specific information among clients.

- ImportExportAnchorManager.cs shows how to create anchors and share them with other clients using the sharing service.

- RemoteHeadManager.cs draws cubes on remote heads of users joining the session.

# Spatial Mapping

HoloLens's spatial-mapping capability maps out the room around the user so that holographic objects can be placed appropriately in relation to the real environment.

# Spatial Perception

To use spatial mapping in your app, the SpatialPerception capability must be enabled in the AppxManifest file. To enable SpatialPerception, do the following:

- Go to Edit ➤ Project Settings ➤ Player to put Player Settings into the Inspector panel.

- Click on the small green Windows Store icon.

- Expand the Publishing Settings section, scroll down, and check the **SpatialPerception** box in the Capabilities list.

---

■ **Note** If you have already exported your Unity project to a Visual Studio solution, you will need to either export to a new folder or manually set this capability in the AppxManifest file. Following that:

- In Visual Studio, right-click on **Package.appxmanifest** in the Solution Explorer and select **View Code**.

- Find the line specifying TargetDeviceFamily and make sure MaxVersionTested="10.0.10586.0

- Save Package.appxmanifest.

---

# Editor

The Editor subfolder of the SpatialMapping folder contains two scripts: SpatialMappingColliderInspector and SpatialMappingRendererInspector. These files are used to adjust the settings for the SpatialMappingCollider and the SpatialMappingRenderer scripts.

# Materials

There are two materials: Occlusion and Wireframe.

# Plugins

In this folder are WSA, x64, and x86 subfolders, each containing an appropriate version of PlaneFinding.dll.

# Prefabs

There are three prefabs: RemoteMapping, SpatialMapping, and SurfacePlane.

The RemoteMapping prefab contains three scripts: RemoteMeshTarget, RemoteMeshSource, and RemoteMappingManager.

The SpatialMapping prefab contains three scripts: SpatialMappingObserver, SpatialMappingManager, and FileSurfaceObserver.

The SurfacePlane prefab contains a Cube mesh filter, a Box Collider, a Mesh Renderer, and a SurfacePlane script. It also includes the Default-Material.

## Scripts

Spatial mapping is a complex problem to solve. Happily, the HoloToolkit provides a large number of scripts to help accomplish this. Within the scripts folder, along with over a dozen scripts, is a subfolder named SpatialMappingComponent.

## Spatial mapping component

The Spatial Mapping Component is a unified set of scripts that provides physics or rendering support for spatial mapping. When you add a SpatialMappingColllider component and a SpatialMappingRenderer component to a GameObject, spatial mapping starts working.

### SpatialMappingRenderer.cs

This script is used for rendering spatial mapping. In rendering mode, it determines how to render the mesh. The default is Occlusion. Occlusion will cause the mesh to occlude holograms behind it. Material will apply the specified material. If you specify None for material, the meshes will not render at all.

The Occlusion material, mentioned earlier in the Materials section, is used to occlude holograms with the spatial-mapping mesh. If a hologram is behind an occluding object such as a table or chair, it will not be displayed.

The Rendering Material, also mentioned in the Materials section, should be set to Wireframe. Its purpose is to render the spatial-mapping mesh. This is only relevant when the rendering mode is set to Material.

### SpatialMappingCollider.cs

This script is used to perform physics collisions with the spatial-mapping mesh. The _enableCollisions variable determines whether to create a collider for RigidBody physics.

## Component design considerations

If you want spatial mapping to work for a user who moves from one location to another, attach the components to the camera, and the spatial mapping will move with the user.

If you want collisions to continue taking place in the user's original location even after she has walked away, leave a second SpatialMappingCollider in the original location.

If you want both physics collisions and to render the spatial-mapping mesh for an area, add both a SpatialMappingCollider and a SpatialMappingRenderer to that area. The component's default values for all the variables work fine in most situations, but are customizable if need be.

By default, removed meshes are cached. They can be restored if the user returns to an area whose mesh had been removed.

## Other Scripts

The following scripts help you to load the spatial-mapping mesh from a file or the network into a Unity scene.

### FileSurfaceObserver.cs

This class is a SpatialMappingSource that loads spatial-mapping data from a file into Unity. MeshFileName is the name of the file when either loading surface mesh data or saving it back to a file.

## MeshSaver.cs

This is a static class that can read and write mesh data to and from the file specified in FileSurfaceObserver.cs.

## PlaneFinding.cs

This script wraps the native PlaneFinding DLL. It is used by SurfaceMeshesToPlanes.cs

## RemoteMappingManager.cs

This script enables the sending of meshes remotely from HoloLens to Unity.

## RemoteMeshSource.cs

This is the networking component that runs on the HoloLens to send meshes to Unity so that it can build up a map of the room.

## RemoteMeshTarget.cs

This script runs in the Unity editor and receives spatial-mapping data from the HoloLens.

## RemoveSurfaceVertices.cs

This script removes spatial-mapping vertices that fall within a specified bounding volume.

## SimpleMeshSerializer.cs

This script is a static class that converts a Unity mesh to an array of bytes. It is used by MeshSaver.cs to serialize and deserialize mesh data.

## SpatialMappingManager.cs

This script manages the interactions between the running application and all spatial-mapping data sources, whether they come from a file, an observer, or the network.

## SpatialMappingObserver.cs

This script adds and updates spatial-mapping data for all surfaces discovered by the SurfaceObserver running on the HoloLens.

## SpatialMappingSource.cs

This script is a class that generates and retrieves meshes based on spatial-mapping data coming from the current source object, which could be a file, an observer, or the network. SpatialMappingManager.cs manages switching between source types and interacting with this class.

## SurfaceMeshesToPlanes.cs

This script finds and creates planes based on spatial-mapping meshes. It uses PlaneFinding.cs and requires the PlaneFinding plugin.

## SurfacePlane.cs

This script generates planes and classifies them by type, whether wall, ceiling, floor, table, or unknown. It should be a component of the SurfacePlane prefab that is used by SurfaceMeshesToPlanes.cs.

## TapToPlace.cs

This is a script you add to a GameObject that enables users to place the GameObject somewhere in the spatial-mapping mesh by performing an air tap gesture. It requires the GazeManager, the GestureManager, and the SpatialMappingManager to be in the scene.

# Shaders

There are two shaders in the HoloToolkit that are used with spatial mapping: the occlusion shader and the wireframe shader. They contain code and instructions for the GPU to execute. When a hologram moves behind a real-world object that has been represented with a mesh, it should be occluded. That effect is enabled by the occlusion shader. A wireframe shader is used to render a wireframe representation of a holographic object.

# Tests

In addition to some additional assets, there are four simple projects that demonstrate some key aspects of spatial mapping:

- The PlaneFinding scene (PlaneFinding.unity) runs in a loop. In scene view in Unity, you will see a visualization of the planes found. This test exposes properties that enable you to manipulate API parameters in real time and observe the impact of your manipulations. When you use the code contained in this scene, call the PlaneFinding APIs from a background thread to avoid stalling the rendering thread and causing a drop in frame rate.

- The SpatialProcessing scene tests the two processing scripts that are available in the HoloToolkit: SurfaceMeshesToPlanes and RemoveSurfaceVertices. If you already have a room file saved, this test will automatically load it and run it in Unity. If you don't have such a file, you can run the test directly in a HoloLens. The scene will scan your surroundings for 15 seconds and then convert all meshes to planes. If a floor plane is found, the scene will remove vertices from surface meshes that fall within the bounds of any active plane.

- The Example scene in the SpatialMappingComponent subfolder shows a static play space that preserves physics around it while maintaining the physics and wireframe rendering of spatial mapping around the camera. You can also tap to drop a cube with a RigidBody component in front of the camera, displaying the effect of gravity.

- The TapToPlace scene demonstrates the TapToPlace capability by attaching the TapToPlace script to a cube. The GazeManager, GestureManager, and SpatialMapping prefabs are also included, as is the BasicCursor. A first tap will move the cube along the spatial-mapping mesh. A second tap will fix it in its new position.

# Spatial Sound Scripts

The SpatialSound folder in the HoloToolkit contains a collection of scripts in the UAudioManager subfolder. These scripts can help you to set up complex sound playback events. You can introduce randomization to avoid sound becoming repetitive and trite. Different audio clips can be played, volume can be varied, and so can pitch, all randomly. Audio events may invoke the playing of multiple sounds, either at once or sequentially.

Spatial sound in Unity uses the SetSpatializerFloat API to set the spatial properties of the AudioSource component. The UAudioManager makes relevant parameter values immediately accessible to the sound designer.

In addition, with UAudioManager events, sounds can be categorized into the bus system of Unity's audio mixer. This enables the sound designer to control the sounds coming from multiple holograms with a single setting.

## Editor Scripts

The Editor subfolder of the UAudioManager folder contains the UAudioManagerBaseEditor, the UAudioManagerEditor, the UAudioMiniManagerEditor, and the UAudioProfiler. These editors enable the sound designer to add sounds when triggered by an event or to modify an existing sound, again, when triggered by an event.

## Other Scripts

The UAudioManager folder contains a collection of scripts that you can use to design and control your app's audio, including spatial sound.

## ActiveEvent

This script controls currently active AudioEvents and their AudioSource components for instance-limiting events.

## AudioClip

This script encapsulates a single Unity AudioClip with playback settings.

## AudioContainer

This class is the sound container for an AudioEvent. It specifies the rules for playing back the AudioClips it contains.

## AudioEvent

This script defines how an audio object should be played back.

## AudioSourcePlayClipExtension

This class is a shortcut to assigning a clip to an AudioSource component and playing the source repeatedly.

## AudioSourcesReference

This class encapsulates a cache of references to AudioSource components on a given local audio emitter GameObject. It is used primarily by UAudioManager. It improves performance by bypassing the need to re-query for a list of attached components for each use.

## MiniAudioEvent

This class is the main component of UAudioMiniManager. It contains settings and a container for playing audio clips.

## SpatialSoundSettings

This class provides a set of methods that simplify making modifications to SpatialSoundSpatializer parameters.

## UAudioManager

This class is a singleton that provides organization and control of an application's AudioEvents. Designers and coders can share the names of the AudioEvents to enable rapid iteration on the application's sound in a way that is similar to the way XAML is used for user interfaces. It enables sound designers to set up audio events with playback behaviors and play AudioEvents via a singleton API.

## UAudioManagerBase

This script provides the base functionality for the UAudioManager classes.

## UAudioMiniManager

This script plays all the AudioEvents in the manager.

# Utilities

The scripts in the Utilities folder are useful tools that you can use in your applications.

## Editor

The Editor subfolder contains several scripts that you can use in building your application.

## BuildCommands

Builds HoloLens applications.

## BuildMenu

Gives developer a menu item to build the current application for HoloLens.

## ConfigureMenu

Applies project settings to the current project.

## EditorGUIExtensions

Sets up the current application's graphical user interface (GUI).

## EditorGUILayoutExtensions

Uses EditorGUIExtensions to produce the GUI layout.

## LayerMaskExtensions

Makes extensions to the UnityEngine.LayerMask class.

# Prefabs

The MainCamera prefab is designed for HoloLens and should be used in place of the default main camera that is present when Unity is launched.

The FPSDisplay prefab displays the number of frames per second an app is running at. This helps you to know whether your app has a frame-rate problem.

# Scripts

There are several scripts that you could find helpful in a number of different situations.

## Billboard

This class keeps a GameObject facing the user.

## DirectionIndicator

This class creates an indicator around the cursor that shows which direction to look to find a GameObject.

## FixedAngularSize

This class causes a hologram to appear the same angular size, regardless of how far it is from the camera.

## FpsDisplay

This class calculates the frame rate and displays frames per second in a referenced Text control.

## Interpolator

This MonoBehaviour interpolates a transform's position, rotation, or scale to smooth animations.

## ManualCameraControl

Attach this class to the MainCamera object to enable manual control of the camera in the Unity editor.

## NearPlaneFade

This MonoBehaviour enables the near-plane limit to be a gradual fade out rather than an abrupt cutoff.

## SimpleTagalong

This script makes a GameObject stay a fixed distance from the camera and always have a part of itself in the view frustum of the camera.

## Singleton

This class finds and returns an instance of an object of a specified type.

## Tagalong

This extension of the SimpleTagalong enables you to specify the minimum and target percentage of an object to keep in the view frustum of the camera. It keeps the Tagalong object in front of other holograms, including the spatial-mapping mesh.

## TextToSpeechManager

This class enables text-to-speech using the Windows 10 SpeechSynthesizer class. SpeechSynthesizer generates speech as a SpeechSynthesisStream. It converts the stream into a Unity AudioClip and plays the clip using the AudioSource that you supply in the Inspector. You can position the voice where you like in 3D space. One possibility is to place the AudioSource on an empty GameObject that is a child of the main camera and position it about 0.6 units above the camera. This is similar to where Cortana's speech emanates from in the operating system.

## VectorExtensions

This class is a collection of useful extension methods for Unity's Vector structs.

# Shaders

Several shaders that go beyond the functionality of the StandardShader are included, such as two variants of the Blinn-Phong shader, two variants of the Lambertian shader, two variants of an unlit shader, two variants of the vertex lit shader, and the StandardFast shader.

## Tests

The ManualCameraControl.unity test shows how to use the ManualCameraControl.cs script. The script is a child of the main camera of the scene. When in preview mode in Unity, the user can move around the scene using the WASD keys and look in various directions using Ctrl + mouse.

The TextToSpeechManager.unity text shows how to use the TextToSpeech.cs script. The script is a child of three cube GameObjects in the scene. An air tap on a cube will trigger a text-to-speech voice from the cube. In addition, the user can ask "What time is it?" and hear a voice intoning the current time. This voice follows the user wherever she goes.

# Designing a Simple App

If you have worked through the tutorials at the Holographic Academy, starting with Origami and working through to sharing holograms, you must have a pretty good idea of how to map a space with spatial mapping, create a hologram and place it in a location, select a hologram with gaze and gesture, affect a hologram with an air tap gesture, affect a hologram with voice, have the hologram emit a sound, and get multiple HoloLens users to experience the same holograms. The code and other assets used in those example applications are available to you for your use or modification, as are the code and the other assets in the HoloToolkit.

You can create 3D objects with a computer graphics package such as Maya, 3ds Max, or Blender and then import them into Unity. Alternatively, you can start with the 3D objects available under the GameObject menu option and modify them as you wish within Unity.

# Setting Up Unity for Holographic Development

You may have a simple app in mind that you want to develop. However, if it needs to be aware of the environment around the user, it will need to include spatial mapping, and that will be one of the not-so-simple things that you are going to have to deal with. The procedure followed in the Holograms 230 tutorial is instructive. Let's follow the sequence outlined there:

- Start Unity and create a new 3D project.

- Go to Edit ➤ Project Settings ➤ Player.

- In the Inspector, find and select the small green Windows Store icon.

- Expand Other Settings.

- In the Rendering section, check the **Use 16-bit Depth Buffers** box.

- In the Rendering section, check the **Virtual Reality Supported** box.

- Verify that Windows Holographic appears in the list of Virtual Reality SDKs. If it doesn't, select the + button, add it to the bottom of the list, and then choose it.

- Scroll down and expand Publishing Settings.

- In the Capabilities section, do the following:

  - Check the **InternetClientServer** box.

  - Check the **PrivateNetworkClientServer** box.

  - Check the **Microphone** box.

  - Check the **SpatialPerception** box.

- Go to Edit ➤ Project Settings ➤ Quality.

- In the Inspector panel, under the Windows Store icon, select the black dropdown arrow under the Default row and change the default setting to **Fastest**.

# Downloading and Installing the HoloToolkit

The HoloToolkit is constantly evolving, so you will want to have the latest version. This means that you should build the Toolkit from source. Follow these steps:

- Go to https://github.com/Microsoft/HoloToolkit-Unity.

- Click the green Clone or Download button.

- From the dialog box that appears, click Download Zip.

- Right-click the downloaded zip file, select Properties, check the **Unblock** checkbox, and click the OK button.

- Unzip the contents of the folder HoloToolkit-Unity-master to a convenient location, such as your desktop.

- Launch Unity and click on the Open icon.

- When the Open Existing Project window opens, select the HoloToolkit-Unity-master folder that you just downloaded and click the Select Folder button.

- After much disk activity and many progress messages, HoloToolkit should appear in the main menu and also in the Assets folder in the Project panel.

---

■ **Note**　In addition to giving you all the cool tools in the HoloToolkit, the menu options under HoloToolkit in the main menu include Launch Sharing Service, Launch Session Manager, and Launch Profiler. You would not get these if you just copied the HoloToolkit files into the Assets folder in the Project panel manually.

---

# Mapping Your Environment

To create a simple project that makes use of spatial mapping, perform the following sequence:

- Delete the default main camera from the Hierarchy panel.

- Find the **MainCamera** prefab located in the Project panel at Assets ➤ HoloToolkit ➤ Utilities ➤ Prefabs and drag it into the root level of the Hierarchy panel.

- Find the **Cursor** prefab located in the Project panel at Assets ➤ HoloToolkit ➤ Input ➤ Prefabs and drag it into the root level of the Hierarchy panel.

- In the Hierarchy panel, select the **Cursor** object.

- In the Inspector panel, click the Layer dropdown menu and select **Add Layer**.

- Name User Layer 31 as Spatial Mapping.

- Save the new scene with File ➤ Save Scene As. . .

- Create a new folder in the Assets folder and name it Scenes.

- Find the **SpatialMapping** prefab in the Project panel via HoloToolkit ➤ SpatialMapping ➤ Prefabs. Drag and drop it into the root level of the Hierarchy panel.

- In the Main menu, select GameObject ➤ 3d Object ➤ Cylinder.

- With **Cylinder** selected in the Hierarchy panel, make the following edits in the Inspector panel:

  - Change the X, Y, Z position to (0, 0, 2). This will put the cylinder two meters in front of the user.

  - Change the X, Y, Z rotation to (45, 45, 45)

  - Change the X, Y, Z scale to (0.25, 0.25, 0.25)

- Click the Play button in the center of the icon line below the menu line to see how the cylinder looks.

- Click the Play button again to return to Development mode.

- Save scene.

# Build and Deploy Project

Build and deploy the project to your HoloLens at this early stage in the process to make sure everything is working as expected so far:

- Go to File ➤ Build Settings to display the Build Settings dialog box.

- Click the Add Open Scenes button to add the **Cylinder** scene to the build.

- Select **Windows Store** in the Platform list and click the Switch Platform button.

- Set SDK to **Universal 10** and UWP Build Type to **D3D**.

- Check the **Unity C# Projects** box.

- In the Build Window Store dialog box that appears, create a new folder named App.

- Select App to put it in the Folder text box and then click on the Select Folder button. The build operation will commence.

- In the File Explorer window that opens up when the build is done, double-click on the **App** folder to open it.

- Double-click on the **.sln** solution file to launch Visual Studio.

- In Visual Studio, in the top toolbar, change the configuration from Debug to **Release**.

- Change the platform from ARM to **x86**.

- Click the dropdown menu to the right of the platform menu and select **Remote Machine**.

- In the Remote Connections dialog box that appears, enter your HoloLens's IP address.

- For Authentication mode, select **Universal (Unencrypted Protocol)**.

- Make sure your HoloLens is on and running.

- Click the Select button.

- From the Main menu, select Debug ➤ Start Without Debugging. Visual Studio will start building your project and then deploy it to the HoloLens whose IP address you entered.

If everything has gone well, you should see a holographic cylinder in front of you, canted at an angle from the vertical and rotated 45 degrees in the horizontal plane. Shortly thereafter, a mesh of triangles should appear, approximating the contours of the walls, floor, ceiling, and furniture in your room. Figure 17-1 shows what this might look like.

***Figure 17-1.*** *Cylinder embedded in spatial map*

The reason you would want an app to perform spatial mapping is so that the app's holographic objects interact realistically with the real environment. If a holographic object falls onto a table, you want it to stop there rather than falling through the tabletop. It can only do that if the app has an accurate map of where the tabletop is. You can give your GameObjects behaviors and then trigger those behaviors with inputs from the user.

# Responding to Inputs

Holographic objects can respond to two kinds of input: hand gestures and voice commands. Responses could be of any nature. For example, as is the case in the Origami sample application, an air tap or a voice command could cause a GameObject to suddenly become responsive to physics in the form of being subject to gravity or colliding with other GameObjects or real objects. A GameObject could also respond to a user input by starting or stopping an animation that gives it a specific behavior.

Before a GameObject can respond to a user input, the user must be targeting it with gaze so that the HoloLens knows which GameObject should respond. To add this capability, we will need to add some assets from the HoloToolkit to Unity's Hierarchy panel. Here are the steps to take:

- In the Create menu above the Hierarchy panel, select **Create Empty**.

- Right-click the new GameObject and rename it Managers.

- In the Hierarchy panel, select the **Managers** GameObject.

- In the Inspector panel, click the Add Component button.

- In the search box above the menu, type "Gaze Manager," then select it when it appears in the menu.

- In the Inspector panel, select the **RaycastLayerMask** dropdown menu and unselect **Transparent FX**.

- Select the **Cursor** object in the Hierarchy panel and expand it.

- If it has not already been done automatically, drag the **CursorOnHolograms** object onto the Cursor Off Holograms property in the Inspector panel and drop it there.

- If it has not already been done automatically, drag the **CursorOffHolograms** object onto the Cursor On Holograms property in the Inspector panel and drop it there.

- Now build and deploy as you did in the previous section. If all went well, your view of the cylinder and the spatial map should be the same as before. In addition, a torus-shaped cursor should now appear at the center of your gaze, conforming to the contour of the cylinder. Figure 17-2 shows this.

*Figure 17-2.* Cylinder hologram, targeted by cursor

■ **Warning** Notice how I keep saying, "If all has gone well . . ." I do this because sometimes things do not go well. As I write, the tool chain we are using is still beta-level software. It does not always behave consistently. Sometimes something doesn't get reset properly between runs. Sometimes a build will just refuse to deploy for no apparent reason. Don't let this discourage you. Persist and you will prevail. It also helps to consult the community on the Windows Holographic Developer Forum.

To enable response to gesture inputs, do the following:

- Select the **Managers** object in the Hierarchy panel.

- In the Inspector panel, click the Add Component button.

- In the search box above the menu, type "Hands Manager."

- Select the search result.

- Select the **Cursor** object in the Hierarchy panel.

- In the Inspector panel, click the Add Component button.

- In the search box above the menu, type "Cursor Feedback."

- Select the search result.

- In the Project panel's Assets ➤ HoloToolkit ➤ Input ➤ Prefabs folder, find the **HandDetectedFeedback** asset.

- Drag it onto the Hand Detected Asset property in the Cursor Feedback (Script) component.

- In the Project panel's Assets ➤ HoloToolkit ➤ Input ➤ Prefabs folder, find the **FeedbackParent** asset, which is found under the CursorWithFeedback asset.

- Drag it onto the Feedback Parent property in the Cursor Feedback (Script) component.

- Drag the **CursorWithFeedback** asset from Assets ➤ HoloToolkit ➤ Input ➤ Prefabs into the root level of the Hierarchy panel.

- Build and deploy the app as you have done before. If things have gone well, when your hand with an upraised index finger enters the field of view, the cursor changes from a torus to a hand-with-upraised-index-finger icon. When your hand moves out of the field of view, the cursor reverts to its original torus shape. This shows that your app is now able to sense the presence of a hand in the "ready" position. Figure 17-3 shows the resulting cursor image.

***Figure 17-3.*** *Hand icon cursor, with user's hand in field of view*

Now, it's time to cause a gesture to affect the holographic object and have the object respond. Let's use an air tap to cause physics to start functioning, which will cause the cylinder to fall to the floor. To do this, we will need a small amount of code in addition to resources in the HoloToolkit. Write the following code and call it CylinderCommands.cs:

```
using UnityEngine;

public class CylinderCommands : MonoBehaviour
{
    // Called by GestureManager when the user performs a Select gesture
    void OnSelect()
    {
        // If the sphere has no Rigidbody component, add one to enable physics.
        if (!this.GetComponent<Rigidbody>())
        {
            var rigidbody = this.gameObject.AddComponent<Rigidbody>();
            rigidbody.collisionDetectionMode = CollisionDetectionMode.Continuous;
        }
    }
}
```

- In Unity, drag the **CylinderCommands** script onto the Cylinder asset in the Hierarchy panel.

- Drag the **GestureManager** script from Assets ➤ HoloToolkit ➤ Input ➤ Scripts onto the Managers asset in the Hierarchy panel.

- Drag the **GazeStabilizer** script from Assets ➤ HoloToolkit ➤ Input ➤ Scripts onto the Managers asset in the Hierarchy panel.

- Build and deploy the app as before. If all goes well, when you target the cylinder with your gaze and the cursor turns into a hand with uplifted finger, perform an air tap. The cylinder will suddenly realize that it is in a gravitational field and it will fall to the floor. Figure 17-4 shows the fallen cylinder.

***Figure 17-4.*** *The cylinder has fallen under the influence of virtual gravity*

In addition to gestures, the other way for the user to affect a holographic object is with a voice command.

# Responding to Voice Commands

To get the hologram to respond to voice commands, we will need to use the KeywordManager.cs script from the HoloToolkit:

- In Unity, drag the **KeywordManager** from Assets ➤ HoloToolkit ➤ Input ➤ Scripts onto the Managers asset in the Hierarchy panel.

We will also need some code to inform the HoloLens of the specific words we want it to recognize and what we want the targeted holographic object to do as a result. The speech-recognition code will go into a script named SpeechManager.cs. Here's the code:

```csharp
using System.Collections.Generic;
using System.Linq;
using UnityEngine;
using UnityEngine.Windows.Speech;
using HoloToolkit.Unity;

public class SpeechManager : MonoBehaviour
{
    KeywordRecognizer keywordRecognizer = null;
    Dictionary<string, System.Action> keywords = new Dictionary<string, System.Action>();

    // Use this for initialization
    void Start()
    {

        keywords.Add("Drop Cylinder", () =>
        {
            var focusObject = GazeManager.Instance.FocusedObject;

            if (focusObject != null)
            {
                // Call the OnSelect method on just the focused object.
                focusObject.SendMessage("OnSelect");
            }
        });

        keywords.Add("Reset World", () =>
        {
            // Call the OnReset method for the targeted object.
            var focusObject = GazeManager.Instance.FocusedObject;

            if (focusObject != null)
            {
                focusObject.SendMessage("OnReset");
            }
        });

        // Tell the KeywordRecognizer about our keywords.
        keywordRecognizer = new KeywordRecognizer(keywords.Keys.ToArray());

        // Register a callback for the KeywordRecognizer and start recognizing!
        keywordRecognizer.OnPhraseRecognized += KeywordRecognizer_OnPhraseRecognized;
        keywordRecognizer.Start();
    }

    private void KeywordRecognizer_OnPhraseRecognized(PhraseRecognizedEventArgs args)
    {
        System.Action keywordAction;
        if (keywords.TryGetValue(args.text, out keywordAction))
        {
            keywordAction.Invoke();
```

```
        }
    }
}
```

- Drag the **SpeechManager.cs** script into the Scripts folder outside the HoloToolbox in the Project panel.

- Drag the **SpeechManager** script from the Scripts subfolder of the Assets folder in the Project panel onto the Managers asset in the Hierarchy panel.

At this point, we must update the CylinderCommands.cs script to accept voice commands in addition to the gestures that we told it to accept it earlier. Replace the CylinderCommands script currently in the project with the one here:

```csharp
using UnityEngine;

public class CylinderCommands : MonoBehaviour
{
    Vector3 originalPosition;
    // Called by GestureManager when the user performs a Select gesture and by SpeechManager
    // when user says "Drop  Cylinder".
    // Initialization
    void Start()
    {
        //Get original local position of cylinder
        originalPosition = transform.localPosition;
    }

    void OnSelect()
    {
        // If the cylinder has no Rigidbody component, add one to enable physics.
        if (!this.GetComponent<Rigidbody>())
        {
            var rigidbody = this.gameObject.AddComponent<Rigidbody>();
            rigidbody.collisionDetectionMode = CollisionDetectionMode.Continuous;
        }
    }

    // Called by SpeechManager when the user says "Reset World".
    void OnReset()
    {
        // If the cylinder has a Rigidbody component, remove it to disable physics.
        var rigidbody = GetComponent<Rigidbody>();
        if (rigidbody != null)
        {
            DestroyImmediate(rigidbody);
        }

        // Put the cylinder back into its original local position.
        transform.localPosition = originalPosition;
    }
}
```

In its current state, the app we have been developing using the tools in the HoloToolkit and a little bit of extra code will do the following:

- Make a spatial map of the user's surroundings

- Place a holographic cylinder in mid-air in the room

- Capture the user's gaze and locate where it hits with a cursor

- Indicate when the user's hand is in the field of view

- Cause the cylinder to respond to an air tap gesture by falling to the floor

- Cause the cylinder to respond to a voice command by falling to the floor

- Restore the cylinder to its initial position in mid-air with a voice command

That's quite a lot of functionality, produced with very little coding by you. You can go on from here to add spatial sound and to refine what we have done to create highly functional applications.

# Summary

The HoloToolkit is a collection of helpful assets that can save a developer much time and effort by performing tasks that are common to many different kinds of mixed-reality applications. This chapter enumerates all the major elements of the Toolkit, with a brief description of each one. It then shows how to use some of those tools to create a simple application with minimal additional coding.

Once you have created an application, the next thing to do is to test it carefully and fully. There are bound to be situations that you did not anticipate or encounter while you were doing the development, which could cause problems to users. You will want to correct these problems before you let your creation out into the world. We'll cover the many aspects of testing in the next chapter.

# CHAPTER 18

■ ■ ■

# Testing Your App

There's no feeling quite like the one you get when you finally get the app you have been working on to run as intended for the very first time. Yay! Success!! Let's celebrate!!! Getting your app to work is indeed worthy of celebration, so, by all means, go ahead and party hearty. However, this does not mean that you are finished. Not by a long shot.

You don't just want an app that works. You want an app that works consistently under all conditions, at all times, for all users. Nothing will kill the popularity of an app faster than word getting out about problems with it. You want to make sure that you have not only squashed all the bugs, but also anticipated and neutralized all the potential usage problems that might make the experience of using your app less than what the user is expecting.

Users have pretty high expectations. They want apps, even free ones, to be polished and ready for prime time. There are a number of characteristics that people expect out of an application regardless of what kind of application it is, as follows:

- It has to do what the developer says it will do.

- It has to be responsive, not frustrating the user with slowness.

- It has to be intuitive and easy to understand and use.

- It has to work consistently, as expected, every time.

- It has to be safe. When holographic objects obscure portions of the real world, people can get hurt.

- It has to be secure. When a person is wearing a computer on her head, apps should not be hackable.

Bottom line: there are a lot of things to consider beyond the question of whether or not the app works. Let's look at each of these other considerations.

## Functionality

Before any software-development project begins, there should be a Statement of Requirements (SoR) that states in detail exactly what the application should deliver. It's a great day when an app runs for the first time with its essential functionality. However, at that point, can you check ALL the boxes for capability that were set forth in the SoR? Probably not. There is usually some additional work, some cleaning up, that needs to be done. You may not even be aware of what some of this additional work might be. To cover that blindside, you should distribute the app to a representative sample of naïve users who you can use as beta testers. They will complain about absent functionality that you never even considered that you might need.

•

© Allen G. Taylor 2016

A. G. Taylor, *Develop Microsoft HoloLens Apps Now*, DOI 10.1007/978-1-4842-2202-7_18

Sometimes, during the course of development, you will discover that an item specified in the SoR is in fact not feasible to include in light of the time and budget that is available. Sometimes the client or the market changes while development is under way. These considerations may cause you to re-scope the project and generate a new SoR in consultation with all stakeholders. In any event, when you are ready to call the project complete, you must be sure that it not only meets up with what you expect of it, but that it also meets up with what your target audience expects.

■ **Bottom Line**   Make sure your app does everything your target audience expects it to do.

# Performance

It's all well and good that an application does what it's supposed to do. Bravo. However, that is not enough to make it successful. It also must perform up to the expectations of its target audience. Are the animations irritatingly slow? Are the responses to the user's gestures or voice commands sluggish or inconsistent? You want to build apps that users return to again and again rather than ones that they try a few times and then ignore or even delete. The experience of using your app must be enjoyable rather than frustrating. If your app is working but has performance issues, deal with them up front, as you do not want it to die a silent death after a brief period of use.

Things you can do include optimizing your code for speed of loading as well as speed of execution. In spatial mapping, you should set the `TrianglesPerCubicMeter` parameter to the minimum acceptable value. Mapping more triangles than you need just takes up valuable time. Always be on the lookout for places where you can eliminate a millisecond here or there. With the app updating 30 to 60 times per second, those milliseconds can add up to a perceptible delay. Make sure your `Update()` loop is as lean as possible.

■ **Bottom Line**   Make sure your app performs as well as your target audience expects it to perform.

# Ease of Use

An application can be functional and performant and still not catch on with its target audience. Once they become familiar with the app, users should be able to navigate it quickly and easily without having to remember a lot of arcane knowledge. The user interface should be intuitive and natural. Users should not need to refer to documentation or online user forums to determine what the functions and capabilities are. To the extent possible, feedback signals coming to the user from the app should have obvious meanings. A trap that developers often fall into is to assume that the user is as interested in the app as the developer is and has the same background knowledge. This is not a good assumption. When choosing between two different ways of presenting information to the user, choose the one that is easier to understand. This is a piece of ancient wisdom that I call Taylor's Razor.

■ **Taylor's Razor**   When choosing between two different ways of presenting information to a user, choose the one that is easier for them to understand.

# Reliability

Some code is more reliable than others. If you are using Unity and Visual Studio as tools in your development, any unreliable aspects of those tools must be considered along with any unreliable aspects of your own code. Vendors of software publish lists of known bugs that they have not gotten around to correcting yet. You should be familiar with such lists for any tools that you use so that you can avoid the problematical areas. No complex software is free of bugs. That is the principal reason that new point releases are made for every software product of consequence. This is certainly true of both Unity and Visual Studio. You need to understand the problems as well as the positive features of any tools that you use and protect yourself and your users by keeping up on what problems are arising, modifying your app accordingly to steer clear of them.

# Safety

Running mixed-reality apps leaves the user subject to some safety concerns that are not an issue for someone sitting in front of a computer monitor. The recent popularity of the Pokémon Go game has highlighted some of these concerns. A couple of people fell off a cliff while searching for Pokémon near the ocean. Someone else was shot at by an irate property owner. Other mishaps have also occurred. People out in the world who are paying too much attention to virtual content in their visual field are at risk.

With HoloLens, the problem is not quite as serious. People are probably not going to be walking out in public while wearing a HoloLens, although they could, and if Pokémon Go ever comes to the HoloLens it will be more immersive and thus more distracting than it is with a smartphone or tablet. The HoloLens device works best indoors, where light levels are significantly lower than is the case with direct sunlight. Even so, there are still risks. Probably users don't have to worry about falling off cliffs or having people in nearby offices consider them a trespasser and fire a warning shot across their bow. But they *do* have to worry about running into things or tripping over obstacles that they don't see because the obstacles are occluded by a hologram.

You, as a developer, want to create apps that do not endanger your users. That may mean leaving enough of the real world visible to the user for her to navigate successfully through it. You definitely don't want to have to defend yourself against a liability claim when a user of your app accidentally falls down a flight of stairs.

# Security

The HoloLens is a Windows 10 device, so it is subject to the same threats as any other Windows 10 device. If it connects to the Internet through its Wi-Fi connection, it is presenting an attack surface to the hackers of the world. This is more of an operating system issue than it is an application issue, unless your application makes use of the Internet connection. If so, then security is your problem too. Your best defense is to stick to creating self-contained holographic experiences. If your app must connect to the outside world, incorporate all the security features that you would use if you were running your app on a Windows 10 desktop or laptop computer. Hopefully, your users will have their Wi-Fi protected by a hard-to-break password and their local area network protected by a strong firewall.

For you as a developer, another security concern is in establishing a trusted connection between your HoloLens and the computer that is paired to it and running the HoloLens Device Portal. Initially, the computer will not recognize your HoloLens as a trusted device. It will issue a warning similar to the one shown in Figure 18-1.

There's a problem with this website's
security certificate

This might mean that someone's trying to fool you or steal any info
you send to the server. You should close this site immediately.

⊟ Go to my homepage instead

⊗ Continue to this webpage (not recommended)

*Figure 18-1.  Connection warning screen*

You will have to go against the warning and recommendation to proceed. You can establish a trusted connection between your host computer and your HoloLens by downloading your HoloLens's security certificate from the Security page on the Device Portal and installing it in the Trusted Root Certification Authorities folder on the PC.

If you want to access the Internet using the Edge browser on the HoloLens, you will have to surmount another hurdle, one also designed to protect your security. Figure 18-2 shows what this looks like.

Microsoft Edge

# Microsoft Edge

The server 10.0.0.8 is asking for your user name and password. The server reports that it is
from Windows Web Management.

moontube

••••••••••••••••

☑ Remember my credentials

OK            Cancel

*Figure 18-2.  Edge browser login*

Any of your users who check the "Remember my credentials" box, as shown in Figure 18-2, will be exposing a potential security vulnerability to anyone who gains physical access to the HoloLens device.

# Unusual User Behavior

When you write an application for the HoloLens, you probably have an idea of how you expect the app to be used. You have a clear idea of how the app *should* be used, and that is what you expect users to do. However, if your app sees widespread use, which of course is what you hope for it, people will try to use it in ways that you have not anticipated. Sometimes these attempts will cause your app to fail in strange ways. Put your app into the hands of as many different kinds of people as possible. They will try what seems logical to them. If you are lucky, some of these people will take your app places you never intended it to go and expose a flaw in the process. Fix as many of these as you can before releasing the app to the wild.

# Unusual User Environments

With HoloLens apps there is a much greater chance that your app will have problems than is true for a normal PC-based app. This is because the environment where the user is located meshes with the holographic content that you have created in ways that you cannot control. The environment may be bare and sterile or it may be cluttered. It may be large or it may be small. Walls may be square or not. The user may be indoors or outdoors. Whatever set of unusual conditions you anticipate, there will be users who come up with new ones that affect the way your app runs. Try to think of and design for any bizarre environment that you can imagine. Someone will probably try to run your app in just such a place.

## Room size and shape

You should test your app in rooms of various sizes and shapes. If a room is too small, your holograms may not appear properly, or perhaps not even at all. If a hologram is at a location that is farther away than the wall you are facing, the hologram will be occluded by the wall and will thus be invisible. Depending on the application, there is probably an ideal size and shape for the room that the app runs in. You may want to suggest to your users what that ideal size and shape is so that they can have the best experience when running your app.

## Lighting conditions

Since you are mixing your holograms with the real world that the user inhabits, you can control how your hologram is lit by your virtual lights, but you have no control over where the environment light is coming from or how strong it is. You want your app to deliver the desired experience across a range of light directions and levels. This means that you need to design it to look good under as many lighting conditions as possible. Testing under many different lighting conditions is crucial to providing the desired experience regardless of the environment in which your users find themselves.

## Movement conditions

HoloLens users are not tied down to sitting in front of a computer monitor. They can turn around for a 360 degree view or even walk from one room to another. This opens up possibilities for you, but also constrains your design. Do you want your holograms to be located at fixed places in a room, or perhaps move along with the user from place to place?

Some users can move pretty fast. Can your holograms keep up? Can they maintain the same level of immersion as the user moves? Will your spatial mapping ensure that holograms are occluded when they move behind real-world obstacles, from the moving point of view of the user? These are all questions that need to be asked, and then answered, by thorough testing.

# Hologram Shape and the User's Field of View

One of the persistent criticisms of the HoloLens is that it has a limited field of view. The display is 1268 x 720 pixels per eye. This is a rectangle that is much wider than it is high. With a visual field in the neighborhood of 35 to 40 degrees in width and somewhat more than half that in height, you will have to consider both the size and the shape of any holograms you create. If you create, for example, an avatar of a person, you don't want the avatar to be chopped off at the knees or, even worse, at the neck. Whenever possible you are going to want to create holograms that completely fit into the visual field. That means they should be wider than they are high, unless they are either small or designed to be viewed from rather far away.

Since the field of view is as small as it is, you may want to use spatial sound as well as visual cues to direct the user's attention to the point in space where your active content is positioned. The Robo Raid and Fragments applications that come with HoloLens use visual cues. Rather than thinking of the limited field of view as a problem, just think of it as a design constraint.

# Heat Generation

In addition to the optics, sound generation, and sensor hardware in the HoloLens, it also contains a full-blown Windows 10 computer, complete with memory, storage, and battery. All this stuff generates heat, which must be dissipated passively, as there are no fans or other active cooling devices. The HoloLens is worn on the user's head, so it's not wise to let it get too hot. People won't want to run your app if doing so burns their brow.

Where you come into the heat issue is with how complex your app is when it is running. If it requires a lot of real-time computation, that will cause the processor to heat up faster than the passive cooling is able to shed the heat. You don't really want your user's head to be the device's heat sink. Test your app by running it flat out and see how long you can wear it in that condition before you become aware that the HoloLens is heating up. When you reach that point, you have gone too far. Decide what you can do to reduce the computational load. You can't anticipate how long a person will use your app at a single stretch. Some of them may run it far longer than you ever imagined. Those people need to be considered too, since the heat will build up over time.

# Battery Depletion

When the computational load is high, you are not only generating heat faster than it can be dissipated, but you are also running down the battery faster than the nominal spec for battery life. For someone using the HoloLens in a professional or industrial setting, wearing the HoloLens for a full eight hour shift is not an option. You need to write your app so that it accomplishes its purpose in less time than that. Microsoft says the battery will last about four hours of what they consider normal use. You probably don't want to write an app that requires users to wear it for more than a couple of hours at a time.

# Summary

While often underappreciated, adequate testing of applications can spell the difference between market acceptance and market failure. Be sure to plan for an extended period of testing after completing development, including adequate time to correct any problems that are uncovered by those tests.

Once you complete your app, unless you are building it for a specific client, you probably want to make it available to the world. The easy way to do that is to upload it to the Microsoft Store. The next chapter tells you what you need to know to make it available and gives some tips on how to promote it.

# Going Beyond App Development

# CHAPTER 19

■ ■ ■

# Becoming a HoloLens Pro

Today, there are several ways to make a living while having fun with really cool tech and developing applications for the HoloLens. In a couple of years, there will be many more ways. Now is the time to get up to speed on the technology so as to be ready when the demand curve rises steeply. All it takes is one killer app to drive a new technology mainstream. With HoloLens, there is the possibility of many killer apps, because the technology can be applied in so many different areas.

There are pioneering opportunities today for beginning HoloLens developers. The field is wide open, because almost everybody who is currently developing for HoloLens is also a beginning developer. The field is that new, and you are truly getting in on a ground-floor opportunity.

One opportunity is to get a job developing for an early adopter of the HoloLens technology, such as Lowe's in the retail business, Volvo in the automobile business, or Trimble in the geospatial-data business. Another is to work for one of the startups that are springing up specifically to develop HoloLens apps for corporate clients, such as Object Theory in Portland, Oregon.

## HoloLens in the Enterprise

Microsoft is selling HoloLens devices to commercial enterprises, and in some cases started doing so before the highly anticipated release of Wave One to developers in March 2016. Lowe's and Volvo are examples of such enterprises. They have developers on staff who work for them as salaried employees. With the many potential uses that the HoloLens has in the enterprise context, and as these use cases become more obvious, enterprises will be looking to hire talent with HoloLens development experience.

If you would like to be in a position to land one of those future jobs, you can prepare yourself by starting now to develop HoloLens apps on your own. You can consider the cost of the HoloLens Developer Edition to be an investment in your future career. $3,000 may seem like a lot, but that is about what it cost back in 1981 (in 1981 dollars) to buy an IBM PC with dual floppy disks and 640 kB of RAM. That was a great investment at that time for anyone who wanted to build a career in the computer business, which was about to explode. In comparison, $3,000 in much-inflated 2016 dollars for a HoloLens seems like a pretty good deal.

With a HoloLens, you can start building simple apps and, as your skill grows, create ever more interesting and useful ones. In the meantime, network with your local HoloLens community. There are bound to be other people in your area who want to get into the development of holographic applications. There may be a Meetup dedicated to HoloLens. If not, you could start one. Existing Meetups for Unity or Visual Studio would also be good places to become active and network. At the beginning of a new field, being at the right place at the right time is not a random chance. You can orchestrate it yourself. When opportunity arises, you will be there to seize it.

© Allen G. Taylor 2016

A. G. Taylor, *Develop Microsoft HoloLens Apps Now*, DOI 10.1007/978-1-4842-2202-7_19

# Startup Opportunities

Existing enterprises such as Lowe's and Volvo are not the only places where HoloLens-related employment might exist. Individuals with an eye to the future are creating startup companies specifically to develop HoloLens applications. In some cases, these firms are co-founded by former Microsoft employees who have worked on the development of the HoloLens and are excited about its potential. In others, the founders are just far-sighted entrepreneurs who sense a major opportunity.

Jobs will become available at these startup development houses as they start to land contracts with enterprises that do not have the staff or the desire to develop apps internally. Microsoft has posted the logos of these partner organizations. Any one of them might be a good place for you to get started as a HoloLens developer.

If, through your networking, you find the right mix of people with complementary skills, you might co-found a HoloLens development shop of your own. It's rare to be able to get in on the ground floor of an industry that is on the verge of experiencing exponential growth. The mixed-reality industry in general–and HoloLens in particular–has all the hallmarks of just such an opportunity. This is the time. This is the place. And you are here now.

# Publishing HoloLens Apps to the Windows Store

You can publish or sell any Holographic application you create any way you want to. For example, a client might contract with you to create a particular app. You deliver the app and get paid for it, and all is good. However, your company brand may not be as well known as is Microsoft's. People who do not know you or other developers and are looking for HoloLens apps will probably go to Microsoft's Windows Store first, just as they would if they were looking for any application designed to run under Windows.

The Windows Store is a great place for you to showcase your apps, and Microsoft makes it easy for customers to buy them. You can get started by building simple apps and offering them for free to build name recognition for your brand. You can move on from there to create apps that address problems that are well suited for holographic solutions.

## Windows Store policies

Any app that you intend to publish on the Windows Store must conform to the policies Microsoft has set out for apps. These policies must be followed or your app will not be accepted for publication. The policies fall under several major categories.

### Function and value

Your app must be fully functional and provide a valuable and quality user experience, and it must be accurately described in its associated metadata.

### Security

Your app must not jeopardize or compromise in any way the security or functionality of the HoloLens or associated devices, and must not have the potential to cause harm to the user or any other person.

### Testability

Your app must be fully testable by Microsoft test personnel.

## Usability

Your app must start up promptly and stay responsive to user input.

## Personal information

If your app accesses user information, you must maintain a privacy policy, which must be accessible from your app at any time. Apps that receive device location information must allow users to enable and disable the app's access to and use of location from the location service API. Personal information may be shared with third parties only with the express consent of the customer.

## Capabilities

To access capabilities such as the camera or the microphone, your app must declare those capabilities in the app's package manifest.

## Localization

You must localize your app for all languages that it supports.

## Financial transactions

You must use the Microsoft in-app purchase API to sell digital items or services that are consumed or used within your app. In-app products sold in your app cannot be converted to any legally valid currency or any physical goods or services.

For purchases of physical goods, real-world gambling, or charitable contributions, you must use a secure third-party purchase API.

## Notifications

Your app must respect system settings for notifications and remain functional when they are disabled. Notifications sent from your app must be related to the app or to other apps you publish in the Store catalog.

## Advertising

Your app must respect advertising ID settings that the user has selected. The primary content of your app cannot be advertising, and advertising must be clearly distinguishable from other content.

## Allowed content

All content in your app must be either originally created by you, appropriately licensed from a third-party rights holder, used as permitted by the rights holder, or used as otherwise permitted by law.

## Forbidden content

Your app must not contain anything that facilitates or glamorizes gratuitous violence, human rights violations, or the creation or illegal use of weapons against a person or animal in the real world. It must not contain anything that is defamatory, libelous, slanderous, or threatening.

# The App Developer Agreement

The App Developer Agreement is a legal document that establishes your relationship to Microsoft with respect to the sale of your apps in the Windows Store. It defines the terms and conditions of the relationship. When you sign it, you will be legally bound by its provisions. The agreement is lengthy and detailed. Painful as it might be, it is a good idea to read it carefully before embarking on a development effort that might result is an app that fails to comply.

# How to pass app certification

Any app published in the Windows Store must pass a certification test given by Microsoft. Some common-sense tips for easing the road to certification include:

- Don't submit your app for certification before it is finished. Everything should work, and all links should go to live and functional places.

- Test your app with the Windows App Certification Kit.

- Make sure your app does not crash without network connectivity. Even if it needs network connectivity, it should fail gracefully.

- Make sure the app's description clearly represents what the app does.

- Provide complete and accurate answers to all the questions in the Age Ratings section.

- If your app uses the commerce APIs from the Windows.ApplicationModel.Store namespace, verify that the app handles all typical exceptions. Use the CurrentApp class rather than the CurrentAppSimulator class.

- Don't say that your app is accessible unless you have specifically engineered it and tested it for accessibility.

- If your app requires a user name and password, be sure to provide a test account so Microsoft can test the app, as well as any steps required to access hidden or locked features.

# Submitting an app for publication in the Store

The procedure for submitting a Windows Holographic app to the Windows Store is the same as it is for any app for either Windows or Windows Mobile. Microsoft provides a handy checklist here: https://msdn. microsoft.com/windows/uwp/publish/app-submissions.

The checklist has several pages:

- Pricing and Availability page: You must specify how you want to price the app as well as where and when you want to make it available.

- App Properties page: What category of app is it and what can your customers do with it?

- Age Ratings page: For what age groups is the app appropriate?

- Packages page: App must be uploaded as one or more packages.

- Descriptions page: This contains all the required metadata in at least one language. Best practice is to provide it in all the languages you claim to support.

- Notes for Certification page: This is optional.

## Uploading your app

Before you can upload an app to the Windows Store, you must put it into a package. There is a list of things that you must do before packaging your app, then you must configure your package, and then you create the package. The steps for doing all this can be found here:

`https://msdn.microsoft.com/windows/uwp/packaging/packaging-uwp-apps`

Once the app is packaged and tested with the Windows App Certification Kit, and once you have registered with Microsoft as a developer, the app can be uploaded. You can register at the Microsoft Dev Center.

## Setting a price for your app

When setting the base price for your app, be aware that Microsoft will retain 30 percent of what you charge in exchange for hosting your app on the Windows Store. Some countries lump a value added tax (VAT) into the cost of the product. That is subtracted from your net income. In addition to that, in a number of countries there is an additional charge, called a Commerce Expansion Adjustment, of 13.9 percent for mobile operator billing. If the customer pays with a gift card, in most countries, including the United States, there is an additional 2.24 percent charge.

You must strike a balance between a price that customers will gladly pay for your app and the net revenue that you would like to receive for it. Coming up with the right pricing is not easy, so give it the thought it deserves.

## Monitoring sales with analytic reports

How well are your apps doing in the marketplace? The data is out there, but how do you access it? Microsoft has this covered for you. You can view detailed analytics for your apps in the Windows Dev Center dashboard. It has statistics and charts that are broken down in all the important ways. How is it selling? What is the demographic breakdown of the people who are acquiring it? How is it being rated by customers? What are the reviews like? All of that plus more is available.

## Receiving payment

After you set up a payout account and execute the necessary tax forms, you can start receiving revenue for your apps. Payouts will occur monthly, provided you have accrued more than a set minimum of credit in your account.

# Promoting Your Apps

Once you have completed your first holographic app and uploaded it to the Windows Store, you have every right to take a moment to celebrate. However, your job is not done. Apps don't get downloaded, even if they are free, if people don't know about them. It is your job to promote your apps to the people most likely to be interested in acquiring them. Who might that be?

Initially, and probably for some time to come, the only prospective customers who will have HoloLens devices are going to be developers such as yourself and enterprises such as Japan Airlines, Volvo, Lowe's, and NASA. You will want to target your promotional efforts toward them. Although it will be possible to run your app on any compatible Windows 10 device, there is not much point to doing so on anything other than a HoloLens.

Where can you find your target customers? They will be in places such as user groups and meetups that are aimed at developers, computer-graphics artists, and techno geeks in general.

Early on, your goal should not so much be to make money by selling your apps but more to get your name and brand out there in the community so that when the market does finally open up you will be positioned to ramp up and take off.

# Summary

This chapter is all about the opportunities that are opening up for you in the brand-new field of holographic development. Mixed reality is slated to become a huge market over the next five to ten years. Some analysts are stating their belief that the HoloLens could change modern life to the same extent that the original iPhone and its successors have changed people's lives in less than a decade.

The road to HoloLens development success runs through the Windows Store. We talked about what you need to do to get your apps published there and what you can expect in terms of compensation for your efforts. This is one of those ground-floor moments that only come along every decade or two. The potential is definitely there to take you to amazing places.

What amazing places might HoloLens development take you to? That's what the next chapter is about.

■ ■ ■

# CHAPTER 20

# Where Is This Technology Taking Us?

It's early days for holographic technology, and nobody knows for sure where it will lead. But recall that when, in December 1974, the Altair 8800 microcomputer was featured on the cover of *Popular Electronics* magazine, nobody had any idea of the tectonic shifts in the computer industry that would follow. First dismissed as a toy to be played with by nerdy enthusiasts, the personal computer went on to displace the "serious" mainframe computers that had preceded it. In the early days of the Internet, called DARPANET at the time, a few select universities were connected to federal government research centers for scientific research collaborations. Few foresaw that it would span the globe, connect billions of people, and even reach out into space.

We probably won't be any better at prognosticating where things will go with holographic computing now than we were with personal computing and long-distance networking then. However, there are a few things that we can foresee even now. One thing that is clear is that there will be career opportunities for people who have skills in the disciplines that go into the production of holographic applications. These skills include computer graphics, computer programming, Unity and platforms like it, Visual Studio and tools like it, computer animation, storyboarding, and many other skill areas that relate to the production of software products.

## Opportunities Opening Up

There are many fields in which a 3D representation of a physical or conceptual item that can be viewed from any angle, including from inside it, would enable understanding on a deeper level than would otherwise be possible. Those who can create such representations, or animate them, or include them in a narrative that tells a story, will always be able to find interesting and challenging work.

### Education and training

Probably the first area in which HoloLens technology will be deployed in any kind of volume will be in education and training. It is said that a picture is worth a thousand words. If that's true, then a hologram ought to be worth a million. If people have a hard time "wrapping their heads around" a concept, with holography they can literally not only wrap their heads around it, they can dive right into it. Carnegie Mellon University in Pittsburgh, Pennsylvania, is an institution that is researching HoloLens devices in a traditional educational context, while companies such as Volvo and Japan Airlines are using the device to train employees in how to assemble or maintain complex machinery. As educators become aware of the way that holograms can make a concept real to a student in a way that a photograph, movie, or description in a book never could, the demand for holographic development in education will multiply.

© Allen G. Taylor 2016

A. G. Taylor, *Develop Microsoft HoloLens Apps Now*, DOI 10.1007/978-1-4842-2202-7_20

## Sales

Lowe's Home Improvement is using HoloLens technology now to sell kitchen remodels. After fitting potential customers with HoloLens devices, the Lowe's associate places holographic overlays on top of a basic kitchen layout, enabling the customers to see how a wide variety of cabinets and counter surfaces would look in their own kitchen. The richer the experience you can give the customer, the greater the likelihood that they will buy. For any sales situation in which it is not possible to allow the customer to directly experience the product itself, such as a test drive of a new car, a holographic view of the product is the next best thing.

## Medical

MRI scans are a wonderful diagnostic tool, but they only show one slice of a subject, such as a human brain, at a time. Imagine how much easier it would be to arrive at an accurate diagnosis if instead of a series of slices, the diagnostician could see an accurate, full-sized holographic representation of the entire brain, along with any pathology that might be present. Every possible view of the subject would be available, including one that penetrates into the innermost parts. Diagnosis could be arrived at quicker and with greater confidence. Dynamic processes, such as the beating of a heart, could also be modeled and viewed, providing greater insight into how both normal and diseased organs operate.

## Game development

The mixed-reality world provided by the HoloLens enables gaming to expand in a major new direction. The instant worldwide popularity of Pokémon Go illustrates this, even though it is not immersive at all in the way the HoloLens is. In addition, game developers are already familiar with the tool chain that Microsoft recommends for development of holographic apps. Many of the skills needed for traditional video game development are directly applicable to developing HoloLens apps, whether or not they are game apps.

The big question mark for game developers is, "Where is the market for my games, and when will it materialize?" At present, the HoloLens is not a mass-market device. It is sold to people who are primarily interested in getting commercial value out of it rather than playing games with it. The Developer Edition costs $3,000, which is a justifiable expense for an organization that has a commercial application, but probably not justifiable for many people who just see it as a gaming device.

A lot depends on Microsoft's plans. They originally envisioned the HoloLens as a gaming platform, as witnessed by the mind-blowing Minecraft demo that they gave in 2015 when they introduced HoloLens to the world. Later, they changed their focus when it became clear that commercial and industrial applications would emerge sooner than gaming applications would. Will they develop and deliver a version of the HoloLens that has a price point that gamers will willingly pay? I think it is clear that they will. The question is, when?

## Holoportation

Alex Kipman's TED talk in February 2016 introduced another mind-blowing capability of the HoloLens–holoportation. Similar to the teleportation foretold in numerous science fiction stories and reminiscent of the holodeck on the Starship Enterprise in the *Star Trek: The Next Generation* TV show, holoportation puts a hologram of a person who is physically in another room into the same room with you. That other room could be across the street, as it was at the TED talk, or it could be anywhere in the world that has a high-speed Internet connection.

## Create your own holodeck

Holoportation is an ingenious use of HoloLens technology, plus some additional optical and computational resources. A person wearing a HoloLens is located in a rectangular room. Video cameras at the four corners of the room and at the midpoints of the four walls image the contents of the room from every angle. Software and external compute power meld this information into a three-dimensional model of the room and the people in it; this model is updated in real time.

Somewhere else, an identical layout is constructed. A HoloLens-wearing person in this second room can see and interact with the people in the first room and vice versa.

## Interact with holopeople

In Alex Kipman's TED talk, a holographic landscape appeared that had been filmed by the Curiosity rover on Mars. Into that context, suddenly a life-sized holographic Jeff Norris appeared. Jeff is one of the scientists at NASA's Jet Propulsion Lab, which built Curiosity. The Martian landscape, viewed with HoloLens technology, looked highly realistic, and so did Jeff. In actuality, Jeff was in a hotel room across the street that had been set up in such a way that he saw a holographic Alex in his room, while Alex saw him on the TED stage.

## The end of business air travel?

In the pre-industrial world, when people wanted to do business with someone far away, they would send a letter with somebody who happened to be traveling to that faraway place. It could be months or even years before they heard anything back. Later, letters could travel by railroad train, and then telegrams could be sent over wires. These methods did not give a person the sense that they were having a conversation with the other person. The telephone added that conversational element, if only for audio. More recently, Skype and Facetime have added a visual element to long-distance communication. None of these things were "real" enough to displace actual physical travel for the most important encounters, and that will probably continue to be the case. However, holoportation comes pretty close to the experience of a real physical encounter. It's possible that many of the less consequential meetings between people could take place holographically rather than in person.

## The Internet of Things

There is a tremendous amount of buzz right now about the Internet of Things (IoT). The IoT goes beyond using the Internet to connect people to each other; it connects sensors, effectors, and other devices to each other without humans necessarily being in the loop. The HoloLens provides humans with a mechanism for getting involved in the IoT loop. Holographic controls of IoT devices can be activated by air taps or other gestures, or by voice commands. There is potential here for a host of new applications.

# Are There Dangers in Merging the Real with the Virtual?

Anything that takes even part of your attention away from what is happening around you is potentially dangerous. People have walked into traffic and fallen off cliffs playing Pokémon Go. Having said that, HoloLens should be quite safe when used correctly. It should be used indoors in an uncluttered room with no dangerous things such as trip hazards, stairwells, or low-hanging chandeliers.

HoloLens can be used outdoors, but that is not its best use. HoloLens works best when ambient light levels are between 50 and 200 lux, which is the range you normally find in indoor venues. As ambient conditions get brighter, the holograms tend to get more and more washed out. On a sunny day, holograms become virtually transparent, even in the shade. On the bright side (no pun intended), people are not going to fall off cliffs playing HoloLens Pokémon Go, unless it is a very cloudy day. The Pokémon characters would be too hard to see. You probably don't want to wear your HoloLens in public anyway, lest you become a social outcast like the people who tried to casually walk around wearing Google Glass.

## Psychological issues

Some people have concerns that people who immerse themselves in virtual reality will become isolated from the real world and the real people who inhabit it. This should be less of an issue with mixed reality of the HoloLens sort than with the virtual reality of Oculus Rift or Vive, but it is still something to watch out for. Susceptible people may have a problem separating what is real from what is virtual.

## Can mixed reality experiences become addictive?

Anything that has a reward, whether physical or virtual, can become habit-forming. This is true for coffee drinking and for playing Spider Solitaire. If you create apps that reward your users in some way, they could become habit forming too. Hopefully this will not cause them to abandon the things that they should be doing so that they can run your app. This is probably not an issue for commercial or industrial apps, but could apply to game apps. If you include some fun, game-like aspects in an educational app, your users might enjoy things more while they learn. They are also more likely to want to acquire more of your work.

# Summary

The future is bright for developers who acquire skills and expertise in creating holographic applications. Wherever your interests might lie, there probably is a way to incorporate holographic development into that field. By learning how to develop holographic applications, you will have a wide variety of application areas to choose from, as well as challenging and enjoyable work.

## APPENDIX A

∎∎∎

# Windows Dev Center Resources

The HoloLens device runs Windows Holographic, a variant of Windows 10, the Universal Windows Platform (UWP). This means that when you develop on the UWP, your app could potentially run on any device running Windows 10. Figure A-1 shows the Platform's family of devices.

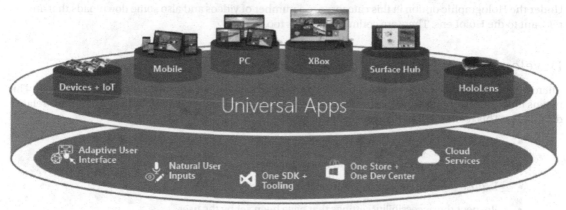

This means that apps originally written for other devices can also be made to run on HoloLens. Conversely, applications written for HoloLens can also run on other Windows 10 platforms, such as PCs, mobile phones, or Xbox. Users may well want to run apps originally intended for other devices on HoloLens. The adaptation should be relatively easy, although any such apps may not show the three dimensionality of an app specifically created for HoloLens.

## The Universal Windows Dev Center

The Universal Windows Dev Center (https://developer.microsoft.com/en-us/windows) is the primary place to look for information and other resources that apply to development for any device supported by the Universal Windows Platform. You will find resources there that are very helpful in your own development efforts. There are several major tabs on the Windows Dev Center menu. Let's take a brief look at each.

© Allen G. Taylor 2016
A. G. Taylor, *Develop Microsoft HoloLens Apps Now*, DOI 10.1007/978-1-4842-2202-7

# Explore

This section introduces the Universal Windows Platform and goes into more depth on what you can do with it.

## What's new for Windows 10

The Windows 10 SDK has been available to developers for a year, and on its first anniversary a new build (Build 1607) was released. A number of new capabilities are provided by this new build.

## Intro to Universal Windows Platform

This is a guide to Universal Windows Platform apps. It covers a lot of what you need to know if you want to develop apps on the Universal Windows Platform.

## Coding challenges

Under the Holographic option in this category are a number of videos and also some downloads that are relevant to the HoloLens. There are coding challenges too.

## Develop for accessibility

Microsoft recommends that, wherever possible, you should design your apps with accessibility in mind. This means including user interface features that can assist people with either visual, auditory, or motion-related disabilities. This relates to four main design principles:

- Use XAML Common Controls whenever possible.

- Include keyboard equivalents to mouse actions.

- Expose the content of your UI through UI Automation.

- Respect the accessibility settings that have been set by the user.

## Build for enterprise

Applications built for enterprises have different requirements than those designed to be sold in the Windows Store. Security is a major concern, entailing authentication and cryptography. Connections to external databases and external devices, either with or without network connectivity, are also important. Deployment of line-of-business apps differs from the Windows Store model, although that may be used too in the enterprise context. Links to pages that address all of these concerns can be found in this section.

## Windows Store opportunities

This page includes helpful tips on how to put apps in the Windows Store, get them discovered by users, and monetize them.

# Docs

This is a treasure trove of links to vital information on the writing and production of all kinds of Windows 10 apps, from games and desktop apps to IoT apps and holographic apps.

## Windows apps

Here's where to look for information that applies to all types of apps running on all types of hardware. From design through development and publication, and on to monetization and promotion, the information you need is all here.

## Games

If you are concentrating specifically on games, how to design, develop, and publish them can be found here.

## Desktop

Specifics for desktop applications regarding design, development, testing, and deployment can be found here.

## Windows IoT

The Internet of Things is a whole new area of opportunity for developers. This section describes how Windows 10 supports IoT development and points to resources that are available to get you started.

## Microsoft Edge

Microsoft Edge is the new browser that is the successor to Internet Explorer. There are tools here to help developers make sure their apps are compatible with Edge on any platform, even a Mac.

## Holographic

This is a link to Windows Dev Center-Holographic, which is discussed later.

# Downloads

This page takes you to all the free downloads that you might need in order to develop for Windows 10.

# Samples

Here we find sample applications that showcase the kinds of things that can be done with Windows 10 applications, and code for the sample apps is available on GitHub. You can use the code as is or modify it to meet your needs.

## Foundational samples

Foundational samples highlight the features and capabilities of the Universal Windows Platform. By studying them, you can learn how to make use of those features and capabilities in your own applications.

## Showcase samples

In this category, we find a photo-sharing app that demonstrates photo sharing on social media.

## Playful samples

This category includes IoT projects that makers have developed around tiny computers, such as the Arduino and Raspberry Pi.

## Other Microsoft samples

Included here is sample code and documentation for things that don't fall into any of the preceding categories, but that could provide valuable learning experiences for developers.

# Support

Microsoft puts extensive effort into supporting developers. Online resources cover most of the questions you might have, and responses to questions on the developer forums generally come quickly and contain quality feedback that will get you going again quickly.

## Windows apps and games

Forums cover a number of topics of concern to all developers, as well as a forum dedicated specifically to HoloLens issues.

## Classic desktop apps

Questions specific to desktop apps would go to the forums found here, as well as any questions regarding the Windows SDKs.

## MSDN subscriptions

MSDN subscriptions are available at several levels and feature different benefits and term lengths.

# Windows Dev Center-Holographic

The Windows Holographic Dev Center (`https://developer.microsoft.com/en-us/windows/Holographic`) contains resources that are specifically aimed at holographic development for HoloLens. This is the place to go to learn about Windows Holographic development and where to find the answers to questions that inevitably crop up. Let's look at the menu tabs that you will find here.

# Get the tools

Below the "Welcome to Windows Holographic" greeting that sits under a photo of a HoloLens device is a small blue Get the Tools button. This takes you to the Install the Tools page, which tells you what you will need in order to develop for HoloLens. There are software packages that you must install. Check here for the latest versions. Even if you have, for example, a copy of Visual Studio or Unity, you will want to download the ones that are linked to from here and use them instead. New versions are being continually issued, and some that are not specifically tweaked for HoloLens will not work at all. If you already have a working stack, read the release notes before upgrading any one tool. Doing so might break compatibility with other tools. You may have to update the entire tool chain to get things working again.

Also listed here are the requirements of the system you plan to develop on. The requirements are extensive and stringent. There are CPU requirements, RAM requirements, graphics requirements, BIOS requirements, and Windows version requirements.

Although there are a lot of requirements to get started as a HoloLens developer, it is not terribly expensive. All the software you need, aside from Windows 10 Pro, is free. A late-model, low-end Windows Pro machine will probably fit the requirements too. Be sure to check the requirements before buying. Even an inexpensive refurbished machine from Fry's Electronics will probably be fine.

## Get Started

The Get Started page gives you an overview of the HoloLens Developer Edition and encourages you to try some of the example apps that come with it. It then directs you to the tutorials to be found at the Holographic Academy.

## Academy

The Holographic Academy, which I describe in Chapter 5, contains a series of tutorials that takes you through the steps of building and deploying example apps that exercise each of the major functions of the HoloLens. Starting with the creation of your first hologram (a cube), the tutorials cover one capability after another, until the last tutorial puts it all together with a fun, game-like app that exercises all the major functions.

## Documentation

The Documentation page contains links to useful information about the development of different kinds of holographic applications; you will find this valuable. It includes tips for designing holograms and even a couple of case studies.

## Community

You DO want to join the community. The Developer Engagement Crew that hangs out on the forums is knowledgeable and helpful. Forum regulars who are not Microsofties are also very helpful to newbies. Everybody was a newbie once, so if you have knowledge that you can pass along, pay it forward by doing so. There is also a HoloLens Twitter feed and a HoloLens YouTube channel, both of which can be sources of valuable information.

# APPENDIX B

■ ■ ■

# Other Resources

The Windows Dev Center is by far the number one place to go for additional information about developing for HoloLens. However, there are other places that also contain valuable resources. Probably the next most valuable resource after the Windows Dev Center is the area maintained by Microsoft on GitHub. GitHub is a code-hosting platform for version control and collaboration. With it, people in different locations can work on the same project. It supports both open-source and private projects. Microsoft has uploaded a lot of information relevant to HoloLens to open-source repositories on GitHub. In this appendix, we will look at some of what Microsoft and other HoloLens developers have posted there. The repositories on GitHub are growing all the time as ever more developers become active in learning and building for the HoloLens.

## Microsoft Resources on GitHub

Resources in GitHub are stored in repositories, and at the present time, there are three repositories in the Microsoft open-source area, which can be found here:

`https://github.com/Microsoft?utf8=%E2%9C%93&query=hol`

Two of the repositories deal with the HoloToolkit that I showed in action in Chapter 17. The other contains all the resources used in the tutorials that I described in Chapter 5.

## HoloToolkit-Unity

This is the HoloToolkit that I describe extensively in Chapter 17. The resources to be found here are specifically designed for use in developing holographic applications for the HoloLens using the Unity platform.

## HoloToolkit

It is possible to develop holographic applications without using Unity. You may want to bypass Unity, and by doing so not have to worry about paying them for the use of their platform. This is only an issue if your app becomes a commercial success, which you probably hope it will. Building on top of the Unity platform, on the other hand, can save you a lot of work. It's a tradeoff. If you do decide to develop outside of the Unity toolchain, there are scripts and components here that you might find helpful.

## Holographic Academy

All the code and other assets that are included in all the tutorials can be found here. These files are being updated as needed whenever improved versions of components are created. The latest versions of all files can always be found here. If you find a problem with any of the code here and can determine that it is an actual bug, you can report it here.

## Resources on GitHub from Developers

Anybody can create a repository on GitHub and put into it whatever files they want. As people become familiar with holographic development, they will create projects and place them into a repository here so as to share their success with or solicit feedback from the community of developers. Early on, many of the repositories contain projects related to Microsoft's holographic tutorials. Other repositories contain simple games. As people become more proficient, the complexity and usefulness of the things to be found here will increase. You may also find value in resources to be found here that are not specific to HoloLens, but are relevant and instructive nonetheless.

## HoloLens YouTube Videos

To get an idea of the variety of things that are possible with HoloLens, you need look no further than to YouTube.com. There are over 100,000 videos up on the site showing things you can do with HoloLens, and more are being added every day. As more developers get their hands on the hardware, this number is bound to explode.

# Index

## ◼ A

Advertising, 231
Air tap, 26–27, 81, 85, 89, 114, 117, 131, 140, 148,
    159, 161, 171, 176, 179, 181, 193, 196, 198,
    204, 212, 215, 216, 219
Animation, 52, 54, 56, 99, 164, 170, 190, 193, 208,
    212, 222, 235
App Developer Agreement, 232
Assets, 5, 22, 55, 56, 61, 67, 75, 77, 102, 104, 110, 112,
    122, 127–128, 130, 148, 162, 163, 167, 173,
    176, 180, 195, 196–199, 204, 209–211,
    213–214, 216, 218, 219, 246
Augmented reality, 3–4, 6–7, 53
Avatar, 25, 134–140, 226

## ◼ B

BIOS, 17, 19–20, 61, 101, 125, 243
Bluetooth, 5, 81, 99, 110, 159

## ◼ C

C#, 22, 23, 70, 75–78, 87, 91–101, 106, 109, 111, 114,
    117, 128, 169, 173, 177, 195, 200, 211
Certification, 30–31, 224, 232–233
Communication
    intergroup, 57
Components, 22, 39, 55, 76, 81, 91–92–100, 120,
    130–132, 134–136, 148, 153, 162, 189, 195,
    197, 202–206, 213–214, 245, 246
Connecting
    via USB, 29
    via Wi-Fi, 27–28
Coordinate systems, 110, 131, 164, 170
Cortana. *See* Universal Windows Platform (UWP)
Cursor, 23, 26, 76, 85, 88, 110, 112–114, 117, 119,
    130–131, 171, 179–182, 196–199, 207, 210,
    213–216, 219

## ◼ D

Developer forum
    Windows Holographic, 18
Device family
    holographic, 14–15
    universal, 14
Device Portal, 25–46, 82–83, 158–159,
    223–224
DirectX 12, 11, 87

## ◼ E

Emulator, 18–19, 21–24, 26, 45, 80, 82–83, 101–102,
    106–109, 113, 116, 119, 122, 124–126, 129,
    130, 161, 169, 195
Event function
    LateUpdate, 99
    Start, 99
    Update, 99

## ◼ F

Field of view, 4–5, 24, 26, 84, 89, 105, 114, 157, 161,
    171, 196, 214–215, 219, 226
Frame of reference, 164–166

## ◼ G

Gaze, 15, 22–27, 74, 79, 82, 85, 86–88, 101,
    110–114, 124, 130, 131, 149, 161–162,
    165, 170, 171, 179, 180, 196–199, 209,
    213, 216, 219
Gesture, 4–6, 15, 22–27, 42, 45, 76, 81–83,
    85–87, 89, 101, 110, 114–117, 124,
    130–131, 140, 149, 161–162, 165,
    170, 171, 176, 181–182, 196, 198,
    204, 209, 212, 214, 215–216, 218–219,
    222, 237

© Allen G. Taylor 2016                                                                                                         247
A. G. Taylor, *Develop Microsoft HoloLens Apps Now*, DOI 10.1007/978-1-4842-2202-7

# Get the eBook for only $5!

Why limit yourself?

Now you can take the weightless companion with you wherever you go and access your content on your PC, phone, tablet, or reader.

Since you've purchased this print book, we're happy to offer you the eBook in all 3 formats for just $5.

Convenient and fully searchable, the PDF version enables you to easily find and copy code—or perform examples by quickly toggling between instructions and applications. The MOBI format is ideal for your Kindle, while the ePUB can be utilized on a variety of mobile devices.

To learn more, go to www.apress.com/companion or contact support@apress.com.

Printed in the United States
By Bookmasters